# It's Not You, It's Us

## A Guide for Living Together Without Growing Apart

by Sophie Winters

ISBN: 978-1-63492-308-8



Published by BookLocker.com, Inc., St. Petersburg, Florida.

Printed on acid-free paper.

Some names and identifying details have been changed to protect the privacy of individuals.

BookLocker.com, Inc.
2017

First Edition – September 2015
Second Edition – March 2017

www.itsnotyouitsus.com

thechachaclub@gmail.com

## Also by Sophie Winters

The Cha Cha Club Dating Man-ifesto

Forty Daze (as Adele Frizzell)

## DISCLAIMER

The disclaimer is the "awkward conversation" we need to have at the outset to ensure we're on the same page.

This book contains my personal experiences, opinions, and advice. I am not a doctor, lawyer, or licensed therapist. Neither my publisher nor I offer medical, legal, or psychological advice, and no contents of this book are to be construed as the advice, care, or treatment of a licensed professional, or as a substitute for such professional services.

This book is offered "as-is", and my publisher and I disclaim all liability in connection with the use of it or its contents.

This book provides content related to relationship topics. As such, use of this book implies your acceptance of this disclaimer.

**For Tex**

*Thank you for giving me wings.*

## Table of Contents

## Dear Reader

In his book, *Things I Wish I'd Known Before We Got Married*, Gary Chapman says that love has two stages. In the first stage, you get caught up in the heady rush of romance, hormones, and sex. You're euphoric, in love, and the rest of the world doesn't matter. You think you've found 'the One'. This stage normally lasts six months to two years. And yet, according to Chapman, the next stage is, "much more intentional than the first stage. And yes, it requires work in order to keep emotional love alive". The rewards are huge though. You become more deeply connected, emotionally intimate and full of love for one another, far beyond the initial euphoria that swept you along.

*It's Not You, It's Us: A Guide for Living Together Without Growing Apart* walks readers through what it takes to build and maintain a deeply satisfying and lasting relationship. It explains how to create a relationship in which both partners feel safe to be themselves, so they continue to grow as individuals, and as a couple.

This is a book to help couples who are planning to move in together, couples who are already living together or couples who are married – to be happier and more successful. It explores multiple topics like the legal differences between living together and being married, mixed-faith unions, having kids and pets, sex and desire, division of labor, money, family issues, personal growth and happiness, emotional distance, privacy and personal space, conflict, and other issues. I haven't come across another relationship book that explores so many subjects in one go. Whole books could be written on just "Money" or "Blended Families" – and have been. Due to the sheer breadth of the topics covered, I provide a list of references and some recommended reading if you wish to learn more about a subject.

*It's Not You, It's Us: A Guide For Living Together Without Growing Apart* draws real world examples from my own relationships, other couples, family therapists, a documentary filmmaker, and other authors and experts. More than an advice book, there are exercises at the end of most chapters so you can immediately take action on what you've learned.

**Feel free to read the chapters in any order you like, and skip sections that you don't connect with.** You can always return to them some other time. However, I recommend you read this guidebook with your partner. Perhaps you can take turns reading each chapter out loud and doing the exercises together. I guarantee that doing this will spark some juicy conversations and increase understanding between you. Think you know your partner? Well, you're about to find out!

If you find this book helps you in any way, please send me an email and/or leave a review. I love to hear from my readers and it would be great to know what parts stood out for you the most. After all, I wrote this book for *you.*

I truly believe in helping people get more love in their lives, starting with themselves.

May you live together without growing apart.

# Introduction

*We are our best selves when we are treated with love, whether it's from ourselves or others.*

– Georgie Fear

After my book, *The Cha Cha Club Dating Man-ifesto* was published, I had the strongest feeling that I would meet an amazing man within a year.

Maybe that's because writing a dating and relationship book made it crystal clear what kind of man I wanted to date and let into my life. I was keenly aware that I had to follow my own advice if I wanted to attract a Quality Man. I don't think it's any coincidence that seven months after I published my first book, I found one.

Tex was unlike any man I had ever dated. He was an American, an oil and gas engineer working and living in Canada. We met through a dating site and dated for a couple of months before going exclusive. He wasn't a commitment-phobe: he told me right from the beginning he wanted to get married again (someday) and thought he was a better man in a relationship. He had a ten-year-old daughter who lived with her mother and new stepfather in Colorado. I had never been married. I had never dated a Dad before. I had never met a man who talked liked that.

Tex was Christian: I wasn't. Tex was from Texas: I was from Canada. Tex was passionate and I was cautious – at first. I felt attracted to him but made him (and me!) wait for sex. I wanted to be sure he was right for me without hormones clouding my judgment. After dating for a couple of months, we decided to be exclusive and take down our online dating profiles. Then we sealed the deal in a tent in Yellowstone National Park. Romantic? I know...but for an outdoorsy Canadian person like me, it was perfect. We had driven across the country to meet each other: he from Colorado, and I on my motorcycle all the way from Alberta, Canada.

After four months of being exclusive, our relationship was tested for the first time. My father died of a massive stroke. Tex drove 600 kilometers (that's about 400 miles for you Americans) to be with me. He took several days off of work to support me at the hospital and at the memorial service. He was there before, during, and after my father passed away. Tex dried my tears, held me, and comforted me through the grieving process. He was my rock, and I knew then, without a doubt, I'd found a man who wasn't just good to me; he was good FOR me.

When Tex's company told him they wanted to move him back to the United States, he asked me to move with him.

I had never truly considered leaving my mountain town – my paradise – for a man before. But I couldn't imagine my life without him.

I said yes.

Seven months after meeting for the first time, we were living together in Washington, DC. Three months later, Tex was having his own personal crisis.

I could sense him distancing himself from me. He no longer reached for me in bed. He no longer texted me during the day. He became prickly. Where was my sweet, adoring man?

I wanted to know what was wrong. We talked, and he told me he was questioning "us" and needed his own space and didn't know how to handle that. It made him feel guilty just thinking about it. He missed the days when we were dating, and only saw each other on weekends and could give each other 100%, because we had our own separate lives all week. He had a lot going on in his head. Had we moved in together too soon? Where was this relationship going? He wasn't even sure he wanted to get married again or was suited for it.

My man had developed a case of ice-cold feet.

Thanks to John Gray[1], I knew this was the "resistance stage" at work in our relationship, so I didn't freak.

*[1]John Gray identifies five stages to intimacy. The five stages are Attraction, Uncertainty, Exclusivity, Intimacy, and Engagement. One of these stages is the "uncertainty stage". It's when you work through inevitable doubts about your relationship. If you don't have doubts, you're probably deluded. John Gray, "My 5 Stages of Dating", http://www.marsvenus.com.*

At the same time, I couldn't help feeling anxious: I had moved to the United States for this man. I had taken a big leap of faith in us. Despite the fact that I had sworn I'd never again move in with a man without a ring on my finger, I'd gone ahead and done it anyway. Why? Because we both knew we couldn't date if we lived 2000 miles apart. Without more time together, we would never know the true nature of our relationship and our level of compatibility. So, we found an apartment and merged our possessions – and lives – together. It was scary. It was exciting. It was what we both wanted. But now he was uncertain!

And he knew all this, and he just felt more guilty. The last thing I wanted was for my man to feel guilty. I wanted him to be motivated and inspired to be with me, not obligated.

So, I decided to be patient and wait it out in the hope he would come around.

It required more faith than I was used to having in a relationship.

I wrote the following diary entry:

> *...Tex and I are re-calibrating. I recently found out that I can't get a work visa, so unless we get married, I have to leave the U.S. in September (for six months). It puts a little pressure on us, which neither of us wants right now. Also, not having an income sucks. I am totally dependent on Tex now. I wish I could contribute in some meaningful way but short of keeping the place tidy (he does his own laundry) and cooking and trying out new recipes (he also cooks), I have a lot of time on my hands. What else? I miss my mountains, my community, and my money. I miss my friends and having a strong purpose each day.*
>
> *My challenge is to recreate myself here and start over. And while Tex is all I have at the moment, it's important I give him some space and not cling too tightly. And so, I go to yoga at night, or a movie, or a meetup, so he can have the apartment and a little time to himself because he works all day and doesn't need to come home and find me here all the time. So right now, things aren't easy, but I am doing my best to settle in, get fit, get a life, and use my time productively.*

# It's Not You, It's Us

We were both in a new city, without friends, new to living together, and trying to figure it all out. We were living together but felt more apart than ever.

Eventually, we figured it out and fell more in love than ever.

Here's how.

# Chapter 1: The Happy Couple

*Most people spend far more time in preparation for their vocation than they do in preparation for marriage. Therefore, it should not be surprising that they are more successful in their vocational pursuits than they are in reaching the goal of marital happiness.*

— Gary Chapman, *Things I Wish I'd Known Before We Got Married*

## Happily Ever After?

In the book *Outliers*, author Malcolm Gladwell states that it takes roughly 10,000 hours of practice to achieve mastery in a field. This theory is currently getting hammered by academics, but the message is clear: spend enough time doing something, and you'll get good at it. If we are to believe Gladwell, after four years of marriage (assuming seven hours a day are spent together), we should all be experts at cohabitation. And yet, that is rarely the case. It would seem that **mindful practice and dedication to a skill are key to mastery.** A so-called perfect union takes dedication to master. And without commitment, practice, or mentors to show us what that looks like, the challenge is impossible.

## Questions: What Does It Take to Live Happily Ever After?

1. Why are some couples happier than others?
2. How did they get that way?
3. Did they simply choose the right partner while others chose poorly?
4. How do they stay connected while other couples seem to drift apart?
5. Do happy people have a greater chance of keeping intimacy, love, and affection alive in their relationships?
6. How can couples help each other become their best, happiest selves?
7. Is some people's lack of marital happiness possibly due to the nearly exclusive focus on extrinsic goals?

These are some of the questions I've asked myself over the years, and the answers are in this book. They may not be complete, but they are the start of a conversation about love and what it takes to live together without growing apart. I invite you to join me. My contact details, including my website and email, are at the end. Let me know how this information lands for you.

I'm not a therapist; I don't have an academic degree in this stuff. However, I do have research and observation skills, as well as wisdom and experience. I have learned from my own parents' troubled relationship and I draw from eight years of a "living together" relationship that went splitsville. I can also draw contrasts to the incredibly loving, healthy relationship I am in now.

I don't have 10,000 hours of experience; I have three decades. I made my share of mistakes along the way. Hopefully, this book will spare you some of those mistakes.

Now you may be tempted to read this book in a few sittings. Feel free to do so but I think you will get more out of it if you come back to it and take the time to read this book with your partner. Designate one day a week to read a chapter together and discuss it. There are 25 chapters, and most will take fifteen minutes to read. You can even take turns reading the book aloud to one another. **Read the book, and do the exercises together, and your relationship could be completely transformed six months from now.** In fact, your relationship could start transforming from the very first chapter.

> *Action expresses priorities.*
>
> — Mahatma Gandhi

## Living Together before Marriage

In my last book, *The Cha Cha Club Dating Man-ifesto*, I suggested that couples not live together before getting engaged or married, if marriage is truly what a person wants. This wasn't for religious reasons, but to provide clarity about a relationship and where it's headed before becoming legally, financially, and emotionally entangled. About 60% of cohabitating couples will not marry within three years. Reading this book will help you more fully comprehend your situation and its risks.

I can see the benefits of living together before marriage: you get to know each other's habits and quirks to a much greater degree. When you're living together, you can only hide the less shiny aspects of your personality for so long. If one of you has a mood disorder or addiction issues, that stuff will come out. Living together means figuring out what you can live with. But there are other reasons to live together first and some of them are logistical.

For Tex and me, living together was simply practical. We needed more run time together before getting married. We had only dated for six months when his company moved him back to the United States. To us, there was no way to sustain a dating relationship with 2000 miles separating us. So, we decided to live together first. It has given us more confidence that we are compatible and right for one another. We're ready now. Life has thrown us some big challenges in the last year – the death of my father; the passing of his father figure; illness; surgery; financial worries; career changes; moving countries; separation for months at a time – and we've never wavered in our commitment to and love for one another. Did we ever question our relationship? Certainly. But only in rare moments, like just before I moved in with him, or after spending months apart had caused us to emotionally disconnect, or when he still hadn't put a ring on it after a year of living together, and I began to wonder where things were going. Normal. Healthy.

*PEARLY WISDOM: There will be times in your relationship, especially if it endures long-distance periods, when you may question your feelings for your partner. You may look at this person you're supposed to love, as if they are a stranger. You may feel disconnected. You may feel a hollowness to the "I love you"s. You may even come to question your relationship. Let me assure you: this is normal. If there is no anger or resentment, just a flatness to things, the feelings and love will come back. Do not think you have to be "on" all the time. Love is like waves, so ride the tide. (And if you can talk about what's happening between you and why, you just may find the love coming back more quickly. That's because nothing is sexier and more energizing to a relationship than authenticity.)*

**Really want to get to know a person? Observe them under stress and see how they handle it.** And that takes time. Very few people consider how important grit is to a relationship when they begin to date someone. As we get older, we learn that suffering is a part of life and misfortune will strike not once, but several times. The ability to bear these events with grace and resilience is an often-overlooked virtue in a partner.

When I was in my twenties, **I didn't consider how important grit was to a relationship**. I looked for things we had in common. If a guy liked the outdoors and had the same music tastes, he was dating material. But I never really considered whether he had the kind of internal strength required in a relationship. **I never considered whether my partner was good *for* me**. The kind of guy who won't run at the threat of conflict. The kind of guy who will stay faithful after three months apart. The kind of guy who will say, "Let me be your rock," when you feel like you cannot bear the pain of grief.

It doesn't always take living together to figure out a person's character. All you need is time to see how your sweetheart deals with life's more painful aspects, such as losing a job, dealing with grief or illness, or struggling with financial hardship. The truly great ones won't succumb to drama, despair, or addiction. The truly great ones will love you through it all and bear it with grit and hope. Living together means you get to experience it all first-hand.

> **Guideline #1: When looking for a life partner, look for someone who is resilient in the face of adversity.**

## Risk of Divorce

Let's bust some myths about living together and divorce first.

## Q: Does living together before marriage lead to a higher risk of divorce later on?

Good news for those who may have heard that living together before marriage increases the risk of divorce: it's BS. In a 2013 study published in the *Journal of Marriage and Family* by associate professor Arielle Kuperberg, it was found that there is no correlation between living together before marriage and divorce.[2]

Current research shows that cohabitation doesn't cause divorce – and probably never did.*

**I have placed all remaining references at the end of the book, in the Endnotes section to maintain readability. You may also notice that I use "he" and "she" interchangeably and use "they" and "their" to be gender inclusive. I bold certain words and sentences. This is not an error: I do it to draw attention to important ideas. Finally, feel free to replace the word, "marriage" with "living together" whenever it suits you.*

## Q: What is the greatest predictor of divorce?

According to several studies, age and income level are the greatest predictors of divorce.[3] **The lower the age and income at the time of marriage, the greater the risk of divorce.**[4] Marrying before the age of 25 is a terrible risk, no matter how "in love" you are right now; half of young marriages end in divorce. The message? Don't settle down too early. Go to school, get some marketable skills, check a few items off your bucket list, and then get married. That goes for both men and women.

Research may indicate that the very best age to marry is between 28 and 32, but it's not so much that there is a magical number that will safeguard you from divorce as much as it's about having the life experience, self-awareness, and financial resources to weather the demands of marriage.

**Q: What about marital satisfaction? Does living together before marriage guarantee greater satisfaction later?**

Sadly, no. It would seem that living together before marriage doesn't contribute to a more blissful union, although there is some data indicating that women are happier married than cohabiting – for social and cultural reasons, and possibly due to greater feelings of security overall. There is also some data to support that married men have more successful careers and live longer than their unmarried counterparts.

**Q: So why live together before marriage?**

Well, for couples like Tex and me, living together is a stepping stone to marriage, a chance to see how compatible we really are and a necessity due to geographical distance. For others, living together is a viable alternative to getting married. However, cohabitation does come with some risks, which I explore in the chapter on "Covering Your Ass(ets)".

## What Can We Do to Be Happier?

Just because a couple is still together after a few years doesn't mean they're happy.

When I look at couples, at least a third of them seem miserable or lacking in love and affection... or just kind of *meh*. Sometimes, I even get the impression they irritate the hell out of each other and wish they could be left alone. I feel pained when I hear these kinds of couples talk to each other. The contempt and disrespect are palpable.

Which makes me wonder: How many of these people are together out of necessity, or for the kids, or due to religious or cultural pressure, instead of love and desire? How many relationships are surviving rather than thriving?

For some people, marriage is such a scary proposition that they would rather live together than risk divorce. But that's avoiding the heart of the issue. To me, the real question is not: Is living together better or worse than marriage? The real question is: How can we live together without growing apart?"

Chuck all the statistics and probabilities; I want a relationship that thrives. And since you're holding this book in your sweet little hands, I'm sure you do too.

We all want to be loved. We all want to be happy. Problem is, we're not always sure what that looks like, or how to get there. This book is a start.

*PEARLY WISDOM: Early happiness determines future success. The better a couple gets along in the beginning of a relationship, the better their chances of continued happiness later on. Research indicates that happy couples, after years of marriage, were far happier at the beginning, while unhappy couples had far more problems right from the start.*

To me, a happy couple is affectionate and respectful of one another. They light up around each other, laugh easily and show enthusiasm in each other's company. Most importantly, they support and respect each other. They constantly share new experiences together. They act like a team.

**Guideline #2: If you're choosing to share your life with someone, give some thought as to *how* you're going to be happy together.**

I don't know about you, but I don't want to just grow old with someone. I want to become more, do more, see more, feel more, love more, and laugh more than I ever would have on my own.

How about you? What does your relationship look like to other people?

Think about every couple you know.

How many of them seem happy together?

What does happy look like to you?

Kiley writes:

> *My parents! They joke about their differences, make fun plans together, but also give each other space to follow their own interests.*

> **Guideline #3: One sure-fire way to spot a happy couple: they laugh together.**

## Like before Love

Many couples who say they love each other actually treat each other horribly. Let me ask you this: Would you complain and talk about your friend behind their back? Would you criticize and belittle them in front of others? Would you avoid spending time with them? This is how some couples behave – like enemies.

> **Guideline #4: You need to like each other in order to properly love each other.**

## Keeping Romantic Love Alive

At one time, I was a bit cynical about love. I used to think that romantic love never lasted. That it was all fun and games until the honeymoon phase was over, and after that it was downhill. Unless you were one of the very lucky ones – like the rare old couple you see still holding hands in public. Seems I was wrong, and that adoration can last a lifetime.

"Romantic love is more common than people tend to think, and it certainly doesn't need to end once a relationship enters its mature years", says Theresa E. DiDonato, Ph.D., in her article "The 3 Simple Habits That Predict Long-term Love".[5] DiDonato summarizes the work of researchers in a study that asks, "Is long-term love more than a rare phenomenon? If so, what are its correlates?"[6]

The study outlines three behaviors and beliefs that lead to feelings of passion and romantic love. Men and women who are intensely in love:

- Think positively about one's partner.
- Think about one's partner when not with that person.
- Have an affectionate relationship (hugging, kissing, holding hands).

A Harvard presentation on the Psychology of Close Relationships[7] draws similar conclusions. In a nationwide controlled study of couples in the United States married at least ten years and an average of 20 years, couples that were very intensely in love:

- Are physically affectionate.
- Think positively about their spouse.
- Share in enjoyable, engaging activities.

While Tex and I have a young relationship, we both know that experiencing new things and being physically affectionate is an aphrodisiac for us. The natural outcome of these activities is to think fondly about one another when we're not together.

The Harvard findings conclude that while some relationships will decline, "the ones that do, tend to be troubled from the start. Couples can and do have deeply happy, passionate, romantic relationships after decades". Indeed, about one in three marriages that have lasted over 30 years are still very much in love. How wonderful is that?

Tex says he'll still slap my ass when I'm 70 years old. I am holding him to it. Because ass-slapping may be one of the keys to a love that lasts.

But it's only one of the keys.

## The Happy Couple

More interestingly, DiDonato says that analysts observed a "relation between general life happiness and intense love for a spouse".

Did you catch that? Happiness with one's life is highly linked to a happy relationship.

It is a cliché to say no one can make you happy but it's an absolute truth. Once you assume responsibility for your own happiness, it becomes the tide that lifts all ships. I talk about this more in Chapter 16 – Personal Growth and the Pursuit of Happiness.

For now, here's a teaser: If you want a happy relationship, you must first be happy with your own life.

Your level of contentment is the result of the choices you make, the thoughts you hold, and the actions you take each day. By cultivating an attitude of gratitude, finding purpose and meaning to your life, and having a positive relationship with yourself, you nurture a joyful spirit and high self-esteem.

**High self-esteem is a huge predictor of relationship and life satisfaction**, since how you see yourself and your partner matters a great deal. Self-esteem influences your perception of events and even your commitment and communication during conflict. If both partners have high levels of self-esteem, your relationship has the best possible chance of long-term happiness.

Like a stone thrown into a pond, happiness begins with you and ripples outward.

*PEARLY WISDOM: It's a cliché because it's true: no one can "make" you happy – that's your job in life. It is a noble calling, and we are each called to it in our own way. The challenge is to find someone who will support your journey, even if they don't share in it.*

**Guideline #5: Long-term happiness and love is an inside job. It starts with YOU.**

## Roko Belic's Lessons about Happiness

There is a documentary film called Happy, which I think everyone should watch. The film explores the "true sources and causes of happiness", according to director Roko Belic. Roko has kindly allowed me to share the following article about the lessons he learned about happiness while making the film. I think his advice could help relationships everywhere.

*A dirt-poor rickshaw puller in a slum in India once told me that he was the luckiest person alive. His hut was made out of bamboo sticks and plastic tarps, with raw sewage trickling out front, but still, Manoj Singh said he was happy, very happy, in fact. Though sometimes he had only a few bowls of rice to feed his family, he said, "I feel that I am not poor, but I am the richest person in the world".*

*How could this be? I have friends who can become unhappy by bad cell phone reception or a delayed flight.*

*For the past six years, I have been making a documentary film called Happy, exploring the true sources and causes of happiness. My crew and I traveled to 14 countries and talked to people from many different cultures. Old and young, rich and poor, they taught us about happiness. We also spoke with many of the leaders in the field of positive psychology, the scientific study of happiness.*

*What I learned changed my life.*

***1. You can Become Happier***

*There are a number of ways we can increase our happiness. The formula for happiness is not the same for everyone, but all of us can make changes to become healthier, more fulfilled and happier.*

***2. Your Happiness is Good For You***

*Happy people are more likely to have better relationships and have happier children. Happy people do better at school and at work and make more money. They are more creative, more resilient in the face of hardship, healthier and they even live longer.*

***3. Your Happiness is Good For the World***

*Happiness is contagious. As you become happier, those around you have a higher likelihood of becoming happier. Happy people are less likely to cheat someone else, commit a crime or pollute the environment. They are more likely to help a stranger in need and stand up for justice and human rights. Happy people create a happy world.*

***Seven Things You Can Do to Become Happier (Roko Belic)***

***1. Get in the Flow***

*Flow is a state of being where you are totally immersed in an activity. You forget about the worries of everyday life and you are completely focused on the experience of the moment. Flow usually occurs while engaging in a hobby like gardening, painting, golfing or surfing, but it can also happen at work. People who get into flow on a regular basis are happier than those who don't.*

***What to do:*** *Recognize your flow-inducing hobbies and prioritize them.*

***2. Integrate Exercise into Your Day***

*We have a chemical in our brain called dopamine that is essential for feelings of pleasure and happiness. It is part of a system of transmitters and receptors that deteriorates as we get older (past teenage years). The best way to maintain the health of our dopamine systems is through physical aerobic exercise.*

***What to do:*** *Find something aerobic that you like to do and prioritize it in your schedule. Some ideas are biking, dancing, running, tennis, basketball, walking.*

***3. Spend time with Friends and Family***

*Ed Diener, a leading researcher in positive psychology, told me that every happy person he studied in over 30 years had strong relationships. Not all were outgoing or necessarily very social, but all had someone they loved and someone who loved them back.*

***What to do:*** *Make time to spend with your friends and family on a regular basis.*

***4. Focus on Intrinsic Goals***

*People who prioritize "extrinsic" values for money, power and fame are less likely to be happy than people who prioritize "intrinsic" values for compassion, cooperation and wanting to make the world a better place.*

***What to do:*** *Shift your priorities and your actions toward intrinsic goals.*

***5. Be a Part of Something that Offers a Sense of Meaning and Purpose***

*Happy people often feel they are part of something bigger than themselves. Whether it's a community service organization, a charity or a spiritual affiliation, participating in a group or identifying a context for your life can increase your happiness.*

***What to do:*** *Participate in an organization that reflects your values or do things that contribute to the legacy you want to leave.*

***6. Act with Compassion***

*Being kind and helping others, even strangers, makes you happier.*

***What to do:*** *Take opportunities to be kind and offer help.*

***7. Practice Gratitude***

*Writing a letter to thank someone can boost your happiness for days afterwards. The amazing part is: it works even if you don't send the letter! If you do send the letter, the positive impact is even greater. The simple act of expressing your gratitude makes you happier.*

***What to do:*** *Make a habit of thanking people who help you, and write a list once a week of things you are grateful for.*

**Guideline #6: The quality of your relationships is a direct reflection of how you feel about yourself.**

* * *

## HOUSEKEEPING: Get Happy(er)

At the end of most chapters, I have included some "Housekeeping" items. Consider this section your homework for the week. If you read ahead, please come back and work on these items with (or without) your partner. Knowledge is nothing without application, and **your relationship will transform if you actually take the time to do the exercises and apply what you've learned.** If your partner is not willing or able to do some of the housekeeping items with you at the end of each chapter, then go ahead and do them yourself. Sometimes, it only takes one person to shift things for the better in a relationship.

Try not to do all the housework at once: one chapter per week is more than enough.

Let me know how it goes!

**Task 1. Watch the movie *Happy* together.**

You can rent it for a few dollars at www.thehappymovie.com. Get inspired!

**Task 2. Get involved in something bigger than you.**

If "happy people often feel they are part of something bigger than themselves", what can you do as a couple, or individually, to participate in something that gives you a sense of purpose and contribution to a community?

For example, Tex and I deliver groceries once a month to cut-off seniors who are facing poverty and social isolation. It's a four-hour time commitment once a month, but our small visit means the world to these lonely seniors. The visits mean a lot to us too. We also feel closer and more connected to each other afterwards.

If you would like to become more involved in your community, consider volunteering through your church or neighborhood, or through organizations like volunteermatch.org, where we found our cause. Volunteermatch has thousands of listings to bring good people and causes together, and there is no cost to join.

**Task 3: Reread Roko Belic's lessons about happiness.**

If you have some juice in you, go back to Roko Belic's lessons about happiness and reread his seven tips on what you can do to become happier. Find a way to implement them in your own life. You might want to journal about this.

I can't stress the importance of finding your own happiness enough. To rely on someone else to make you happy is giving your power and destiny away. **When you become the best person you can be, you are on your way to deep personal satisfaction with life. As you blossom, so do your relationships.** You become your wisest, happiest, and most loving self when you commit to your own happiness and find ways to be of value to others.

## Guideline #7: Good relationships help you become your best self.

# Chapter 2: Communication - Good Talk, Bad Talk

*Much unhappiness has come into the world because of bewilderment and things left unsaid.*

— Fyodor Dostoevsky

Ask most therapists, and they will tell you that good communication is at the heart of any successful relationship. How you relate – or don't – affects every aspect of your well-being and relationship health. You want to feel comfortable talking to your significant other, the most trusted person in your life, about most things. Couples who don't talk are at greater risk of health problems and divorce.

## What Does Healthy, Good Communication Look Like?

1. It means you may not find the right words to express what you want to say but you try anyway, and you give your partner the same courtesy, knowing your partner may not express things perfectly either.

2. You are willing to be vulnerable and expose parts of yourself, including your needs and desires. You do so knowing that vulnerability can sometimes lead to rejection but most often leads to greater intimacy.

3. You feel that your opinion is valid but you are willing to listen to other viewpoints.

4. You seek to understand your partner's actions; you check in when something seems amiss.

5. When your partner brings up a problem, you listen and explore a solution together – perhaps not immediately, but at a time that is convenient for both of you.

6. When discussing a subject, you stay on topic and don't bring in other complaints about your partner. If you can't resolve the situation in that one conversation, you table it for discussion at another time.

7. While you may pick your battles, you also realize that negative feelings don't go away until addressed.

8. You don't pretend to feel something you aren't. If you're angry, you don't pretend you're okay. If you're hurt, you don't act as if nothing has happened.

9. You don't avoid telling your partner something because you think it might hurt or offend them. You know that in the long run, a truth gently told is better than a lie exposed.

10. You're humble enough to apologize when you've hurt someone, even if it's unintentional.

Contrary to what some experts say, couples who bring up issues as they occur often have fewer problems than couples who willfully try to minimize the conflict in their relationship. As the African proverb says, "If you think you're too small to make a difference, try sleeping in a closed room with a mosquito". Couples who are good at communication aren't afraid to deal with the mosquitoes in their relationship. They deal with pesky problems quickly so they can relax again.

## What Is the Mosquito in Your Relationship?

Let me share one of our mosquito moments, something I'll call the T-shirt incident. Tex had been saving a pile of T-shirts for donation. They had lain in a pile on the bedroom floor for days. I could look down the hallway into the bedroom, and the first thing that would catch my eye was the small pile of T-shirts just lying there. Suddenly, I was tired of looking at it. Sure, I could just toss the pile of clothes somewhere out of sight, but what would happen the next time? My man was rather fond of leaving piles of things around the house. I didn't want to spend the rest of my life "sweeping" behind him and knew this would just make me resentful in the long run, so I made a mental note that I would talk to him about it. That night, when Tex came home, I greeted him at the door as usual. We hugged and kissed and chatted about our day. Suddenly, I recalled the T-shirts. "Can I show you something?" I asked. "Sure", he replied. I pointed down the hallway. "See that? When I look down the hallway, the first thing I see is the T-shirts on the carpet, and it doesn't look good. Everything looks so nice and clean, but the first thing you see when you look in the bedroom is the T-shirts..." I didn't have a chance to finish.

"Oh", he said. "I'll clean that up. You're right". And he scooped up the shirts. "Thank you for telling me that it bothered you". And just like that, it was over. I'd been prepared for a longer conversation, but his attitude disarmed me. Instead of getting defensive, he thanked me! (Yes, this man actually thanks me when I communicate with him, good or bad. He loves knowing where he stands. Every time he thanks me for communicating with him, I feel humbled by his ability to take in criticism and not take it personally.) "Thank you", I said. I kissed him and, in a conciliatory gesture, asked, "Is there anything I'm doing that bugs you?" He patted my bum. "Can't think of anything". And we went back to enjoying our evening.

What happened there? Well, I shared something that was bothering me – in a warm moment, so he was receptive. It didn't wreck our night. He didn't take it personally. We swatted that mosquito and went right back to enjoying our evening.

When something bothers you and you can't let it go, then it's time to bring it up. Not addressing it will just cause things to fester and come out awkwardly at some weird time. It only has to bother one of you to be worthy of discussion. So, check in with your partner whenever you perceive a mosquito in your relationship.

> **Guideline #8: Check in with your partner whenever you perceive a mosquito in your relationship.**

One of my readers, Vanessa, read this chapter and had some good comments worth sharing with you:

> *I totally agree that one should not be afraid to tackle a difficult conversation. But maybe taking a day or two or even a week to reflect on why something is important to you will help you get clear on what you really want. Using your T-shirt example, what if Tex didn't react so positively when you broached the subject? You were pretty clear on why you wanted the pile moved. But I might ask myself, in your shoes, why didn't I just put the shirts in a bag for him? Does that turn me into his domestic slave? Does he leave stuff all over all the time, or is this an isolated incident? Can it wait till he gets around to it? Can I help him get around to it? Do I not feel this is my house too? Would I be overstepping my bounds to move it? Or does that violate one of the*

> *principles we've agreed on, that as mature adults we are each responsible for our own stuff....*
>
> *I have sometimes found there are really big personal identity questions behind the littlest pile of T-shirts, with all kinds of unarticulated "rules" we adopt without challenge.... and they may or may not be working for us. A little time challenging those notions ourselves before we bring it up, might open our minds. When I do that, I end up in a much more secure, happy place, as usually I find my happiness does not depend on what someone else does.*

Vanessa is absolutely right. When I decide to have a conversation like this, I ask myself a few questions:

1. Is this a trend, or a one-off situation? (A trend means the situation has occurred at least three times; or, as Tex says, "One or two data points is not a trend.")

2. Is this trend something that bugs the crap out of me?

3. Why does it bug the crap out of me?

I pride myself on being an easygoing person but not a pushover, and this capacity to overlook the trivial and annoying stuff that crops up in a relationship is one of my finer qualities. But if I see the same stupid stuff over and over, I will say something. In this case, I try to treat the other person as innocent until proven guilty. I've learned through experience that **there's often a good reason for stuff happening and you're just a discussion away from finding out why.** This approach worked well when I was a supervisor, and it works just as well in my intimate relationships. When you take a non-confrontational approach, you can find there are valid reasons for certain behaviors.

For example, an employee I was supervising started coming into work late. I let it go the first couple of times, but then I realized a trend was starting. We talked about it, and I learned she was taking night school and having a hard time getting going in the morning, so we agreed to let her start work 30 minutes later and leave 30 minutes later. It was a win–win. Sometimes a conversation will yield new psychological insights into people if you just ask, "Why?"

Why does Tex leave piles of things out in the open? Things like mail, keys, clothes and even food? Because if something is out of sight, it's out of mind for him. He kept the T-shirt pile going so he would remember to donate it to Goodwill. Tucked away in a closet, it would be forgotten. What he didn't account for was the impact his habit of leaving piles of things around the house would have on me. When you ask why something is happening and try to see the situation through another person's eyes, you often realize it's not personal.

**Healthy relationships stay away from criticism and complaints and focus on desirable outcomes.** In a healthy relationship, you are free to express anger and hurt, but do it kindly. We don't say things like "Could you stop being a slob", and make it personal with name-calling and labelling. Instead, we shine a light on the problem and request a change in behavior. **We ask for what we want. No drama.**

### Guideline #9: Ask for what you want. No drama.

Is there something your partner is doing that bothers you? Are you fed up with the shoes not getting put away in the closet? Tired of waiting for her to get ready and always being late to arrive somewhere? All you have to do is ask for what you want.

Example: "So, I have a favor to ask you..." and then go on and put your request in. If it's a small thing, such as that they put their shoes away in the closet when they get home, or pick their underwear off the bedroom floor, then they should be receptive. You could also follow up with, "Is there anything I do that you would like me to change?" Because fair is fair and relationships are about meeting your partner halfway. It shows you're a good sport, too. You might be amazed by the response you'll get. It takes humility and vulnerability to offer yourself up like that, but meeting your partner halfway gets you 100% more love, respect, and appreciation.

**Relationships are about relating.** Communicating. Asking for what we want. Telling each other what we don't like. Trying to understand the "why". If you want someone who thinks, acts and is exactly like you, then you might as well be alone.

So, what about those times when you don't feel comfortable communicating? Usually, it's when you're unhappy with something your partner is doing. That discomfort with speaking up could manifest in different ways. Maybe you hold your tongue in order not to hurt anyone's feelings. Maybe you second-guess yourself and rationalize that something is no big deal. Maybe you're afraid of an argument, so you avoid bringing up issues that could lead to a fight. Maybe you've simply lost hope in finding a resolution. Regardless, if you're feeling bad about something, or even a little resentful, it's important to discuss it. Don't pretend you're okay with something when you're not. Things need to be said – or they'll come out, eventually. Not speaking your truth is like setting the detonator on a ticking bomb. Eventually, it's gonna blow; you just don't know when. Wouldn't it be better to defuse the bomb now?

The way to defuse the bomb is to speak your truth. For most people, speaking their truth in a non-critical, non-heated way takes practice. **The good news is, the more you practice speaking**

**your truth, the more relaxed and fantastically level-headed you'll feel.** Expressing strong emotions and having courageous conversations becomes much easier. You become an expert at defusing bombs.

So, what happens if you ask for something and you don't get the response you hoped for?

Just you wait. We're going to cover that in the coming chapter, "The Art of Difficult Conversations". But first, some exercises.

* * *

## HOUSEKEEPING: Get Better at Communicating

This week, I would like you to focus on your communication skills. Here are some tasks that will help you to improve. Remember, you do not have to be perfect; you only have to practice. Communication skills may be the hardest relationship skills to master. Indeed, they can take a lifetime.

### Task 1: Speak your mind.

The next time something bothers you, bring it up at an appropriate moment. By appropriate, I mean not when you're super-angry or it's 2 a.m. in the morning and you're both exhausted. Make sure you do it in a timely fashion and when you're in the right frame of mind. Don't wait for the perfect moment, because perfect moments are almost non-existent. In fact, you create a perfect moment just by sharing requests in a non-confrontational way.

Speak your mind to clarify things in your relationship and avoid future drama. Some people have great difficulty speaking their mind (this was me, years ago). If this is you, then you need to practice this skill more than anyone. Sure, the first few attempts may come out awkwardly, and that's okay. You can laugh about it later.

Be firm but gentle, and own your feelings. For example, "I am feeling upset about..." or "I don't understand why you..." works well.

**Task 2: Ask for what you want.**

If you choose to, you and your partner could sit down sometime this week and each of you could bring up one behavior you would like each other to improve upon. Remember to keep the request simple. One example of this might be, "I'd love it if you cleaned up your whiskers around the sink after you shaved". That kinda thing.

**Task 3: Fulfill requests immediately.**

Satisfy your partner's request immediately, and see how much lighter and better things feel. Do not put it off.

**Task 4: Show appreciation.**

Thank your partner when you see them making an effort. Use specific language. Although saying, "Thank you" is lovely, using specific words to address the action has much more impact. For example, "Thank you for unloading the dishwasher" is more specific and clear. It doesn't hurt to throw in some praise too! For example, "Thank you for unloading the dishwasher so quickly. I really appreciate your thoughtfulness", is bound to give your partner the feelsies. It also goes a long way to reinforce the behavior. Praising an action usually encourages repetition; just ask any elementary school teacher.

If this seems fake at first, know that anything new feels awkward in the beginning. Over time, these kinds of requests and conversations will come more naturally.

# Chapter 3: Communication - Kindness and Love Languages

*No act of kindness, no matter how small, is ever wasted.*

— Aesop

## The Five Relationship Builders

Extra! Extra! Read all about it! "**Science says lasting relationships come down to – you guessed it – kindness and generosity**", according to a 2014 article from theAtlantic.com called "Masters of Love".[9]

Are you surprised?

In her article "Masters of Love", Emily Esfahani Smith says that only 3 in 10 marriages are happy. The glue that holds happy couples together? Kindness. According to Smith's article, "Kindness (along with emotional stability) is the most important predictor of satisfaction and stability in a marriage. Kindness makes each partner feel cared for, understood, and validated". And only 3 in 10 couples are masters at being kind to one another, meaning they know how to be kind even when arguing. If you'll recall from the previous chapter, this is the same number of marriages that are still intensely in love, decades later. Correlation?

So now we have the following ingredients for a happy relationship. Couples that are very intensely in love:

- Are physically affectionate
- Think positively about their spouse
- Share in enjoyable, engaging activities
- Are kind to one another
- Have emotional stability

If affection, positivity, activity, kindness, and emotional stability are what bind couples together, then what pulls them apart in 7 out of 10 marriages?

## The Four Relationship Killers

To respected psychologist Dr. John Gottman, the biggest destroyers of relationships are contempt and criticism. Dr. Gottman has spent four decades researching thousands of couples, trying to discern what behaviors are common in happy couples and what behaviors are common in unhappy couples. With this knowledge, Gottman claims he can predict which couples will divorce with 94% accuracy.[10] He is able to do this based on certain destructive behaviors he sees over and over again.

Dr. Gottman calls these destructive behaviors "the four horsemen of the apocalypse". They are:

1. Criticism – "You're so selfish".

2. Contempt – "You're a moron".

3. Defensiveness – "It's not my fault; it's yours".

4. Stonewalling – emotionally withdrawing, not responding.

Contempt is considered the worst of all. In fact, it is the number one predictor of divorce. It's when we treat others with disrespect and say things like, "You're a moron". We act superior to our partner and mock them. Gottman says the presence of these "four horsemen" in a marriage almost always leads to divorce, an average of 5.6 years after the wedding.

The key takeaway here is that kindness and positivity matter a great deal. When you are focused on your partner's good qualities and show them the same kindness, warmth, respect, and generosity of spirit that you would your best friend, your relationship has the greatest chance of not just surviving but thriving into its later years. And if criticism, contempt, defensiveness, and stonewalling are issues in your relationship now, take them as signs that you are headed for divorce unless you learn to be kinder to one another.

**Guideline #10: The secret to a long and happy marriage is an abundance of kindness.**

*PEARLY WISDOM: You can be kind when arguing. In fact, it's when you are arguing that you need to be at your kindest. You don't lose any power by choosing to be kind when things get heated. Being kind keeps you grounded and in control of your darker emotions. If you can't be kind in the heat of the moment, take a time out until you're more in control of yourself. I have some strategies on this later in the book, where I talk about "safe words" and "The Art of Difficult Conversations".*

## Relationship Killers: A Reader Shares His Story

Sean writes:

> *Some demons I have learned about in my last relationship.... Insecurity, control, criticism, lack of trust, lack of openness (not sharing because you think it might hurt). Also, honesty with yourself and your needs (compromising yourself for your partner). But the biggest relationship killer of all in my marriage was criticism. I think it was a major reason for my withdrawal and consequent divorce.*

Sean sent me an article which I link to at www.itsnotyouitsus.com/chapterlinks. It's called, "I Wasn't Treating My Husband Fairly and It Wasn't Fair" by a woman who goes by the name MissFranJan. This confessional article should be required reading for couples who are feeling the drag of criticism in their relationship. Sean saw this same dynamic play out in his previous marriage and wanted me to share it. Here is an excerpt:

> *I asked my husband to stop by the store to pick up a few things for dinner, and when he got home, he plopped the bag on the counter. I started pulling things out of the bag, and realized he'd gotten the 70/30 hamburger meat – which means it's 70% lean and 30% fat.*
>
> *I asked, "What's this?"*
>
> *"Hamburger meat", he replied, slightly confused.*
>
> *"You didn't get the right kind", I said.*

*"I didn't?" he replied with his brow furrowed. "Was there some other brand you wanted or something?"*

*"No. You're missing the point", I said. "You got the 70/30. I always get at least the 80/20".*

*He laughed. "Oh. That's all? I thought I'd really messed up or something".*

*That's how it started. I launched into him. I berated him for not being smarter. Why would he not get the more healthy option? Did he even read the labels? Why can't I trust him? Do I need to spell out every little thing for him in minute detail so he gets it right?...*

Read more at www.itsnotyouitsus.com/chapterlinks.

Essentially, MissFranJan comes to the realization that the problem with her husband isn't that he's an idiot for not picking up the right leanness of hamburger meat; it's about criticism and nitpicking and how it was destroying their marriage.

When you're having fights about hamburger meat, or how the toilet paper roll goes, what you're really fighting about is a need to control things. The more a person needs to control things – people, events, conversations and even environments – the more fearful and insecure they are. Some personal work is needed to get at the root cause and restore harmony.

*PEARLY WISDOM: News flash! There IS one correct way for the toilet paper roll to go. Basically, the person who replaces the toilet paper is the one doing it right. End of story. (Who wants to be boss of the toilet paper, anyway? Kind of a crappy job to give yourself, if you ask me.)*

I cringe when I witness couples being critical of one another. I suppose it triggers childhood memories of my mother criticizing my father. It killed me to watch it, because I sensed, even then, a venom at work. Criticism slithers its way into the heart and turns it cold. It destroys the love between two people.

Harriet Lerner, Ph.D., talks about this in her book, *Marriage Rules*[11]. She says that in the beginning, when couples first get together they know how to make each other feel loved and special and there is an abundance of praise. The longer a couple stays together, the more they notice and comment on things they don't like. (Like the hamburger meat that hubby buys, for example.) Dr. Lerner calls this "selective attention" and it flips 100% from loving to critical. I don't believe all couples do this, just the ones that are running on autopilot – which probably describes most couples.

Dialing down the criticism goes a long way, but so does specifically acknowledging what you love and admire and appreciate about your partner**. Saying "I love you", is beautiful, but it isn't enough to sustain a relationship.** Kindness, respect, gratitude, and consideration are essential for living together without growing apart. It's how we show up for our best friends, and it's how we should always show up for our partners in life. It's a terrible thing to save our best selves for other (shiny, new, less important) people.

## "Define the Relationship" Moments

Even married couples need to have DTR (Define the Relationship) moments. In dating, DTRs are considered "first-time events" such as "first kiss", "first road trip together", and "first time you say, 'I love you,' to one another". These milestones tell you exactly where you stand and possibly where you may be headed as a couple.

But here's the kicker: Define the Relationship moments also exist in long-term relationships. These are one-time occurrences that have a lasting impact. The experience leaves you changed in some way, for good or bad.

Since DTR experiences can be positive or negative, the goal should be to focus on the good moments that make you appreciate your partner. Is your relationship defined by kindness? Do you share a mutual respect? So often we focus on the negative aspects of when a partner didn't come through for us – that time we were sick and didn't get quite as much support as we wanted, for example. But we downplay or forget those everyday moments that help define the relationship. Things like your partner bringing home a pizza, or making coffee for you every morning. If you ever feel disconnected from your partner, or unloved or taken for granted, I urge you to make a list of things that your partner has done for you that signaled love. Below, I share some examples of things Tex and I do for each other that make us feel cared for. Maybe you will recognize yourself in some of these situations.

**Examples of Positive DTR Experiences in My Relationship:**

- Telling me to rest while he kept unpacking boxes at the new house
- Giving up the aisle seat on an airplane
- Getting up quietly and keeping the lights dim so I could keep sleeping
- Making his lunches each day
- Opening doors
- Foot rubs
- Letting me select the paint for the house
- Texting articles that may help with research
- Bringing home three different kinds of cough drops when I was sick

Once you've made your list, feel free to share some of these moments with your partner. **It's important to acknowledge kindness whenever it shows up in a relationship.**

## Love Languages

On our very first date, Tex mentioned he had read a book called *The Five Love Languages* by Gary Chapman and asked me if I had read it. "You've read *The Five Love Languages*?!" I exclaimed. "It's one of my favorite books!" I was excited because understanding your own love language (and that of your partner) is like cracking the code to you and your partner's heart. After reading the book the first time, I suddenly made sense to myself. My previous relationships made sense. My ex. My mother. So many things suddenly clicked.

"What are your two love languages?" I asked. He replied that they were touch and verbal. I couldn't believe it: Tex and I spoke the same love language! It's no wonder our relationship has always felt so easy – we give and receive love in the same way.

If you haven't read *The Five Love Languages* by Gary Chapman, I urge you to check it out. It's a great book for discovering how your partner feels most loved and cared for. "Speaking" your partner's love language has the power to completely transform your relationship.

## Late Bloomers: A Personal Story

Tex and I came to find each other later in life. Sometimes, it makes me a little sad that I lived so many years without him. Being with him gives me so much peace and happiness.

A couple of years before I met Tex, I used to practice visualization techniques to attract the love I wanted. I'd been single for a long time, so it wasn't easy. I imagined myself climbing up a mountain ridge. It was like watching a movie. From a distance, I could see myself climbing, using my hands and feet to scramble over the rocky ridge. Sometimes there was a close-up of pebbles falling, and of my hands on the rock. Then there would be a faraway shot of a figure (me) silhouetted on the ridge and making its way up. It was misty. I climbed by myself, silently and with the summit slipping in and out of view. When I finally reached the top – a small knob of rock with barely enough room for two people – I sat down in relief. "I'm waiting for you", the narrator in my head would say. And I would picture Him climbing the same ridge to join me at the top.

I didn't know what he looked like.

I only felt him, working his way towards me.

That visualization was a great metaphor for the two of us.

We were on separate journeys, moving at different speeds to the same destination. We would meet when we had each climbed our mountain.

And not a minute sooner.

In fact, I'm not sure that my younger self would have dated Tex. The things we were looking for when we were younger were not the same things we looked for in a partner after we did the work on ourselves. We had both suffered heartbreak. We had both experienced failed relationships and subsequent pain. This pain motivated us to read and deeply reflect on ourselves and where things had gone wrong in our previous relationships. We did a lot of soul-searching to understand what we would do differently the next time love found us.

Only then were we ready.

I remember Tex saying to me, “The man you see before you is not the man I was 10 years ago. I’m a better man now”.

And I’m a stronger, happier woman.

Elizabeth Gilbert talks to Oprah about this subject. After a difficult divorce and some soul-searching, she wrote her book *Eat, Pray, Love*. It was during this soul quest that she met José Nuns, the man she would marry a year after her book became a bestseller. Gilbert asks a friend how she “won” this life she now enjoys. Her friend tells her it’s because she blossomed into the kind of person who would attract a man who would treat her as well as she learned to treat herself.

What does soul-searching look like to you?

For a start, it’s the book you’re holding now.

You are doing the work, by reading this book.

You are trying to understand your soul, and your beloved’s. You are trying to find a better and more profound way to love.

Thank you for being part of this journey.

* * *

## HOUSEKEEPING: Love Languages and Appreciation

How’s that Communication coming along? Have you been able to speak your mind, ask for what you want, fulfill requests immediately and show appreciation? Keep practicing.

It's not easy to stay calm and centered and loving in the heat of the moment, but that's what masters of love do.

In the meantime, here are some other communication skills you can practice. They have to do with expressing appreciation in specific ways. As I said earlier in this chapter, kindness, respect, gratitude, and consideration are vital to living together without growing apart.

**Task 1: What makes you feel loved?**

What kind acts has your partner done for you that make you feel loved? For example, was there something you were too tired to do and your partner did it for you? Or did they compromise on an activity to make you happy? Note it in your journal but also bring it up with your partner. Share with them how you felt loved in that moment. Use specific examples.

**Task 2: What makes your partner feel loved?**

Discover what it is that makes your partner appreciate you. Ask your partner if there is something you've done, either in the past or recently, that moved them. That's the stuff you want to do more often. That stuff is like credit in the bank, generating interest. You want to keep adding to that account because chances are high that, one day, you're going to screw up, and it won't matter much because your relationship will have so many positive DTR (Define the Relationship) moments invested in it that a bit of jackassery will be forgiven. (In other words, karma.)

**Task 3: Do the Love Language quiz.**

Visit my website at www.itsnotyouitsus.com/chapterlinks and look for the "Love Language" quiz by Gary Chapman. Each of you should do this quiz on your own, and not discuss it until you've finished it. Once you know each other's love languages, try communicating in your partner's love language, the way that makes *them* feel most loved. Watch how powerful this can be.

For more information about *The Five Love Languages*, visit www.5lovelanguages.com.

**Task 4: Listen to Zig Ziglar share marriage advice from his book *Courtship after Marriage.***

There is A LOT of wisdom packed into this audio clip. Sure, it's old-fashioned and Zig sounds like a preacher, but I guarantee you'll get something of value out of it. Give it 10 minutes – I'm sure you'll be hooked.

BONUS: Listen to it together: fix a hot beverage and cuddle on the couch. Link provided on my website at www.itsnotyouitsus.com/chapterlinks.

## Chapter 4: Love Agreements

*There is a candle in your heart, ready to be kindled. There is a void in your soul, ready to be filled. You feel it, don't you?*

— Rumi

We've talked about the courage it can take to ask for what you want. Perhaps the most courageous conversation of them all is a Love Agreement. Love Agreements are not just about asking for what you want; it's declaring it and writing it down. They are a way for a couple to reach written agreement on the kind of lifestyle they want to live and the behaviors they want to reinforce. Love Agreements are unique to each relationship; some agreements even spell out repercussions for not doing something – for example, not having sex at least once a month, which would allow a partner to find sex elsewhere. (No judging.) If the goal of a relationship is to build your Happily Ever After together, consider a Love Agreement your blueprint for success.

**Guideline #11: It's HOW you love each other that matters. Love Agreements help you figure this out.**

I first heard about Love Agreements about four years ago, when I read David Viscott's 1970s book *How to Live with Another Person*. I came across the idea a second time when I read *Fifty Shades of*

*Gray*. In case you haven't read the book, or seen the movie, I'll fill you in. Basically, the two protagonists draw up a BDSM contract that spells out what sexual acts they are willing to perform together. Some acts are absolutely out of the question, and others are marked off as to be considered. The submissive is also required to see a doctor once a month, go on birth control, eat regularly, work out, etc. The contract is very descriptive, but the thought of writing out exactly what you want in a relationship and from a partner intrigued me. When Tex and I started to date, we made our own. It was short and sweet, and a lot more vanilla. It had things like "Take Sophie on fun and interesting dates", and so on. We were camping and drinking when inspiration hit, so we wrote everything on a scrap of paper using a big felt pen.

As our relationship matured, we made changes to our original Love Agreement; we even used a proper pen.

## What Is a Love Agreement?

Love Agreements are written agreements about what each of you needs to be happy in your relationship – sexually, emotionally, physically, financially. Anything is on the table for discussion, preferably over a bottle of wine because *In vino veritas*, as they say (Latin for "In wine, there is truth").

Allow yourself time to think about yourself. Write down both what you want and need from your relationship with the other person and what you want out of life. After you have a list, go over it carefully, asking yourself about each item. "How much does this mean to me? Do I really need this? How long have I wanted this? Why haven't I gotten this before?" Your partner should be making a list and thinking about it in the same way. When you finally discuss your lists together, don't rush or pretend to understand something you do not. Don't allow your partner to pretend for the sake of pride that something is unimportant to him when you know differently.

*Each of you must look out for the other's rights as well as your own.*

— David Viscott, *How to Live with Another Person*

Love Agreements do several things:

1. They make us more aware of our own (sometimes latent) needs and desires.

2. They let us explore new attitudes and ideas and give us permission to abandon ones that don't work anymore.

3. They're surprisingly sexy conversations.

4. They breathe fresh air into a relationship.

5. They lead to greater intimacy.

Love Agreements can be changed at any time. In fact, they should change, as people mature and gain life experience. Tastes change, people change, and so must the terms and agreements of your union. If you expect your partner to remain the same person year after a year – a perfect fossil of their younger self – then you're in for a big disappointment. After all, what doesn't grow, dies. That's true of plants, people, and relationships.

*A man who views the world the same at fifty as he did at twenty has wasted thirty years of his life.*

— Muhammad Ali

## Changing Your Love Agreement

Updating a Love Agreement makes a couple stronger because it leads to deeper intimacy and greater understanding with every passing year.

Tex and I made our first Love Agreement in Yellowstone National Park, when we decided to be exclusive with each other. We sat at a picnic table and I waited while Tex wrote down a few things that he wanted and then folded the paper so I couldn't see what he had written. I wrote my bit next, and then we unrolled the paper and had a good laugh. Reading things aloud and talking about it was very, very sexy.

Our second Love Agreement came nine months later. I was now living with Tex in the United States, and our relationship had changed. In fact, Tex and I had been feeling a little prickly around each other and I sensed we both needed a little space. Well, we ended up pouring a glass of wine and having a conversation about the need for personal time. That conversation led to Love Agreement #2.

Now we've moved again, to Houston, and we are much closer to his family, which means juggling family time, personal time, and Sophie-and-Tex time. We are also talking about getting married, and a trip to Europe in the fall. As a new chapter begins, I sense Love Agreement #3 is on its way.

Your Love Agreement can be as simple or as detailed as you like. Here's an example of our second Love Agreement, along with the notes I made. We began the conversation by reviewing the previous Love Agreement and deciding what was working/not working for us. We then used this information to craft a new one; it's always good to look back before looking forward.

As you'll probably notice, our Love Agreement focuses on what we want – not on what we don't want. We like to keep it positive. I truly believe that the more positivity you have in your relationship, the more it crowds out the negative.

## Our Second Love Agreement

*CHANGES:*

*Meals – Once a week, we cook a meal and eat together at the dining room table, alternating chefs. One night a week, we also try a new restaurant (Tex's idea).*

*Personal Time – Allow for 10 hours of "personal time" each week (This represents 25% of total free time after work and sleep are factored in.)*

*Sex – Yes, we put a number down. (Let's just say it's important to not let it slip.)*

*Personal hygiene – Tex agreed to manscape once a month. He said he would do this the first of every month.*

*Hobbies – Sailing once a week for him is important. I want more music in our life: in the house, live concerts, etc.*

*Couple time – Tex likes it when I read to him, and I like discussing ideas. We'll keep doing this.*

*SPIRITUAL/ARTISTIC TIME:*

*Volunteering – Tex brought up volunteering once a month to help people who have less.*

*Nature and animals – I need a weekly dose of this. Walking the neighbor's dog, for example, or hiking.*

(After updating our Love Agreement, Tex honored my need for nature in a beautiful way. He found us a place to live in Houston near Buffalo Bayou, which has biking trails and wildflowers.)

> *WHAT'S WORKING:*
>
> *Date night – Keep doing one date night a week and a weekend activity. I love it!*
>
> *Getaways once a month – New York, the mountains, camping, etc. Doesn't have to be expensive. Just want new scenery.*
>
> *Exercise routine – Keep working out together in the morning; we both love it.*
>
> *New things/foods – I need to have new experiences to be happy and so does he, so we will be mindful of this.*

It was a wonderful evening. After this really authentic conversation, we felt very connected and in synch. The prickliness was gone: **we had an understanding and an action plan.**

Tex and I talk all the time, whether it's about the groceries that we need to buy or how we're going to spend the evening. That's communication at a superficial level. When we talk about family or friends or share something interesting on a TED Talk or on NPR (National Public Radio in the United States), that's a deeper conversation. The Love Agreement goes deeper still: it allows us to imagine how we want to live our lives – as individuals and as partners. It's a road map to greater love. Of all the levels of communication, it may be the deepest and most authentic one of all.

*PEARLY WISDOM: Your Love Agreement is highly personal and doesn't need to be shared with others. If you're concerned about the information getting out in a public way, you can do one of two things: 1. Don't write down anything sensitive; 2. Include a confidentiality clause. If the threat of humiliation crosses your mind, you may wish to engage a lawyer. Don't want to use a lawyer? Then adhere to point 1, especially if your Love Agreement is sexual in nature.*

## Putting Together Your Love Agreement

Anything and everything is on the table when it comes to a Love Agreement. Here are some ideas:

- How much quality time you will spend with each other per week
- How much video-game time your partner wants per week
- How much sex you want each week
- Vacations: separate and apart
- How much time to spend with the in-laws
- Churchgoing: Will you go separately or together, and how often?
- Food and nutrition: junk food, alcohol consumption
- Body weight: goal of not putting on more than 20 pounds
- Monogamy
- Pornography
- Personal goals
- Private time
- Boys' night out or girls' night out
- Privacy
- Hygiene
- Division of labor

By creating space for conversations like this, you would be surprised at what bubbles up.

> *A good agreement does not try to change reality but provides for adjusting to the truth as it is and as it changes.*
>
> — David Viscott, *How to Live with Another Person*

The very act of writing this stuff down makes Tex and me take our own – and each other's – desires seriously. More importantly, it holds us accountable. Have I made dinner this week? Whoops! We haven't been on a getaway in a while... better start planning something.

Being taken out on fun dates and sharing new experiences is one of my core needs. To this day, Tex and I plan something fun to do together every week. I actually think he's taken it on as a kind of personal challenge. One weekend we went for lunch – Southern comfort food – in the basement of a church in Washington, DC. This Canadian gal had never eaten fried catfish and collards before! Another time, we went to a drive-in theatre and pigged out on junk food and laughed at the commercials from the 1950s. We've done a scavenger hunt at the Museum of Natural History and been to New York to see a Broadway show. We've gotten tipsy at Whole Foods, and ordered five desserts at a restaurant – just because.

I really do believe that in a healthy relationship, you want to make each other happy and fulfilled. So why not tell your partner exactly what you need to thrive? Better yet, why not write it down?

### Interview with Warren and Betsy Talbot

My friends Warren and Betsy Talbot, co-adventurers over at *Married with Luggage*, are very fond of Love Agreements, which they call "Love Contracts". They wrote about their own life-changing Love Contract in their fabulous book *Married with Luggage: What We Learned about Love by Traveling the World.* Spelling out exactly what each of them needed to be happy led to a big surprise: they both realized they hated living in suburbia and wanted to see more of the world. They ended up quitting their corporate jobs to travel. Several years later, they've settled down – in Spain – with no plans to return to the United States and the corporate world any time soon. And while their Spanish villa is home base, they still get plenty of travel in.

**Q: Would you say that a Love Contract saved your marriage?**

Warren and Betsy: *What the Love Contract did for us was solidify the plans we made to save our marriage. Without the Love Contract, it would be too easy for us to fall back into the same unhealthy habits and routines that got us in trouble in the first place. We wouldn't credit the Love Contract with saving our marriage by itself, but it is glue that binds us to our promises and keeps us on track with the relationship we want to have with each other.*

**Q: You do "Annual Love Contracts". Can you explain why?**

Warren and Betsy: *Our lives have changed dramatically over the years. We aren't the same people as we were when we met. The Annual Love Contract takes this personal growth into consideration, as well as the lifestyle, career, financial, and health changes that occur over time. This annual review and renewal of our relationship allows us to consider where we are, if we like the direction, and to make any minor adjustments to maintain our happiness. We want our relationship to grow and change as we do, and reject the notion that a one-time agreement has enough bandwidth for a lifetime of experiences and challenges.*

**Q: In what ways have your Love Contracts changed over the years?**

Warren and Betsy: *In the early years, we tackled a lot of deeper problems. Now that we've been doing it for a while, the changes are relatively minor. We've aired our major gripes, and the plans we make now tend to be toward growing our life together instead of fixing big issues. There still are challenges, of course, but the focus is largely on the positive now.*

**Q: Is there anything else you would like to add?**

Warren and Betsy: *What we love most about this type of contract is that it is customizable to any couple. You can be as formal or informal as you want, as specific or as broad as you need. It can be a one-time conversation over dinner, a written contract, or a poster of rules to live by that you post on the refrigerator. It's a one-size-fits-all solution because it is so flexible, and any couple that uses it will see how it changes over the years as the relationship becomes more like a team, achieving more lifestyle goals together. We love this kind of thinking – that we're a team striving toward the same goals, working hard to eliminate the negatives in our lives. The longer we live and love like this, the more invincible we feel as a couple.*

Warren and Betsy have a fun podcast on the events that led up to their first Love Contract. You can listen to it by visiting www.itsnotyouitsus.com/chapterlinks and clicking on the link "Betsy and Warren's Love Contract".

* * *

## HOUSEKEEPING: MAKE (a) LOVE (Agreement)

Ready to find out *how* to love each other better? It's time to design YOUR Love Agreement.

**Task 1: Craft a Love Agreement together.**

You don't have to make it perfect. In fact, our first Love Agreement was written on a scrap piece of paper with a felt pen. The point is to get started; you can always modify it later.

What you'll need: Reflection. Honesty. Paper. Pen.

Optional but recommended: Alcohol.

If you need some help to get started, you can download a Love Agreement template at www.itsnotyouitsus.com/chapterlinks.

# Chapter 5: The Division of Labor - Fairness and Respect

*There is nothing especially wonderful about having a spotless home and a cluttered or empty mind. This means that housework, cooking and shopping can be the man's work as well as the woman's. Because tradition has assigned different roles in the past does not mean that they are right for today. Some men need to be protected from stress and some women need to be in open, aggressive competition in the world. The roles each person fills in any relationship should be determined by his abilities and needs, not by society's expectations.*

— David Viscott, *How to Live with Another Person*

## You Don't Need Ovaries to Unload the Dishwasher

No one should be doing certain tasks just because of their genitalia. As if loading and unloading the dishwasher requires ovaries!

If you're falling into certain gender roles when it comes to the division of household chores, ask yourself why. Are both of you working full-time jobs? If one of you is working from home, that still qualifies as a job. It's not 1965 anymore. Women should not expect the majority of housework to fall on them, nor should men expect the dishwasher to unload itself.

### Guideline #12: No one should be doing certain tasks just because of their genitalia.

The purpose of splitting up the chores is to allow each other to do what you prefer to do, and to do this by spoken agreement, not outdated expectations of gender roles. If the woman prefers to do house repairs and the man prefers to cook, then why not adjust your living arrangement to accommodate your talents and inclinations? To make someone do a chore he or she hates, using tradition as an excuse, is a recipe for resentment.

**In fact, one of the three major sources of conflict when living together is the division of labor.** Save yourself the inevitable blowout and agree on who is responsible for which tasks. Even better, get your list of chores in writing and post them on the fridge until these tasks become habits. Then adjust as needs and circumstances change. For your convenience, I have created a list that you can use. Simply visit www.itsnotyouitsus.com/chapterlinks to download it.

I find it interesting that research shows that women who divorce in middle age often thrive post-divorce while the men struggle. Google "Are divorced women happier than divorced men?" and you'll see a ton of literature to support this. In fact, according to the Pew Research Center, a 2014 study shows that previously married women are much less likely than previously married men to say they would like to get married again someday (15% of women compared to 29% of men).[12] This may be due in part to the fact that women are suddenly liberated from the burden of caring for someone else and doing most of the household chores. This automatically frees up energy for more pleasant activities. Head to a yoga retreat, and you'll be amazed by the number of divorced women enjoying their new-found freedom and reconnecting with their chakras.

## Less Housework, More Sex

Would you like a more satisfying sex life? Then split the housework fairly. According to a 2014 article in *The Washington Post*, "Couples who split the housework fairly are the happiest between the sheets. They have the most sex, are the most satisfied with their sex lives, and express the highest level of sexual intimacy".[13] I link to the full article at www.itsnotyouitsus.com/chapterlinks.

While I dislike the expression "Happy wife, happy life", because it sounds as if the woman is holding the man emotional hostage to the happiness of the relationship, let's just agree that BOTH partners need to be able to clock out and relax at some point. I guarantee that the happier you are as individuals, the happier your partnership will be. **Happy *life*, happy wife.**

Disputes over domestic responsibilities like housework and child care are less about tasks and more about fairness and respect. If both of you are working full-time, then it's only fair that you split the chores. If one of you has more free time than the other, it only makes sense that that individual does more around the house. Tex is up at 5:30 a.m. to go to work, and home at 6:15 p.m. You can bet your sweet ass that this work-from-home gal is making his lunch and dinner most of the time. It's not because I'm playing housewife. I do it because a relationship is about teamwork and I have more free time than he does. I'd rather we spend our evenings doing something enjoyable and relaxing. I do it because it's the fair thing to do.

*PEARLY WISDOM: Feminism, at its heart, is about equality and fairness between the sexes, and men can be feminists, too. If you're splitting household duties fairly, you are showing that you support gender equality. Don't consider yourself a feminist? Then just think of it as the fair thing to do.*

## Be a Conscientious Objector

If your partner is doing the lion's share of work around the house, you must step up and offer your help, even if they object. They may object because they think they can do better, and they may be right; they have the benefit of practice. Ask them to show you how they like something done. Do not offer this half-heartedly, to assuage your guilt or sabotage the task in the hope they will release you from future responsibility. They may also refuse help because they view domestic responsibility as a kind of badge of honor or an expression of love. This happens a lot with new couples, but I promise you: it gets old fast. Women are mostly guilty of "wifing up" in the beginning of a relationship, and then becoming resentful as time passes. Coax your partner out of that mindset. **Treat your partner as you would wish to be treated, and your relationship will be better off.**

## Note to Control Freaks

If your partner doesn't do something exactly the way you like it done, tough. He (or she) tried. That might be his first attempt. He can only get better if you let him practice. Thank him. Then the next time you see him doing X, Y or Z, provide kind and gentle correction at the appropriate moment. Practice leads to mastery, if not perfection.

As I've said before, praise and gratitude are valuable currency in a relationship.

> *A burden shared is half a burden.*
>
> — Swedish proverb

## Clutter

Looks like there is a link between clutter and anxiety. A team of researchers at UCLA's Center on Everyday Lives and Families conducted a detailed study on 32 California families and the thousands of objects in their homes. They found a link between the high density of items in a home and high cortisol (the stress hormone) in the female home owners. The more stuff in the house, the more stress. Interestingly, the men didn't seem bothered by the mess. Still, men would do well to pay attention to this fact: if the woman in a man's life is feeling anxious, one of the best things he could do is help declutter and clean the home.

If your garage is so full that you can't park your car in it, take it as a sign that you have too much stuff. If you're like one in 10 American households, and you rent a self-storage unit because you can't fit everything in your home, it's time to downsize, especially if you haven't looked at that stuff in over a year. If you need some inspiration, watch the movie, *Minimalism: A Documentary About the Important Things*.

## Divvy It Up

Some people like to let others do the heavy lifting whenever possible, but a relationship is no excuse to escape chores you would have to do if you were single. Discuss what needs to be done for the proper care and maintenance of your household, find out what tasks each of you prefers to do, and divide up the rest. If you don't do this, you will quickly find your mate becoming more resentful.

For example, Tex likes vacuuming. I think vacuuming sucks. Therefore, he vacuums. We both like grocery shopping, so we do this together. I sweep and wash the floors and recycle. We each clean our own bathrooms. One of us empties the garbage when it's full. Same goes for the dishwasher. When it comes to bed making, the rule is that the last one out of bed makes the bed, but if we both exit the bed at the same time, we make it together. We do our own laundry. He likes to wash the car. The kitchen is mostly my domain.

We've had to talk through all this.

## Use the Tidiness Scale to Reach Agreement

Women may have more of an affinity for a cleaner home, but you two need to agree on an acceptable standard of clean (a 7/10 on weekdays, an 8/10 on the weekends, a 9/10 when guests come over) and follow through on that.

I'm an 8 on the tidiness scale; Tex is a 7. We compromise. He comes up a half-point and I go down a half-point. We meet at around 7.5. If I were a 10 and he a 4, I think cleanliness and tidiness would be constant sore points with us, as we both would feel we were compromising too much for comfort. I would be cleaning all the time and nagging him to do more around the house, and he would be annoyed. Both of us would be bitchy. Being well-matched on many levels, including the most important ones like a willingness to pitch in and hold things to the same standard of cleanliness, makes life a lot simpler and smoother. Which is awesome.

> **Guideline #13: The more polarized you are on things, the more tension there will be in your relationship.**

*PEARLY WISDOM: People talk about the importance of the two Cs – Chemistry and Compatibility – but if you had to choose one over the other in a long-term relationship, which would you choose? I say, choose compatibility. If you're a 9 in compatibility and a 6 on the chemistry scale, you'll be a lot happier than if you're a 6 in compatibility and a 9 in chemistry. Why is this? Because after a couple of years, you may only have sex a couple of times a week. When you're not between the sheets, you have a whole lot of time together, to either spend fighting or enjoying each other's company. And let's be real: a fight can make for great make-up sex in the beginning of a relationship, but too much fighting wears you down eventually. Not many people want to get naked when they're feeling annoyed and resentful. Trust me, when you're well connected and compatible, your relationship hums – in and out of the bedroom*

.

* * *

## HOUSEKEEPING: Divvy Things Up

A lot of couples get into fights about household chores. In fact, most people in relationships overestimate how much they contribute to responsibilities. Well, that's not going to happen to you. Why not? Because you're going to get another chance here to implement the lessons you learned about speaking your mind, asking for what you want, fulfilling requests immediately and showing appreciation. As a special bonus, I provide a list of chores on my website so you can divvy things up fairly. Let's get started.

**Task 1: Settle on a number for your tidiness scale.**

What's an acceptable level of cleanliness you can both agree on during the work week? How about on weekends? When company comes over? Pick a number between 1 and 10 for each of these. It should be a number that is realistic for both of you. (You could add this to your Love Agreement.)

Can you compromise in certain areas? If you can't compromise, why not? A relationship will blow up eventually if it's just one person always getting his or her way.

One of you may have to do more around the house at certain times. Can you live with that without fighting?

**Task 2: Identify the stuff you hate doing.**

Can you swap duties?

**Task 3: Identify skill sets.**

What's the stuff you're good at? Discuss so you can use your different abilities for the benefit of the relationship.

**Task 4: Recognize if you are you falling into certain gender roles or patterns.**

If so, why not swap once in a while, in order to gain an appreciation of each other's tasks and prevent monotony? (I really appreciate it when Tex makes breakfast on the weekends!)

**Task 5: Divvy it up!**

Download a list of chores from my website at www.itsnotyouitsus.com/chapterlinks and take turns initialing a task until all the tasks are assigned. This way, no one is stuck with the crappy chores or burdened with the majority of tasks. Pin this list on the fridge so you are both accountable for your selections.

**Task 6: Get clarity.**

Clarity is queen. Occasionally review your checklist and make changes as needed. Talking about this stuff each week doesn't have to be a big deal; a chat over breakfast should set you up nicely for the week ahead.

## The Division of Labor: A Poll

While researching this book, I sent out the following questions.

## Poll Question

> *Hi, I'm Sophie Winters. I'm doing research for my second book, which is about living together without growing apart. I'm writing a chapter about the division of household chores – things like cleaning, cooking and shopping for groceries – and I want to hear from you. Yup, if the two of you don't discuss and agree upon who will do what around the house, this sort of thing can become a major source of conflict. So, what I want to know is: What is your experience with who does what around the house? Who has the stronger urge to keep the place clean and tidy? Does a messy partner make you feel resentful? Does it impact your sex life or your feelings towards him or her? I am very curious about process and how you resolve these things – or don't! Feel free to answer any or all of these questions. Your contribution will help future couples.*

I asked that only people who were married, or living with someone, respond. Here are some of the responses, mostly from the United States.

Note: Only one man responded. Basically, he said he was grateful that his wife took out the trash, a chore he had loathed since childhood. *Ahem.*

You are about to hear women tell it like they see it.

## Excerpts from the Responses

Note that the following has been edited for readability while preserving the character and meaning of the written responses.

### 1. Rose

*My husband George and I have been married for 12 years. We have three young children. Children have a large impact on division of labor and a to-do list for housework. The mess of two people – dishes, laundry, vacuuming, dusting, scrubbing and grocery shopping – is doubled or tripled when kids enter the picture.*

***In my house the division of labor is lopsided. My husband and I both work, but I do 90% of the housework.*** *This problem stems from two sources. First, when we started living together I had no problem taking care of everything for both of us. Our home at the time was about 900 square feet, we had no kids and we both led busier social lives.* ***By the time we were married and the kids came, I tried to renegotiate this division but was unsuccessful.***

*And the second source was how we grew up. My husband was tended to like a prince by his mom and sisters. They did all domestic chores for him. When he moved out on his own, he took his laundry to the cleaners, ate out or ordered in for meals, and housework was done by his mother.*

*Yes, lack of sharing these daily drudgeries led me to resent my significant other and short-circuited my interest in sex because I am always behind the eight ball when it comes to keeping the house clean and getting my chores done.*

**2. Helen**

*I'm a 53-year-old female and my husband is a 56-year-old male. We grew up in households where the mom didn't work so she did most of the housework. When we got married (26 years ago) I made it clear that things would be different.* ***The first thing we did was hire someone to clean our home, because I didn't want to do it. I worked both day and evening shifts and weekends.***

*I love cooking, so I enjoy coming home and cooking, but I have a one-hour commute. So, I call him and tell him things he can do to help me get started. He also does his own laundry and will do sheets and towels too. He handles most of the yard work, although I will periodically pull weeds or deadhead flowers.*

***We've got a good system – if something needs to get done, it's both our responsibilities.*** *I also think the key is doing something for the other person so that you appreciate him/her. I'll pick up items that I know my husband needs for his lunch without him asking. Or, I take care of all the bills and all the finances. He washes my car and takes care of the car maintenance, since that's not something I like to do.*

*It's a work in progress – even after 26 years.*

**3. Diana**

*When my husband and I moved in together, we were both working. Initially, he was content to allow me to do the majority of household chores (since it was my house we were moving forward in). However, I decided to make a list of all the chores around the house, and the time it took to perform each job on a weekly basis. I presented the list to him, and asked him to choose which chores he wanted. This included everything from mowing the lawn, to cleaning the house, the laundry, cooking, and doing the dishes.*

***Once we both knew and understood our expectations around the household, everything went smoothly.*** *I feel that communication is the cornerstone to any good relationship, including discussions regarding finances, religion, raising children, and household chores.* ***No surprises equates with no arguments.***

**4. Beth**

*My husband and I were best friends for 13 years before marriage and had previously lived together. We were in different states when we decided to get married and made a specific decision to discuss these very issues before marriage and combining our lives, knowing there was a specific issue with clutter that needed to be addressed.* ***Clutter, piles, and messes make me edgy, nervous, and unable to relax. My husband, on the other hand, hardly notices them.***

*I work almost two hours away from home and he works mostly out of the home, so we have to be careful that neither one of us feels taken advantage of or disrespected. In some cases, it has required changes to lifestyle or home to maintain that balance. We would rather have all tile and wood floors than disagree over floor care. If one of us is feeling resentful, we discuss how to change things.*

***We maintain a list on the refrigerator of things that need to be done daily, weekly, biweekly, and monthly.*** *This is mostly a reminder, not a hard rule or something we check religiously. Some items have been taken over wholly by one or the other of us, simply based on our care of the other. I have immune system issues, so he took the cat litter box as his own without me asking. By the same token, he does not enjoy financial or organizational problems, so I handle finances and scheduling and make the decisions for major expenditures. Overall, this is a delicate balance and we are very aware of the risks involved. I was previously* *married and the household tasks were expected to be mine and the financial tasks his, and it was a major issue. We have made a conscious decision to be aware of our communication and how we treat each other's skills.* ***It is a constantly shifting balance that is critical to our marriage.***

**5. Lisa**

*Both my husband and I work hard and believe that our hard work translates into our home. Our home is one of our largest assets, and therefore taking care of it is important to both of us. In our home, my husband and I have strategies that help us manage the household chores, but keeping the house clean and tidy is definitely more important to me.*

*We used to argue over the hours invested into cleaning and the number of chores each of us performed, and then* ***I started realizing that cleaning was just not that important to my husband and that his level of dirty was not at my level of dirty.*** *Trying to remember all the activities needed to maintain our home was becoming more difficult as both of us needed to travel more for our careers. We realized that we needed a better system to get us on the same page.* ***Once a week we have a quick 30-minute meeting*** *to go over all the personal tasks, finances, chores, and other activities to make sure we are both on the same page with our personal life. This also helps define who is doing what, and basically the habits are formed. My husband takes responsibility for our sprinkler systems and our pool, while I focus on the actual landscaping and the inside of our home. I also make the cars my husband's responsibility, which works because he actually loves cars. I love to cook, so dinners are generally cooked by me, and my husband assists with the cleanup. Now, we don't have any more arguments about cleaning.*

## Seven Takeaways on the Division of Labor

I loved reading these shared stories, and I got quite a few takeaways from them. How about you? For me, these were:

1. Resentment builds, and sex life and intimacy suffer, when the woman feels unduly burdened with the chores.

2. The lack of a fair and equitable division of labor is a major source of tension in couples. Often, the woman must advocate for change.

3. People have different ideas about "clean" and what it takes to run a household.

4. Arguments can be avoided with simple checklists and agreements about household responsibilities. (Notice how it all comes back to healthy, goal-oriented communication and asking for what you want?)

5. It's important to recognize what each of you does. Some chores are not so obvious, like banking or washing the car or gardening, but these are time-consuming activities that bring value to the relationship.

6. Adherence to outdated notions about gender roles and what qualifies as "woman's work" or "man's work" puts stress on relationships and often leads to unhappiness.

7. If you both hate to do a certain task, free yourself from it and hire someone else to do it if possible. Who says money can't buy happiness?

# Chapter 6: Hygiene - Behind Closed Doors

*Tolerate no uncleanliness in body, clothes, or habitation.*

— Benjamin Franklin

When you first started dating, you probably put more of an effort into your appearance. You were trying to "attract" each other, and you were very conscious of what you wore, how you smelled and how you carried yourself. Once you started living together, things probably slid a little. This is entirely normal as couples become more relaxed around each other. But just how far downhill have things slid? Be honest: have you stopped trying to "attract" each other? According to a survey of 22,619 men and women in long-term relationships, "Poor hygiene was the factor most frequently cited as reducing initial attraction"[14] by both men (84 percent) and women (94 percent). And 88% of respondents said that sexual attraction is critical to a successful marriage. Therefore, keeping yourself sexually attractive to your partner is as simple as keeping yourself well-groomed. Here's a refresher on how to stay desirable.

## Bathroom Rituals

In the beginning, you were a bit of a mystery to your man or woman. He didn't watch you shave your legs or clip your toenails – you just showed up with pretty feet. She didn't have to smell your bathroom smells, or watch you scratch your balls. Now that you're living together, it's harder to keep the mystery going, but you really must try. Keeping some of your beauty rituals mysterious means you get to keep your allure.

So how do you go about keeping your allure?

Number one: Close the bathroom door.

This is the single most important thing you can do.

Try to have separate bathrooms.

And if you can't have separate bathrooms:

- Close the door when you're using the toilet.
- Keep the door closed for personal grooming.
- Keep the sink, toilet, and shower clean of hair and nail clippings.
- Keep your things in a separate area in the bathroom.
- Have an air freshener handy, for both your sakes.
- Keep dirty clothes separate and have separate laundry baskets.
- Empty the garbage regularly.

As reader Peggy says, when it comes to personal hygiene, "Discretion is the better part of valor. Men know that there are areas of your life that they don't need or want to be included in."

Unfortunately, we live in a world of TMI. Do you think Beyoncé brags when she has a massive bowel movement? Not everything needs to be shared. Nor should it be.

This goes for the men too.

The male equivalent of allure would be charm or appeal. There's a bit of an art to it. Mostly it's about holding certain information back.

Bowel movements, farts, belches – some people think these things are funny. Especially men. But let me ask you this: would you have shared this stuff when you were courting? Why not? Because it's gross; that's why!

Number two – and this is for the women – don't share the details of your "lady day". He really doesn't need or want to hear when you're having a heavy-flow day. Nor should he be exposed to the evidence.

> **Guideline #14: Don't mistake sharing *everything* for true intimacy.**

## Put Some Effort In

Ladies: Put some effort into how you look, in and out of the house. Don't save the pretty for other people. When you were dating, you probably made an effort to look your best. Don't let yourself slip away.

Men: That goes for you too. Some women have no problem dating cavemen, but not many.

> **Guideline #15: Your appearance matters to your partner.**

In my first book, I wrote a section called "The 8 Secrets to Understanding Men". Here's one of them: "Your appearance matters more than he'll admit". A few of my male readers also weighed in.

> *Sophie: You know that thrill you get from seeing your guy get all dressed up? Your guy feels exactly the same way when you make an effort to look good. He cares about how you look. He wants to show you off. It*

*gives him status with other men to have an attractive woman at his side. It makes him feel powerful. It feeds his ego. When you stop trying to attract him and impress him, it kills him inside. When you gain weight, and wear stretch pants and don't bother with your hair or makeup, it makes him feel less loved. Put some effort into your appearance – around the house and when you go out – and watch him light up.*

*Caesar: BOOM! Yup.*

*Brent: I would agree. I smile or smirk when I see other men check out my wife. I love it when men tell me how beautiful my wife is. Is that about possessiveness and ego? Probably. I didn't marry her for her looks, but it certainly did help get my attention.*

*Robert: Appearance does matter. Mary and I both don't dress up often. Just the other night she was dressed to the nines for a banquet. I remember vividly my sense of jealousy over the men who would have more time to admire her beauty than I would.*

Although *The Cha Cha Club Dating Man-ifesto* was written for women, the advice still applies to men: **Your appearance matters to your partner.**

I'll confess, I've been guilty of letting it slip. Sometimes, I just feel like being comfy – especially when I've put on some pounds and the jeans are a little tight. But when I do make an effort, it's appreciated. My man notices, and I notice him noticing. He tells me I'm beautiful every day, but I certainly see his eyes light up and his gaze linger when I put in a little more effort.

Sure, you don't always have to get dressed up. You're home and you deserve to relax. You shouldn't always have to put on a show for each other. Maybe you just want to chill out in sweatpants and a T-shirt at home, but please, put in some effort when it comes to hygiene and personal grooming. Don't wear stained and dirty clothing. Find a cute T-shirt or hoodie that flatters you. You can be comfy and still look good.

Like most men, Tex loves a sporty look, but he also loves a skirt. I have one that is long and comfortable and it looks so much better than sweatpants around the house. In fact, it's probably comfier than 99% of the things I own – and it's pretty. Never underestimate the power of pretty.

*PEARLY WISDOM: When Eva Mendez said that sweatpants were the number one reason for divorce, people flipped in social media. (Proof that very few people have a sense of humor on the Internet.) Oh, how we love to be righteously indignant! How shallow! How superficial! As if marriage was that simple! While she hastened to say it was a joke, I think I understood what she meant. Sweatpants are a symbol of how much people value their marriage and themselves. How willing we are to continually work at things. If you once cared about your appearance by dressing well and working out, and this preening helped you to attract a mate, and then you slipped into a "I don't give a crap, take me as I am", kind of attitude after marriage, well, you've kind of sold your partner a false bill of goods. Nothing says, "I've given up", or "The romance stops here", like the North American "marriage uniform" of soiled T-shirts and stretchy pants or boxers. Put a little effort into your appearance, and watch your partner light up. And – trust me on this – YOU will feel better about yourself when you spend a little time on your looks.*

I love my man in a clean, snug T-shirt and jeans. Why not ask each other what sort of outfits turn each other on?

The most important takeaways for both of you: clean clothing, good hygiene and some personal grooming go a long way. You can stay attractive just by taking care of yourself and having a little pride in your appearance. No plastic surgery or major gym time needed.

## Daily Habits

People may have different standards when it comes to basic hygiene, but here are some daily habits to consider:

### Washing

I used to shower in the morning before work, usually every couple of days. It helped me wake up and it was how I was raised, so I never gave it much thought. Now I have a warm bath before bed each night, and it helps me sleep. But that isn't the only reason I've switched my schedule.

I first became accustomed to the habit of nightly bathing when I lived in Japan, because that is what Japanese people do. It struck me as a strange ritual at first, but that's only because it was the opposite of what most people in North America do (shower in the morning). And really, bathing or showering before bed makes more sense. You wash, and then you slide your night clothes onto clean skin. Your freshly washed body lies down in a clean bed. When you shower in the morning, you carry the debris and germs from an entire day – the gym, the subway, the office – into your clothes and bed and into the arms of your lover. Your pajamas and sheets get dirtier and dirtier. It's kind of gross when you think about it.

There's also another reason why I wash before bed: my relationship.

Those 15 minutes of lying together before falling asleep may be one of our most intimate moments of the day. It's nice to smell good for each other as we hold each other close. "Your hair smells so good", Tex will say. Or, "Mmmm, you smell delicious", when I wear the coconut-scented body lotion that he adores. Smelling good for each other is important. Smelling bad is a sure-fire way to kill the mood.

Some people don't wash their bodies every day, and their partner is fine with that. But sometimes that's only because they don't know any better and don't know what they're missing.

**Your Kisser**

Kissing isn't fun if one of you has stinky breath. You probably brush your teeth first thing in the morning and at night, but if you care about your dental health and breath, you may also want to floss and use a tongue brush every day. Mouthwash is not as important as brushing and flossing every day. In fact, studies have shown that the alcohol in mouthwash can dry out your mouth and contribute to bad breath. If you have a problem with the floss getting stuck between your teeth, look for dental tape. It glides in and out much more easily.

Also, have some gum or breath mints handy and throw them into your mouth before you come home to kiss your loved ones or head into a business meeting. It's a temporary cover for bad breath, but one that is appreciated.

If you want to keep your lips looking good, gently brush them with your toothbrush each night to ex-foliate them, then smear on some coconut oil or moisturizer before bed. Products containing coconut oil, olive oil, beeswax or cocoa butter seal in moisture and don't come with the health risks associated with petroleum jelly products.

## Hands

With all the nail salons around, it's clear that women care more about their nails than men do. Still, if you're a man and reading this, consider your hands. In fact, have a look at them right now. Are your hands and nails clean? Are the nails trimmed? How are the cuticles? Nails – especially toenails – should be clean and trim to prevent snagging your lover in bed. A file isn't a bad idea, either, or hand lotion. Look for products containing natural ingredients like shea butter.

If you have calluses, you can keep them to a minimum by gently running a razor over them in the shower. A few strokes should do it. After a week, you'll see and feel a noticeable difference. Tex and I both have calluses from lifting weights, and he taught me this trick – it works like a charm.

## Hair

Short or long, the most attractive thing about hair is that it's clean, styled and healthy-looking.

Now, some women love beards and moustaches; I'm not one of them. When I first met Tex, he had a beard. I think this may have been the reason I was not super-attracted to him in the beginning. He shaved on date number two, and it made a huge difference in his looks – at least to me.

Tex and I negotiated very early on that he would shave for my sake – and probably his too, as he'd rather turn me on than off. But as on most things, we compromised: Tex takes weekends off from shaving and I thought that was fair, because it's kind of a pain in the ass to shave all the time. We also agreed to a few more conditions. He always shaves on date nights, even if it's the weekend, but he lets it grow when we're on vacation. The funny thing is, now that he's in the habit of shaving, he prefers the clean look and he notices it's better for his skin. Shaving has become voluntary rather than obligatory.

Whenever I don't want to shave my legs, I think about Tex shaving his face each morning and I suck it up. Just as I love how soft his face is to kiss, he loves how soft my legs feel. **Being in a relationship means doing the little things to please your partner.**

While we're on the subject, you may want to talk about other kinds of hair. The "down there" kind. Some people like things neatly trimmed, while others like a landing strip. Some people like the genitals shaved bare, and others like a '70s-style bush. If you haven't talked about it, now is a good time to discuss your wants and desires. I remember reading about a couple who had been married for a very long time, and how he enjoyed going down on her but hated all the bush he had to get past, especially the hair in his teeth. Years of muff diving and picking out pubic hair, and he had never discussed it with her and didn't even know how. Talking – it seems like a simple fix for most problems.

*PEARLY WISDOM: Asking your partner to shave their pubes doesn't make you a perv; it just makes you someone with a reasonable request. I know a few women who feel squeamish about the idea since it makes them think their guy is into prepubescent girls, but I assure you, that is not the case for the majority of men. For a lot of women, shaving/trimming themselves down there is just "cleaner" and less smelly. Think of it as the female beard. Some folks just prefer things clean-shaven.*

In my opinion, what happens between two consenting adults behind closed doors is their business, as long as no one is hurt or coerced into doing something reprehensible to them. A relationship is all about having hard and soft limits, and being willing to explore those limits together in a sexy, safe way.

### What's That Smell?

Farting is normal; apparently, we fart 15–20 times a day, and more if we eat certain foods (which should probably be avoided for intimacy's sake). We tend to fart more in our sleep because the sphincter relaxes and we're not really aware of passing gas, so we can't be blamed. But people who proudly fart in front of others – or belch – are being disgusting, in my opinion.

> *My ex has severe digestion issues, yet he made no effort to conceal his horrible gas. I actually burst into tears once after he farted, because I felt that having asked him 100 times not to do it and he still did, it was a clear indicator that he didn't respect me enough to make an effort.*
>
> — Melanie

> **Guideline #16: Being in a relationship means doing the little things to please your partner.**

Excessive gas and super-smelly farts can signal poor digestion, food allergies, infection, an ulcer, or a condition such as irritable bowel syndrome. Basically, the plumbing isn't working and you should find out why. You may have a food intolerance to things like dairy. In fact, it's believed that MOST people are lactose-intolerant. If you're of African, South American or Far East Asian descent, you are 75%, 85% and 95%, respectively, more likely to be lactose-intolerant than those of Western European descent.

If you're like me, you may have problems digesting vegetables from the cabbage family, such as cauliflower and broccoli. If you get bloated and gassy from certain foods, try switching to organic versions. Amazingly, I could consume broccoli with ease in Ecuador (possibly because they have a constitutional ban on genetically modified foods or possibly because they use different pesticides). I can't eat the normal stuff without stinking up a room, so I avoid it a lot of the time. Experiment. If you still have issues with organic foods, try eliminating suspicious items completely from your diet for 21 days. Do the smells go away? Do you have less bloating and flatulence? This is proof your body is better off without these items in your diet. Fix your gut, and your health will improve. In fact, you may find that your skin is clearer and that your mood and energy are better off as well.

*PEARLY WISDOM: It's now believed that more than 70% of our immune system is related to our gut health. As Hippocrates said 2,000 years ago, "Let food be thy medicine". Popping pills doesn't necessarily "fix" the root cause of digestion issues; it only makes the symptoms you experience more bearable.*

Often, we accept unpleasant situations because we have no idea how to fix them. Don't become complacent. Almost everything is fixable.

**Eau de Man**

There's a difference between smelling like a man and smelling like a bum. Have you ever travelled to a developing country where people don't use deodorant? Yeah. The smell is so thick, it's overpowering. Ever camped for a few days without showering? Kinda like that.

Steve Jobs used to go without bathing for several days, sometimes weeks. He thought that he was special and that his fruit-based diet kept him from smelling, but his co-workers could barely stomach the stench. Amazingly, no one spoke up. Don't be Steve Jobs.

Shower and use deodorant. Your co-workers will be delighted. Your lover will be relieved.

*PEARLY WISDOM: Disgust is also known as revulsion, which Charles Darwin described as "a basic biological motivational system" to protect us from harm. When we gag from a strong smell, we may be trying to protect ourselves from bacteria and illness. This can be instinctual or culturally conditioned.*

**Cologne/Perfume**

Have you ever been assaulted by the smell of someone wearing too much perfume or cologne? It's a tricky thing to get right. As people wear a scent over time, they become desensitized and tend to slather more and more on. Or they use a good smell to cover up a bad smell, which is never a good idea.

Here's some advice: bathe regularly, wear deodorant and err on the side of too little cologne/perfume. People with fragrance allergies can smell things at lower levels than others, and a strong scent in a closed environment can trigger hostility along with allergic reactions. If people are scowling or sneezing around you, it's a sure sign you're wearing too much scent.

You don't want to apply a fragrance to every pulse point. One or two pulse points should suffice: neck and wrists, for example. Keep it subtle. You may wish to buy a couple of scents – one for day use and one for evening. You don't need to wear it all the time, either.

If you're already using a scent, ask a few people for their opinions on whether you smell too strong.

Tex has two colognes that I adore, and he wears them for different occasions. I'm sensitive to a lot of fragrances, so it's harder to find something I can wear. If you're like me, know that it is possible to find an aromatic oil or perfume that doesn't make you sneeze and stuff up. Usually it's the highly floral ones that cause the most problems, so look for a citrusy, single-note scent that is uncomplicated and easier on the nose. Personally, I like to wear Lavanila Pink Grapefruit. It's a soft fragrance that doesn't make me sneeze, and I get nice compliments on it.

### Guideline #17: Smelling nice. It's not just for first dates.

My Facebook page is where I interact with readers the most, and exchange ideas. So, I asked them the following question: "Fill in the blank: You know you've given up on your relationship when you..." These were some of the responses:

- Stop grooming down there. Anywhere below the neck, in my opinion.

- Are wearing curlers while watching TV!

- Leave the door open to do anything involving a specialized hand tool, like tweezers or a razor. Obviously, blowing out your hair doesn't count, because you can see that happen at the mall.

- Squeeze anything around each other. Not entirely sure why, but men seem to think that popping their zits in front of me is OK.

- Go to the bathroom with the door open.

- Farting should never be acceptable. Ever.

- A friend of mine said her husband stopped brushing his teeth for a couple of days at a time. I don't think anything says you've given up quite like trench mouth.

- Clip your toenails in a common area (bad enough) and then leave the clippings out, using the excuse "I'll clean them up later". Inexcusable. This is personal grooming that should be confined to the bathroom, and there should not be any evidence left behind.

- Spit in the shower and don't clean up afterwards.

- Clip toenails and drop them behind the couch for the wife to find when pulling out the couch to vacuum. True story! Not my story. And not surprisingly, this one didn't end well...

Some of these responses made me cringe, but others made me shrug and think, "That's not so bad". We all have different thresholds. Wearing curlers around the house is totally acceptable for some couples. Talk it over so you're not inadvertently turning each other off. Some things are cultural or boil down to how we were raised. For example, blowing your nose in front of others is considered disgusting in Japan, and I find it hard to take at a dinner table when people are eating. Find out what works for you and your relationship so that you don't lose respect and attraction for each other.

* * *

**HOUSEKEEPING: Rev up the Attraction Factor**

When you were in the first throes of love, all of your senses were alive with the sight, smell, taste, touch, and sound of your lover. How many cylinders is your relationship firing on now? This should rev it up:

**Task 1: Bring back a little mystery into the relationship.**

Keep the door closed when you're using the bathroom.

**Task 2: Keep the bathroom free of human debris.**

Hair around the sink, pee on the floor, toenail clippings and used tissues… 'nuff said.

**Task 3: Bathe or shower before bed.**

Talk about bathing and showering daily, and possibly doing this before bed for a fresher experience.

**Task 4: Smell good.**

Find a skin lotion you both think is dee-lish. Buy it. Try it. Wear it to bed.

**Task 5: Hair and pubes.**

What do you like? Bushy or trimmed? Why not try something new for each other? Scandalous, I know.

**Task 6: Shop for a new scent together.**

Make it a date! Find a scent you both enjoy; after all, you're going to be smelling a lot of each other over the years.

**Task 7: Make an effort to look nice around the house.**

That means hair, makeup, clothes, shaving, whatever. You'll also feel better about yourself.

**Task 8: Discuss this chapter together.**

Is there anything not covered that you would like to change? Why not create some ground rules around farting or personal grooming? One reader writes:

> *We have clear farting rules. Not while someone is eating (like snacking during TV, obviously it never happens at the table). Never on the same piece of furniture. Not while touching. If you have to in the car, and you will, then give notice and roll down the window. If you know it's going to be a rough night, offer to sleep in the other room – if we're both suffering we just crack the window and turn on the ceiling fan. Otherwise, we come up with creative ways to blame it on something else, or if it's really loud, "Wow! D'you hear that? Pretty sure it was me." Farting is the final frontier of intimacy; if you can laugh at each other while respecting boundaries, your relationship has staying power.*
>
> — Peggy

**Guideline #18: Never stop courting each other.**

# Chapter 7: Money, It's a Kick (in the Ass)

*Too many people spend money they haven't earned, to buy things they don't want, to impress people that they don't like.*

— Will Rogers

## Why Is It So Hard to Talk about Money?

For a lot of people and cultures, money represents power, status, and success. Not having it, or enough of it, can make people feel like failures: very often, it is tied to a person's sense of self-worth. Discussing money problems is painful because it brings up our deepest fears, insecurities, and frustrations. In one survey polling 2,000 American men and women, **money was the most common conflict for couples.** Think about that for a second. Money is a bigger issue for couples than sex, children, or in-laws.[15]

When you're living together, you can't avoid discussions about money, because it's what puts the roof over your head, food in your mouth and gas in the car. It's what pays for school, vacations, and dreams. It's ever-present, and one of the hardest things to talk about.

*PEARLY WISDOM: Many people spend beyond their means and purchase cars and houses they can't afford, because they want to impress others and show the world – and themselves – they've "made it" in life. They may even be fooling themselves into thinking they've made it, while racking up huge credit card debt. When you're single, you can live in denial for quite a while; after all, it's a "party of one". When you're in a relationship, you've got someone else to write you a reality check.*

You must talk about money in your relationship. This means honestly addressing things like joint debt, living wills and other grown-up stuff. Listen, I know this stuff is difficult. Tex and I didn't have the money talk – what he made, what I made, and how much we each had in savings versus debts – until I moved to the U.S. with him. It just felt uncomfortable bringing it up when we were still testing the waters. But as time went on, I got more uncomfortable not knowing the status of our financial situation and future. So rather than dancing around the issue and find out bits and pieces over time, I asked him point-blank what he made, what he paid in child support each month, total outgoing expenses, and investments – all of it. It wasn't an easy conversation, but he answered all my questions. We were walking down the street:

> *Me: "Is there anything else?" I asked.*
>
> *Tex: "No, that's everything." He took a deep breath and exhaled.*
>
> *Me: "Are you okay?"*
>
> *Tex: "That was hard. I never talk about money."*
>
> *I nodded. "Thank you."*

It wasn't that he had anything to hide; it's just that he holds those cards close to his chest. Talking about money was a serious milestone in our relationship.

*PEARLY WISDOM: You know the joke: "I asked my trainer at the gym what machine I should use to impress beautiful women. He pointed outside and said, 'The ATM machine.'" It's a horrible joke, but it underscores an important point: money IS security for a lot of people, and women especially crave a feeling of security in a relationship. At the heart of it, I think, is that women crave feeling safe with a man. Money is one way for them to feel safe. Sure, some women want designer handbags and other frivolities, but fundamentally, I think most women want to feel that their welfare and that of their children will be provided for. It's almost instinctual: My man is a good hunter/provider... We won't starve... My children and I will flourish... And because many women earn less than men, especially if they have children, they are more vulnerable in this world. A man with money helps them feel safe.*

## The Money Talk

Some people are savers, and some people are spenders. Some people respect money, and some people only respect what it can buy them. **The more polarized your attitudes are about money, the more tension this will create in a relationship.** If you like to have "nice things" and your spouse is more restrained in their purchases, it can cause disagreements.

If both of you are savers, you're probably going to have fewer arguments about money, but if you're both spenders, beware! You might be risking your financial future. You need to prepare for misfortune, because when things are good, no one can imagine harder times. And yet, harder times always come.

Maybe your partner loses their job. A relative has a health crisis. Your investments collapse. The value of your property tanks. Your Pension Plan or 401K dries up. **Enjoy your years of plenty, but put aside for leaner times.** How much and how you do this is for you to determine as a couple.

## An Eye-opener

Tex and I volunteer with an organization that delivers groceries to isolated and impoverished seniors living in the inner city. I remember the first day I got the list of seniors we would be visiting. The names were 90% female. I felt a wave of sadness wash over me as I read the names: so many widows living in poverty. Here's a diary entry from that first day:

> *Spent half a day volunteering, dropping off groceries to isolated seniors in inner-city Washington, D.C.. First, we met with 40 other volunteers at a church, where we bagged and loaded hundreds of groceries. After loading all the groceries, we split up to deliver the food.*
>
> *Tex and I went to some project-like housing and people were very welcoming and grateful for the groceries and human contact. Some of the seniors are in rough shape, health-wise, and you could see the poverty in their small apartments. Most of the dwellings were bursting with possessions, and I wondered if people were hoarding or holding onto things out of fear of scarcity or just plain sentiment. In many of the apartments, things were piled haphazardly on chairs and the floor so there was hardly a clutter-free surface. Some places were very dark, and the blinds had been pulled down and a few seniors greeted us in their pajamas at noon. It seemed a bit dismal. The building was also a bit rough, with some kids selling drugs in the stairwell and the smell of urine in the hallway. We were told to stay together (there were three of us – me, Tex and another fellow). We knocked on doors and dropped off a bag of food to help folks make it to the end of the month. Many of these seniors are widows. Without these groceries, some of these seniors would be faced*

> *with tough decisions, like going without food to pay for meds, or shutting off the electricity. With so many elderly females on our list, it made me think about couples who start a life together, rarely considering that the wife may outlive her husband by twenty years and how they may not save enough money for her to survive financially. Our groceries contained rice and beans and a few tinned items, plus grits and a block of Velveeta-like cheese – how long would that last? Does anyone really imagine their final days like this?*

In his book, *MONEY – Master the Game: 7 Simple Steps to Financial Freedom*, Tony Robbins says that half of married couples will have at least one spouse who will live to the age of 92. That's a lot of retirement to plan for.

## Twenty Questions Couples Should Ask before Moving in Together

Here are 20 questions to ask each other, and I recommend you do this before moving in together. If your relationship is new, questions 11 through 20 may feel too personal. Feel free to ask them, but also respect that your partner may be uncomfortable answering all of them now. I recommend starting with questions 1 through 10, and finishing the rest later. If you're engaged, or have been living together for at least six months, this is a conversation you need to have, stat! Set aside time to answer each of these in honest detail. Let no stone be left unturned!

Questions 1–10 are light questions you should have no problems discussing. Questions 11–20 are more probing.

1. What does money symbolize to you? Power? Status? Freedom? Security?

*Note: The reverse of these things reveals your hidden fears about not having enough money. For example, if money makes you feel secure, not having enough will make you feel insecure. This could be the underlying emotion that gets triggered when you're arguing about money. It's also a good insight into your partner's money personality.*

2. Would you rather spend money on things or experiences?

3. Would you rather spend money now and enjoy the present, or save for the future so you can retire early and enjoy a comfortable life later?

4. What kind of house or neighborhood do you want to live in three years from now?

5. What kind of car do you want to drive? Would you be okay with a used car?

6. Are brand names and designer labels important to you?

*Note: Many people feel that luxury items convey status; they get a boost from knowing that others notice what they're wearing or driving.*

7. Have you ever been unemployed? For how long? What happened?

8. What were your parents like with money? What did you learn from them?

*Generally, our parents have a huge influence over our views on money.*

9. What would you do with a million dollars?

   *If a person just talks about what they would spend it on, you have a good insight into their money personality. If they describe spending some, investing some and giving some away, it's a good sign.*

10. Would you be willing to work a job you hate to support the household if your partner couldn't work? How do you feel about the woman being the main breadwinner or making more than the man?

**More-probing questions:**

11. How much do you make? Do you feel secure about your job?

12. How much debt do you currently have in credit cards, line of credit, loans, etc.?

13. What are your total savings?

14. Do you have any assets?

15. Do you have any ongoing financial obligations, such as investments, charities, alimony, legal settlements, child custody or unofficial debts? When do those end?

16. Do you find it easy to save money? Do you have an automated savings plan?

17. Do you receive a monthly allowance, royalties, or other sources of income?

18. What is your credit score like? Look up and share your scores with one another.

19. What's your five-year money plan? Do you plan to start a business or anything that will require a substantial capital investment? How do you plan to get the start-up money?

20. Do you have a retirement plan? Health insurance policies?

Finally, you need to discuss how you are going to spend money as a couple.

Did you know that the late Sam Walton, founder of Wal-Mart and one of the richest men in America drove around Arkansas in an old pick-up? Isn't life funny? People without money acting like they have it, and people with money acting like they don't. I've had some very rich acquaintances who regularly wear jeans and T-shirts, and you would never know they owned their own private plane or TV station or group of hotels. And then I've had friends who look like a million dollars, with the expensive shoes and handbags and cars, but are deeply in debt. Because of this, I am always suspicious of glitter. A conversation about money helps cut through the pretentions.

### Guideline #19: Treat your personal finances like a business; beware of bad investments.

*When I was dating my ex of seven years and he bought his house (we had been together six years already), I refused to put my name on the mortgage even though he kept saying if I did, we could get a more expensive house. I knew that if I signed my name on that paper, I would be tied to him and I just couldn't do that to myself.*

> *I made the mistake once of getting a cell phone in my name that my boyfriend at the time used. Then when we broke up, I found out the bill was over $300 (the nice debt collector informed me of that). I had zero money and was moving back in with my parents, and they ended up paying it for me. I learned the hard way from that one.*
>
> *Other than that, I've never had a joint account (and never will) and I wouldn't put my name on a mortgage with somebody unless we were married. I wouldn't put my name on anything for anybody, if I wasn't either using it myself or able to make any and all payments on my own. I watch Judge Judy – I know exactly what happens if you do these things.*
>
> — Kass

## How to Handle Expenses

Once you move in together, your financial futures become intertwined. How do you expect to handle expenses in your relationship?

If you're already living with someone, have you worked out an agreement for rent, bills, groceries, and personal spending? Will you maintain separate bank accounts but have one joint account that the bills come out of?

*PEARLY WISDOM: When you open a joint bank account, both of you have access to the funds in it. If things go south in your relationship, your partner could potentially withdraw all the funds and leave you high and dry. The bank won't help you get it back. Your partner can also leave you on the hook for any bills in both your names. For example, if you opened a joint utility account, have a shared cellphone plan, or leased an apartment or vehicle together, you are now 100% responsible for any bills that he or she can't pay. Your relationship might be over, but those bills could haunt you for years.*

Some of my married friends keep separate bank accounts but share one joint account that they each contribute to, for the mortgage/rent and household expenses to come out of. Having their own accounts and spending money allows them to build personal credit scores and maintain some independence. They can buy things for themselves (up to a mutually agreed-upon limit) without having to discuss the purchases with their partner.

The point is, they have a plan that works for them.

So how do you determine how much each of you pays for joint expenses? Here are some scenarios.

### 1. A 50–50 Split

Some couples split the mortgage and household expenses straight down the middle, and whatever is left over they keep for themselves. This seems more like a roommate thing, and unfortunately, these couples often end up nickel-and-diming everything. "You owe me $12.81 for the groceries", can feel unromantic and even petty. When you're going 50–50, what happens to date night? What happens to joint savings and investments? Plans for retirement, and travel? Who pays for upgrades and repairs to the home? What happens if one of you loses their job or wants to go to school – do you borrow from your partner?

*PEARLY WISDOM: If you're too afraid to talk about your financial future, is it because you don't see a future? If you're not talking about money because you're worried about starting an argument, you have communication problems, not money problems.*

**Guideline #20: Money problems in a relationship are often communication problems in disguise.**

### 2. A Percentage of Earnings

Some people pay into a joint account based on a percentage of earnings. Let's say June and John have drawn up a household budget and calculated they need $48,000 a year to cover all household expenses, vehicle expenses, groceries, utilities, and health insurance. They've decided that if they each pay 80% of their salary into the joint account they can cover their expenses, and whatever is left over they keep for themselves. In this scenario, June clears $20,000 a year and John clears $40,000 a year, so June ends up putting $16,000 a year into the household expenses and John puts $32,000. Although each of them contributes exactly 80% of their earnings, June contributes less money to household expenses and savings because she makes half as much as John.

Does it seem fair to you that June pays less because she makes less? Keep in mind that she also has less money left over for personal spending and personal investing ($4000 compared to John's $8000). Is this fair? If she wants to go to school, start a business, buy a new bike, or go on a ski vacation, then she may have to ask John for financial assistance. How would you feel, asking your partner (or being asked) for money? There are no wrong answers; it is simply what feels right for you as a couple.

If you think June and John should have equal amounts of money left over for personal use, then John should put in $34,000 and June should put in $14,000 so they each are left with $6,000 of personal funds.

Does this seem fair to you: John pays more because he makes more? What if June isn't very ambitious and isn't tapping her earning potential? What if she could get a promotion or go to night school and earn more money but isn't motivated to do so? Will John start feeling resentful over time that he has to pull most of the financial weight around the house? What if John hates his job but feels obligated to keep it because June doesn't make enough? What if June feels pressured by John to leave a job she loves?

This is where resentment can set in.

*PEARLY WISDOM: A person's sense of self-worth is often tied to how much money they make, but a person's happiness if often tied to how much they enjoy the work they do.*

## Sacrifices Must Be Made

When I left Canada, I left a high-paying job. I asked Tex if he could support me while I looked for work in the United States, and he said yes. He said he could pay for all the household expenses – transportation, food, rent, everything. I felt reassured. I had some savings that I could use for personal expenses and entertainment, so I felt we could make it work. My savings were small, though: I put myself on a strict budget and stopped eating out. I went from having a $200 salon haircut and color every three months when I was working, to buying $10-boxes of hair dye from the pharmacy and doing my own hair. Sacrifices had to be made so I could be with the one I loved, and I didn't mind buckling down.

Unfortunately, neither of us realized just how hard it would be for me to get a working visa, and my savings dwindled away in a matter of months. Finally, I had to come clean and let him know I was running out of money and needed some help. It was very, very hard for me to ask for help. I even cried. But I was completely transparent about my expenses and listed them all in a spreadsheet for him. For the first time, he saw what debts I owed and what I required to survive. I didn't want to burden him with anything non-essential, so I trimmed all the fat from my budget. What was left was enough to meet expenses but not enough to save anything towards my future.

I remember his serious face so clearly as he reviewed the spreadsheet of expenses, and I remember thinking, "Am I too expensive for him to keep?" I was afraid he wouldn't be able to afford me. Or worse – he wouldn't want to, and I'd have to return to Canada. **It was the little voice that says, "I'm not lovable. Deserving. Worthy". Talks about money can bring that out.**

Fortunately, Tex had a good job and could support me. He wrote me a check each month to cover my expenses and some very modest entertainment. And his generosity expanded: He bought me clothes and shoes and a gym membership and other things as they came up. He paid for me to travel back to Canada. He covered all my expenses and gave me a little cash each week to have fun. We joked about him being my "sugar daddy". Truth was, we both would have liked it if I could have been earning my own living – not just for the money, but for the social aspects and my own self-esteem.

> *Each partner needs to have some money he is not obligated to account for and each should have an equal voice in managing the finances. While it may not always be possible, each partner should also contribute to the support of the household, not just out of need but to preserve financial as well as personal independence and dignity.*
>
> — David Viscott, *How to Live with Another Person*

I'm still not permitted to work in the United States so I'm not earing an income or saving for retirement, but my needs are met, I'm with the man I love, and I'm writing and building my own business. It's enough, for now, and more than most people have.

*PEARLY WISDOM: When couples break up, they land in court over money and possessions – the car, the couch, the dog, etc. For example, a man buys his girlfriend a computer, but when they break up he claims it's his and takes it back. She claims it's hers and he stole it. You can prevent future drama by documenting things. It doesn't hurt to keep the receipt and write "GIFT" or "LOAN" on it. And if one partner gives the other money, it's good to specify whether the money is a loan or a gift and to get that in writing, too, dated and signed by both parties. I know that couples want to operate from a spirit of generosity, but when breakups happen, people can get weird if not downright greedy and dishonorable.*

I asked Tex for a loan so I can grow my author business. He wanted to gift me the money, but I prefer to keep this part of my life separate. It has to do with pride, and needing to feel independent. I told him we would track everything and I would write receipts and pay him back in a year. For me, it's important to have something that is 100% mine. He loves me and wants to see me succeed; he would have accepted any conditions. I love him enough to never want to take advantage of that.

## Sacrificing Your Career

Being single means you can pursue professional ambitions without compromise, but being in a relationship can mean putting career goals on hold. What happens if one of you gets a promotion that requires you to move to a new city? What if both of you are flourishing in careers that are taking you in different directions? Something must give. How do you decide whose ambitions should take precedence?

For example, Tex's job requires him to move every few years. I've accepted that moving around and having to make new friends in new cities or countries every few years will be in the cards. I will not be able to live in my beloved mountains, and I may not get to live in places I always enjoy. I also accept that I will struggle to build a photography business if I am constantly moving, so I should perhaps focus on writing, which allows me to work from anywhere. This is because my fortune is really tied to that of Tex as the primary breadwinner. Again, sacrifices must be made. For an independent woman who built a solid life, community, and reputation back home in the Canadian Rockies, it's a big sacrifice. However, I can no longer imagine life without him, so the sacrifice doesn't feel too big.

*PEARLY WISDOM: When people say a relationship is work, what they really mean is that being in a relationship requires conscious effort, humility, compromise, and the courage to move outside your comfort zone. Expanding your comfort zone could be learning to trust someone else, learning to communicate authentically or learning to share your things. Your comfort zone is personal, and it will be tested, again and again and again. Relationships have the power to put us in touch with our souls, and to make us better human beings.*

## Kids Are Money Pits

If you have kids, you already know this.

> *It's so important for couples to consider the financial impact when planning a baby. I am not sure how paid maternity leave is in the U.S. and Canada, but Australia is pretty crap at it. A lot of families in Australia are doing it on one income for a long time – till the kids are in school or even after that. Child care costs are pretty huge. Anyway, when a baby just happens, there's not*

*much you can do about it; just love the little one and be happy. But if a baby is planned, I cannot stress how important it is to have some serious savings before having a child. The baby industry is quite expensive these days and they do trick the new parents into the guilt trip. You feel obligated to get things for the safety/wellbeing/good development/etc. of your child.*

*No woman likes to let herself go. I personally don't know one single woman who does. But motherhood shifts perspectives. Suddenly, baby is the most important thing. Especially if you're on a budget, baby's needs are first. So, the luxuries are the first to go. No more $300 hairstyles, no more designer shoes, eating out... You know, it's suddenly Kmart and Target. The lifestyle will change dramatically and the financial stress can impact the relationship – especially if the couple just signed for a mortgage and then, boom, they are hit with the news that they are expecting.*

— Anna

**Kids are expensive, and the time required to raise them can stall a career.** Priorities change as new dads and moms must decide between investing in their work or their kids. It's almost impossible to be a superstar parent and a superstar employee at the same time. **You must decide where you are going to pull time from.** As a society, we revere CEOs and heads of companies, but their success often comes at a price: their family life, and health, usually suffer in proportion to their ambition.

## Wills

Do you have a will? It's not something you want to put off. You can hire a lawyer, or download a kit from the Internet and create your own will. Creating your own is still better than nothing, since nothing is exactly what you might be leaving your partner with if you're not careful.

Tex and I were walking back from the library:

> *Me: "So, if something happened to you – if you died – what would happen to me?" I was thinking about the fact that all my stuff was in the U.S., in his apartment, and I had no job and almost nothing in my bank account.*
>
> *Tex: "Well, that's part of the reason I'm working on a new estate plan. If we take it to that next level, then Hope (his daughter) and you will get it all".*
>
> *I nodded, but I was thinking about the present, not about what would happen when and if we got married.*
>
> *Me: "But if you died suddenly, I'd be hooped. I'd have to go back to Canada. How would I get my stuff back?" It wasn't very tender of me. I regretted the way it came out. It probably came out this way because I'd kept these questions inside for too long.*
>
> *I think Tex said, "You'll be taken care of".*

I needed more than a pat on the back. I needed to know there was a plan in place to get me and my stuff back to Canada, without bankrupting me, if I were to lose my "sugar daddy".

And what if something happened to me? Just the previous week, I'd seen a woman step off the curb and get hit by a car. She was walking across the zebra-striped pedestrian crossing. I heard a scream and a crunch and saw her on the ground. She was okay – but the car bumper had crumpled and her flip-flop had flown away.

I was stuck on the visual of her flip-flop, lying on the ground several feet from the accident.

That could have been me.

What if I got hurt or injured or sick in a country where I had no health care? What if I had to go home to get treated, and leave him and everything I owned back in the United States?

After that conversation, I gave Tex a copy of my emergency health care policy, and some numbers to dial in case something went wrong. I showed him where he could find my will, directive and living will – what should happen if I can no longer make decisions for myself – all stuff I had purchased in a kit online and filled out. It had cost me less than fifty bucks and taken a few hours to do.

It was a start, but until we were married and I was under his health insurance policy, until I could legally work and make my own income in the United States, until I had some savings in my own account and until he had a proper will and estate plan with me in it, I would always feel a little vulnerable in this country and in my relationship.

In the chapter "Covering Your Ass(ets)", I bring in some lawyers who go over this topic in more detail.

## Living Wills

When my father passed away from a major stroke, the doctors asked me if there was a will. None could be located. They asked me if I knew what his final wishes were. I vaguely recalled a conversation my parents had when I was a kid, where they didn't want any "heroic" efforts made to keep them alive. My mother was adamant that she not be kept in a vegetable state, so I assumed my father felt the same. With the little information I had, I made the difficult and painful decision to have him unplugged from life support.

Don't make your loved ones second-guess if they are making the right decision to unplug you. Spell out a living directive so they know precisely what to do if you die, and what to do if you don't die and must be kept on machines just so your lungs will fill with oxygen and your blood will continue to circulate, even if it means you won't be able to speak or move again.

* * *

## HOUSEKEEPING: MoneyMoneyMoney!

If you've ever heard the expression "champagne tastes and beer budget", it means someone is living beyond their means. This can cause strain in a relationship. Couples fight about money in all kinds of ways: spending it, saving it, investing it, earning it and budgeting. Some couples even try to outspend each other by buying themselves expensive gifts, because they have deeper issues around entitlement, anger, insecurity, and self-worth. These couples operate like enemies, trying to take all that they can get, instead of loving partners working towards a common goal. You can minimize the drama by working through the following questions together. You may even wish to write some of these items into your Love Agreement.

### Task 1: Define the lifestyle goals each of you has.

What kind of lifestyle do you want for yourself? How do you see yourself living in five years? When you retire? Do you dream about driving a luxury car, having a maid, dining in fine restaurants and enjoying vacations to Europe? Write it down. Maybe put the word "want" beside some items and "need" beside others. I recommend you keep a journal as you go through this entire book, and come back to this chapter later.

**Task 2: Once you've defined your lifestyle, ask yourself how you are going to support it.**

Is this lifestyle realistic, given your current financial situation? What has to change so you can live your dream lifestyle? Are both of you willing to make those changes?

**Task 3: Discuss how you will handle major purchases together.**

Make a deal that anything beyond a certain price must be agreed on together. For example, spending more than $200 on anything (services or products or memberships) must be approved by both parties. When one partner spends money on something the other doesn't approve of, it can cause a big financial strain and breach the trust you have built.

**Task 4: Take your time and do the "Twenty Questions Couples Should Ask before Moving in Together".**

Be honest and open with your answers.

**Task 5: Schedule a time to work through a budget together.**

Sit down, crack a beer, and come up with a budget you can stick with for a month. Review all your household expenses and personal spending. Figure out how much you want to save each month, and what things you can do to support your individual lifestyle goals. Discuss any upcoming major purchases. At the end of the month, review your budget. Tweak as needed. Then make a three-month budget. Meet every three months to review things.

After a few meetings, it will become quite natural to talk about money, and you'll be working as a team, not as adversaries.

You can download worksheets and a free budget template on my website at www.itsnotyouitsus.com/chapterlinks.

*PEARLY WISDOM: Regarding love nests, the ideal situation is one where you decide on a place that you can afford on one person's paycheck. Which means, if one of you lost your job, the other partner could cover all the expenses. If, however, one person absolutely insists on a more luxurious home than their partner can afford, then the person insisting should bear the burden of the cost, according to their salary. The terms should be written out. But beware: If both your names are on the lease and only your partner can afford the rent, you are vulnerable. A landlord won't care about your financial woes; if your name is on the lease, you're on the hook – period.*

**Task 6: Have separate bank accounts, even when you are married.**

It's important to maintain and build personal credit, just in case your future (single/widowed) self needs it. Get your own credit card, buy your own vehicle, and invest in some things of your own, but don't hide anything from each other.

**Task 7: Become financially literate.**

Read some books. Tony Robbins' book *MONEY – Master the Game: 7 Simple Steps to Financial Freedom* is a good one. It's a meaty 600 pages, so if you're short on time you can get the audiobook and listen to it when you're driving or cooking.

*PEARLY WISDOM: Couples often leave one person in charge of the finances because the other person feels uncomfortable or dislikes budgeting. This is risky because it leaves a lot of room for assumptions, overspending and denial.*

## Parting Thoughts

You can take steps to protect yourself from financial destruction, like maintaining your own bank accounts, setting spending limits, documenting gifts and loans, and agreeing that you won't go Dutch on anything "big" until you've lived together for 12 months and/or gotten engaged. By "big", I mean a pet, whose life would be disrupted if you split up, or a mortgage or car loan, which could wipe you out financially if one of you moved out and refused to contribute any longer. Imagine splitting up and being on the hook for the car your sweetheart used to drive off in! Broken credit can take longer to mend than a broken heart.

Money, it's a kick. In the ass.

*PEARLY WISDOM: You may have heard of emotional and physical abuse, but there is also something called financial abuse. This is where one person in the relationship controls the other person using money as a threat by rewarding or punishing behaviors. It can also occur when one partner forces the other to sign a loan, possibly destroying their credit. Victims can feel trapped when their credit is destroyed or they have no means to set themselves up in a new life. It really is a form of domestic violence because the behavior is abusive and aggressive and doesn't come from a place of love, just control.*

# Chapter 8: Property and Possessions

*Home is the nicest word there is.*

— Laura Ingalls Wilder

When you decide to move in together, it's best if you can find a brand new love nest to move into. This is because merging households is hard. The partner who moves in can feel like a guest, while the other person can have moments where they feel like they are being invaded. A new home can reduce flare-ups around privacy and personal space: it's a chance to start fresh, on neutral ground.

If you do end up shopping for a new home together, here are some topics to explore.

## Walkability

How close do you want to be to shops, nightlife, the gym, and local restaurants? Tex and I, we want a very walkable neighborhood. We use the website walkscore.com to find places to rent that fit the lifestyle we are looking for. We look for a score of 75 or higher.

Once we've found a few promising neighborhoods, we turn to Google Maps to calculate walking distances to grocery stores, movie theatres, local attractions, and public transportation. We look for a 25-minute walking radius for most things. Having things close by means less driving and more living.

## Safety

Ask each other: On a scale of 1–10, how important is it to you that the neighborhood feels safe and that you feel free to walk around at night or park your car on the street? Women are usually more concerned about personal safety, and their partners should take this to heart. You can look this information up on the web. For example, if you Google "Crime stats, Houston", you'll see a link to the Houston Police Department website where you can download crime statistics by neighborhood and street. You can view numbers of cases of rape, robbery, auto theft, burglary, aggravated assault and so on. Try it for your city. A lot of municipalities are making crime data transparent and open to the public now.

If you're looking for apartments, you can also go to Yelp and read the reviews by residents. If you notice a lot of comments from residents about break-ins, keep looking.

## Access to Green Space

I need to feel close to nature, and the more trees the better. This isn't always easy in a big city. If I had a dog, I would look for a dog park close by. Dogs need to run and play and socialize, and dog parks let them do this off-leash, which is good for their physical and emotional health. More and more cities are providing dog parks, and some of them even have dog water parks. Look for something within easy walking distance.

## Transportation

If you bike, are there bike paths and bike lanes? How bicycle-friendly is your community? You can generally tell that a city is bicycle-friendly if it has designated bike lanes and public rental bikes available.

If you hate to drive, is there easy access to public transportation? Ideally, you want to be within a 10-minute walk to public transportation. No metro? With one call to City Hall you can find out if there are any plans to expand the metro in your area.

If you drive, what is an acceptable commute to work? How long will it take you to drive to weekend attractions and visit relatives or friends? Look for easy on-ramp access to major roads.

Because driving to and from work each day takes such a big chunk of time, Tex gets in his car and tests the morning commute before committing to a rental agreement. For him, anything less than 45 minutes is acceptable; he listens to podcasts and audiobooks to pass the time.

Again, Google Maps is your friend in all this.

## Cost

How much house can you afford? If you live in an area served by public transportation, you may be able to afford a better place, or a more desirable location, if you ditch the vehicle and take the metro. Cars are expensive, and when you factor in the cost of insurance, fuel, and repairs, you're looking at several hundred dollars a month. When you need wheels, you can always use a ride or carpool service or rent a vehicle for special trips.

*PEARLY WISDOM: The more compatible you are in your lifestyle and interests, the easier it is to find a love nest you'll both enjoy sharing.*

## Summary

When house or apartment hunting, talk about the lifestyle you want to live, and then go shopping. Use walkscore.com, Google Maps and Yelp to help you in your search.

Fortunately, Tex and I are extremely compatible about the kind of lifestyle we want to live. We are not suburb people. We value location and walkability because we like doing things outside the house. We are willing to live in a smaller place and go without a backyard if it means living in an interesting neighborhood, one where we can enjoy different experiences without the drive. Being able to walk to the gym or write in a coffee shop next door is not a "want" to have but a "need" to have. If one of us wanted a big house in the suburbs and one of us craved a more inner-city bohemian lifestyle, it would be a very tough compromise and one I don't think we could sustain for long. In fact, we might become one of those happily married couples who are committed to a life together but live apart. They're called LATs (Living Apart Together). I have an aunt who was deeply in love and committed to one man for more than 31 years until he died. The love and affection they had for one another was palpable, even though they lived apart. Despite the fact they never married, there was no question that they were made for each other.

## Merging Possessions

Although I'd sold nearly all my possessions before I moved in with Tex (actually, I sold them about a year before I met him, to follow a dream of traveling the world), I still had a bunch of stuff when we moved in together. Our combined possessions were too much for the apartment, so we put most of my stuff in storage for safekeeping. We knew that living together was a trial and that if it didn't work out, I'd head back to Canada. It was a comfort knowing

I wouldn't have to start all over from scratch; my heart might be broken, but at least I'd have kitchenware.

Merging possessions has its moments. Here's one of mine:

> *Virginia Day 10: Unpacking.*
>
> *My boyfriend and I each have our own closets. Problem is, he has AT LEAST FOUR TIMES the amount of clothes I do. So, he tried to poach mine.*
>
> *Right.*
>
> *This apartment is now divided into zones. Tex's bathroom and Sophie's bathroom. Tex's closet and Sophie's closet. Everything else is Switzerland.*
>
> *Well, the rest of the apartment might have been Switzerland, but the truth of the matter was, when I looked around, it was all Tex's furniture and his things decorating the walls. I felt like a guest in our new home.*
>
> *So, to feel more at home, I decorated my bathroom and office with my stuff.*

**Guideline #21: Men need man-caves, and women need lady-lairs.**

*PEARLY WISDOM: Moving in with a person can feel like a loss of identity as you merge your lives and possessions. Finding visual ways to express your unique identities can keep you anchored to yourself.*

After living together for a year, Tex and I moved from Virginia to Houston, and it was time to purge ourselves of a lot of things that had been in storage. We had two sets of cutlery, towels, pots and pans, and so on. We decided to keep the best and donate the rest. Well, of all the things I said goodbye to, it was towels that reduced me to tears. Logically, my towels weren't worth keeping. They were old and scratchy, and his were much nicer. But I remembered buying those towels in my twenties and how grown-up I felt to buy a set of matching towels. It was the first time in my life I had nice big towels. (I had a humble upbringing.) I clutched those towels in my arms and shed a tear while Tex looked on in amazement. "Honey, you don't have to get rid of the towels", he said. I nodded. **"I feel like I'm losing my identity", I said.** He hugged me and said, "Keep the towels".

I thought about holding onto them a little longer but realized the time had come to let them go. "I like your towels better. I'm just having a moment", I mumbled, and put them in the donation box. I know it sounds dramatic, and it was: I felt like I was saying goodbye to my youth and independence.

I consider myself an emotionally stable woman who is not very materialistic, but getting rid of stuff and merging possessions can bring a lot of unexpected emotion into the equation. Fortunately, I'm with a guy who gets the emotional side of things.

* * *

## HOUSEKEEPING: Feather Your Nest

Does your home reflect your individual personalities? Whether you've just moved in together or have been living together for a while, here are some ways to feather your nest for more privacy and personality.

**Task 1: Divide the home into neutral and private zones.**

Allow each other to decorate personal spaces that reflect your own unique personalities. For example, when Tex and I merged possessions, I claimed the second bedroom and made it my office. I hung up art from my old home and placed cherished objects on a bookshelf. I placed my old desk and chair in the corner and decorated the bed with my old quilt. The space felt like my own little oasis in the apartment, a private creative retreat that reminded me of my roots and identity.

**Task 2: Have separate bathrooms.**

If at all possible. And decorate these to your own satisfaction.

**Task 3: Discuss art and how to decorate, together.**

As our personal living space grows smaller, we must find ways to preserve our individuality. Art is one way to express our unique personalities. Art provides a way to breathe some life into your living space. It's a way of saying this house is a home, and decorated by the people who share it. Perfectly matched sofas, chairs, curtains, and lampshades may signal elegance but little else in way of personality.

**Task 4: Discuss your man-cave and lady-lair.**

Talk about how you want each space to be respected. We all need a place where we can keep it as clean or cluttered as we want to, simply because it's ours.

## Property and Possessions Bonus: It's Not about the Cup

After about a month of us living together, Tex caught me using his favorite coffee cup, one he got from a coffee chain in Canada called "Second Cup". It happened to be my favorite too. I liked the size and shape of it. It reminded me of Canada – the same reason he was fond of it.

> *"That's my favorite cup", Tex said when he saw me sipping my tea.*
>
> *"Oh. I didn't know. It's my favorite too".*
>
> *"Take care of it, okay? Don't drop it or anything".*
>
> *For whatever reason, the ceramic cup was clearly important to him. "Okay", I said, but what I thought was: He's being kinda weird. It's only a cup.*
>
> *The more I thought about his reaction, the more insulted I began to feel. My internal monologue went something like this: Drop it? Why would I drop it? I've never dropped anything. Why is he being so protective about his stuff? Doesn't he want to share his stuff with me? Tex interrupted me just as I started feeling rejected.*
>
> *"I'd be upset if it got broken", he explained.*
>
> *I nodded my head but felt disappointed. This wasn't about the cup. This was about property. About sharing his toys. To me, it felt like he didn't want to share.*
>
> *The next day I talked to him about it.*

*"You know that thing about the cup – it wasn't about the cup".*

*He listened. I continued.*

*"It's not about the cup. It's about sharing your stuff with me".*

*"You might be right", he said.*

*"I won't use your cup", I decided.*

*"Go ahead. Just be careful. I can't get that cup here if it breaks. I remember when I got that cup. It reminds me of my time in Canada. It's my favorite cup".*

*"There's lots of other cups I can use. I want you to have your cup". I meant it.*

*We hugged.*

*A couple of months later, Tex made me some tea. I noticed he brought it to me in his favorite cup.*

*"Hey, you made me tea in your favorite cup!"*

*He shrugged, like it was no big deal.*

Progress. It doesn't happen overnight.

When you merge possessions and come to live under the same roof, understand that both of you are going to have moments where you feel territorial. Sometimes you'll feel like you're three years old, and you may not want to play nice or share your stuff. This has to do with issues of personal identity and control. As your relationship matures and you become more secure and comfortable with living together, concerns about "my stuff" and "your stuff" will fade away. A year later, Tex says those issues are gone for him and he wants to share everything with me. I don't feel like he needs to share *everything*, but the thought is sweet.

* * *

## HOUSEKEEPING BONUS: What's Mine Is Mine and What's Yours Is Mine, Too?

**Bonus Task: Have a conversation with your partner about objects that you're emotionally attached to.**

What do you have a hard time sharing? What is your version of "the favorite cup"? Can you understand what is at the root of your partner's attachment to this object?

Respect the fact that you are two individuals living under the same roof. While most things are yours together, some things just need to be his and some things need to be hers... until they no longer need to be.

> **Guideline #22: Everyone deserves something to call their own, even if it's just a favorite cup.**

## Chapter 9: Living Together versus Marriage - How Committed Are You?

*A thousand half-loves must be forsaken to take one whole heart home.*

— Rumi

Some people just sort of drift into a live-in relationship. Maybe they figure it's "cheaper" or more "convenient" to shack up than to live apart while seeing each other. This tends to happen a lot in expensive cities like New York. The thinking goes like this: "Hey, we're at each other's places all the time – why not just live under the same roof and save some money?"

Don't buy into it.

These kinds of arrangements, sprung from convenience, can have unintended consequences that can alter your lives forever. Like children. Like pets. Like financial destruction once the honeymoon period is over and couples realize they aren't that compatible after all.

**Guideline #23: Don't build a romantic relationship on convenience.**

I speak from personal experience: I lived with a man for several years before I met Tex. I should have recognized then that a reluctance to commit usually means someone's heart isn't in it. The hard part is knowing if someone's heart isn't in it, or if they just need more time to get comfortable. How much time? Well, it varies but there is some data to indicate an ideal length of courtship exists for marriage success. According to Ted Huston, a professor of human ecology and psychology at the University of Texas, the greatest marital success occurs between men and women who have courted an average of two years and four months.[16] Of course, couples can (and do!) have happy marriages regardless of how much time they spend dating or living together first, but to Dr. Huston, the data is clear; dating less than one year results in a higher divorce rate, and more than three years of courtship also increases the chances that the marriage is doomed. In fact, the longer the couple takes to get married, the quicker the divorce. It would seem there is a kind of Goldilocks principle at work in courtship: couples should be neither too hot or too cold when it comes to getting wed.

## Cohabitation Agreements

When Tex asked me to move to the United States, I asked him if he would help me get my stuff back if it didn't work out. He said yes. I paused and added, "Will you put that in writing?" He laughed and said, "If that's what it takes to make you feel comfortable, yes".

That's the kind of response you want. If you get any flak when you ask for anything in writing, to protect yourself if things don't work out, then consider it a red flag.

You know that old saying "Look before you leap"? That's because if you don't make it to the other side, you can fall pretty hard. I don't recommend taking huge leaps of faith. I recommend building a bridge to the other side. Bridges let you go back, safely.

How do you build a bridge?

By structuring a cohabitation agreement, a form of legal agreement between a couple who choose to live together, whether they are heterosexual or homosexual.

## The M-Word

I advocate having a cohabitation agreement laid out before you move in together, with a plan to discuss marriage in six months to a year, if you're at all marriage-minded. Otherwise, you could find yourself testing the waters indefinitely. With every passing year, you could become more committed to someone who won't commit to you.

Tex calls testing the waters "run time". When U.S. Immigration would question me at the airport about my visits to see him, I'd say, "We just need more run time to see if we want to get married". How much run time you want to give your relationship is personal, but when you start getting antsy about the status of your relationship, you're out of run time.

For me, I started to stress about where things were headed after living together for six months. Although living together got better and better all the time and our confidence in "us" grew, this little voice in my head would start wondering when and if Tex would pop the question. Many times I'd ask myself, "My life is on hold. I'm out of the job market. I'm living in a foreign country with no friends or family. How long should I give this live-in relationship?" I didn't want to waste my time in a live-in relationship that wasn't going to end in marriage, because for me marriage was a true test of commitment. Rightly or wrongly, I wouldn't feel safe or secure until there was a ring on my finger. U.S. Immigration was also forcing us to make a decision: I was only allowed in the U.S. for 182 days out of the year. If we got married, we could be together as much as we liked. I decided I'd give living together about a year, and I told Tex that. He got it. That's the kind of conversation a guy doesn't forget.

PEARLY WISDOM: *No guy should feel forced to propose. You want him to want to marry you, without any reservations. But it's completely reasonable and responsible to share a timeline for marriage if you have always dreamed of getting married. You can do this respectfully, and ideally before moving in together. If your man says he never wants to get married, and you have always cherished the idea, you have a deal breaker on your hands. Don't settle for what he wants and deny yourself something essential to your happiness, just to preserve the relationship.*

Bottom line, when you're talking about moving in together, you should also be discussing the M-word, to see where you both stand on the subject of marriage. As painful as it might be, you may find one of you more committed to a future together. If you can't agree on a reasonable timeline, it may be time to cut your losses. That expression "Why buy the cow when you can get the milk for free?" is never more applicable than when couples shack up.

> *My brother and his wife lived together for nine months before they got married, and the time they spent living together was beyond stressful; they almost split up because of it. I've talked to my sister-in-law since, and she says that the hardest part of living together is not having a long-term plan or knowing how to base your success on it, since you are essentially roommates who have sex.*
>
> — Peggy

## Marriage and Timelines

As individuals, it's normal for people to have different emotional timelines for marriage. When did I know I wanted to marry Tex? Six months after we moved in together. I'd always been afraid of marriage before, but after living with him, it felt right. I trusted him. I liked who I was with him. I could see us having a long and happy life together. He felt these things, too, but he needed more time to be sure about getting married.

If I'd had poorer self-esteem, I could have taken his hesitation as a sign that he didn't love me enough to commit. Instead, I tried to understand where he was coming from.

Tex confided in me that getting married and then getting divorced was the biggest regret of his life. He'd felt pressured into his first marriage because his ex was very strong-willed and he loved her and didn't want to lose her. Unfortunately, the troubles started as soon as they got married. Then they had a baby girl. Inevitably, they got divorced. Now, every time he visits his daughter in Colorado, his heart fills with joy, only to be broken into a million pieces when he has to say goodbye again. It's rough on him, and it's rough on his daughter. Tex said a second divorce would break him in half. He needed to be absolutely sure this time. I softened and relaxed. This wasn't about me; it was about him.

I told Tex I loved him, I told him I respected his need to not rush things and I wanted him to be 100% confident before he proposed, but I also told him I would be moving back to Canada in June if we weren't applying for a Fiancée Visa by then. I couldn't – for the sake of my mental health – continue to play house without knowing a marriage date was in the foreseeable future. I couldn't keep Ping-Ponging between Canada and the U.S.. We had given it 12 months of run time; I would give it six more. No arguments. No tears. No drama. I simply told him I couldn't wait forever, and we went back to enjoying our lives together.

It was January when we had this conversation.

A couple of weeks later, Tex told me he didn't feel right proposing without introducing me to his daughter, so we flew to Colorado.

We applied for a Fiancée Visa in March.

Moral of the story? **Have soft limits and hard limits in a relationship.** The soft limits are things you don't like but are willing to compromise on. Hard limits are non-negotiables, items that you simply can't compromise on without being untrue to yourself and your ideals. **Hard limits allow you to keep your self-respect. They keep you safe and happy.** Any partner worth his salt will respect your hard limits, even if he doesn't like them.

*PEARLY WISDOM: If you find yourself bumping into arguments and hard limits a lot in your relationship, it's either because one of you is too selfish and uncompromising, or you're in the wrong relationship and need to find one that is more compatible.*

**Guideline #24: Have hard limits and soft limits.**

## Are You Playing House?

I realize that not everyone wants to get married. Some couples are deeply committed to one another and have no desire to ever get married. Other couples are living together first to decide if they're compatible enough to get married. As long as both of you are on the same page, there shouldn't be a problem. But what if one of you is living in a fantasy relationship and the other is just enjoying roommates with benefits? How awful it would be to find out that you aren't in the deeply committed relationship you thought you were in.

Here's a checklist to determine where you're at on the commitment continuum. The more boxes you tick, the more you're just playing house and it might be time for one of you to move out.

## Commitment Quiz

1. You sleep in separate rooms.

2. Your partner is barely accountable for his actions, including how he spends money, and he does what he wants when he wants.

3. Your partner focuses primarily on herself and her hobbies or personal goals.

4. You split all expenses 50–50, regardless of what each of you earns.

5. You don't talk about saving money for the future: a car, a house, kids.

6. You don't talk about the future in any detail, and there are no concrete dates and plans involving the two of you.

7. You rarely shop, cook, and eat together.

8. You don't have date nights together where you get dressed up and do something romantic.

9. You spend at least half your free time doing things separately, with your own friends.

10. You haven't met each other's relatives or you don't spend much time with them.

11. You've discussed the M-word but still have no plans to get married.

12. You don't feel like a priority in your relationship.

13. You share a bed and roof but don't feel emotionally connected.

14. You rarely, or never, have sex.

15. You don't encourage each other to become better people.

16. You don't share a spiritual outlet, whether that's volunteering together, going to church, or doing something that stirs your souls together.

17. Your partner pays the rent and bills, but you have no idea how they spend the rest of their money.

18. You don't look into each other's eyes very often.

19. You hear the words "I love you", but you don't feel very loved.

20. You were happier single and living on your own.

If you check several of the boxes, your relationship status is more like roommates than couple-with-a-future-together. I hope this doesn't depress you too much. If so, you really have two choices: you can try to improve the situation (just remember, it takes two to tango), or recognize that you may not be compatible after all. Not wanting to communicate and discuss matters openly is only playing at living together.

When we live with someone, we learn whether we are spiritually, intellectually, emotionally, socially, AND physically compatible. If we're not, then the experiment is over. You tried each other out and found you weren't suited to a life together. Next!

Thank goodness we don't have to marry someone anymore just to figure this stuff out! If you're not happy and you're not compatible, marriage won't make you happier or more compatible. In fact, it will just make things worse.

### Guideline #25: Compatibility is more important than chemistry in a long-term relationship.

*PEARLY WISDOM: Statistically, 75% of women will shack up with a man by the time they're 30, sometimes serially; so in my opinion, a ring is a greater symbol of commitment than cohabitation. A ring is a symbol of intent to marry, but living together – not so much. Some people are quite happy living together and not getting married, and yet they are as devoted to one another as any married couple. However, there are far more people living together and just kind of winging it. If you're a woman of child-bearing age who wants children, you may want to think carefully about the commitment level of your partner. To me, a ring shows some skin in the game. I link to a great article on the topic of engagement rings at* www.itsnotyouitsus.com/chapterlinks.

## Marriage: It's Not Just a Piece of Paper

I've heard people refer to marriage as "just a piece of paper". Hell, that's what my ex said when I broached the topic of marriage after we had lived together for three years. (His response should have been a big red flag that we weren't going to make it.)

If you still think marriage is "just a piece of paper", then you're fooling yourself. My guess is you don't know your rights, or lack of rights, when you choose to live with someone. If you did, you would realize that you need a lot more pieces of paper in addition to a certificate of marriage to protect yourself legally.

In the next chapter, I teach you how to cover your ass(ets), and the legal differences between living together and being married.

* * *

## HOUSEKEEPING: Put a Date on It

Have you talked about marriage and your feelings about it? Have you ever discussed a wedding date? It's a conversation couples should have before moving in together. If you've never broached this topic, or it's been awhile, now is a great time to get clear on your future together.

**Task 1: Discuss your timelines for getting married.**

If neither of you ever wants to get married, fine. Just don't assume it's in the cards if you've never talked about it in a specific way.

**Task 2: Discuss the wedding itself.**

If one of you wants a quickie drive-through wedding in Vegas and the other wants a $40,000 blowout with 200 guests, then let me refer you back to Chapter 7: Money, It's a Kick (in the Ass).

# Chapter 10: Covering Your Ass(ets)

*Your legal rights as a partner may depend on whether you are married or living together. Living together with someone is sometimes also called cohabitation. Generally speaking, you will have fewer rights if you're living together than if you're married.*

— Adviceguide.org.uk

## The Legal Differences between Living Together and Being Married

Let's play a game. Let's see how well you know your legal rights when it comes to being married or living together. What happens to your estate, children, next of kin, and decisions about medical care, support payments, government benefits and tenancy should you and your partner terminate your relationship?

I recruited two American lawyers for this chapter: family law attorney Jacqueline Newman and an estate lawyer we will call Yvonne. Yvonne wishes to use an alias because she feels that the information we provide, while useful, should not be relied upon as blanket advice. Your local laws will vary, and situations are certainly not always black and white.

Therefore, be advised that the legal information provided in this chapter is not going to be accurate for everyone and every situation. So why did I bother to include this chapter – the most difficult to write, and the most complicated? I wrote it because I think people are rather clueless as to what they're getting themselves into when they live with someone, and I haven't found a general relationship advice book that deals with the legalities of living together. Even Judge Judy's book *What Would Judy Say?: A Grown-Up Guide to Living Together with Benefits* doesn't go into this kind of detail. After writing this section, I understand why! This stuff is not easy to read, and it's not easy to write. Most people will probably gloss over this chapter, and that's okay. If one person finds value from the information, and it helps them to cover their ass(ets), then it's been worth it.

Bottom line: The information included herein is only meant to raise awareness. Don't go making big legal decisions regarding your estate based on something Sophie or Jacqueline or Yvonne said in a relationship book. If something you read concerns you, investigate for yourself and consult with your own lawyer.

Now let me introduce our two legal experts.

**Jacqueline** specializes in negotiating pre-nuptial agreements and litigating high-net-worth divorce cases. She is an expert when it comes to matters of alimony, custody, child support, property division and post-divorce actions.

**Yvonne** specializes in international and domestic estate planning, contested matters, and estate administration. She provides comprehensive tax and business advice.

The game we're going to play is called True or False. As I said, the answers are applicable to the state of New York and may vary according to your state or country. **If an answer scares the hell out of you, it's worth looking into to see if the same thing pertains to your area and if it still pertains to New York State.**

**Keep in mind that laws change and that they are also subject to interpretation.**

For the purpose of this game, a "common-law" marriage refers to a couple who lives together in an arrangement similar to marriage, but without legal documents or an actual ceremony.

## Rings

True or False?

**Q. If an engaged couple breaks things off and cancels the wedding, the fiancée gets to keep the engagement ring.**

Answer: False. In almost every case, the gift of an engagement ring is a conditional gift. The ring was given on the condition that a marriage will take place in the future. No marriage, no condition met, means no ring.

Bottom line: Legally, the girl must return the bling. Of course, if a couple marries, the condition is lifted and the engagement ring is considered hers to keep even if they divorce later on.

**Q. A wedding ring is considered marital property and should be treated as a joint asset to be divided up fairly during a divorce.**

Answer: True.

Bottom line: If you're Frank Frugal or Cindy Cynical, you might want to spend less on the engagement ring (which she keeps) and more on the wedding ring (which you split).

## Common-law Marriage

True or False?

**Q. Common-law marriages are the same across the country.**

Answer: False. Common-law marriage is not recognized in many U.S. states, nor in some Canadian provinces such as Quebec.

## Banking

True or False?

**Q. Living together: You will be unable to access your partner's bank account if he or she dies.**

Answer: True. Unless you have a joint account – or a payable-on-death trust account (also known as a Totten account), in which one party places money in a bank account with instructions upon the settlor's death to pass the money on to a named beneficiary.

**Q. Married: If you're married with separate bank accounts, and your spouse dies, their funds will become your property even if you weren't listed on the account.**

Answer: It depends. It's not automatic. It depends on what the spouse's will or revocable trust says. If the spouse dies intestate (with no will or other planning done), it depends on the state's intestate statute or whether there are children.

**Q. Living together or married: If you share a joint bank account, then both of you own the money in it. This means that one person can withdraw as much or as little money as they want from the account at any time.**

Answer: True. It will be hard to stop someone from going to the bank, unless you have a condition on the account that states that both signatures are required for withdrawal of funds. That said, each person may not be entitled to those funds.

Yvonne: *Not necessarily. This is actually a complex issue. Under the laws of some states, each spouse is really only entitled to one half of the account.*

**Q. If one partner dies, then the funds in the account become the property of the other.**

Answer: True.

**Q. Living together: Debts are not inherited.**

Answer: True.

Yvonne: *Unless there are extenuating circumstances, such as a joint debt, there should be no inherited debt when living together.*

**Q. Married: Debts are inherited.**

Answer: True.

Yvonne: *I'm not an expert on this particular issue. It depends on if there is a pre-nup which governs things, and on state law. Best to check with your lawyer.*

Bottom line: If you separate from one another, you should make a clean break of things and also close any joint accounts in order to avoid having your ex access your funds and run up debts that will be your responsibility. It happens.

## Children

True or False?

**Q. Living together or married: If you are the birth mother or father, you are financially responsible for your child's life until he or she emancipates (is legally released from your care). In**

**New York, this is 21 unless there is an earlier emancipation event.**

Answer: True.

**Q. Living together or married: If you aren't the biological parent and there is no adoption, you won't get parental access to the child after you and your partner separate, unless you have a written agreement to that effect.**

Answer: True.

Jacqueline: *I represented the husband in a divorced couple. The couple was together for five or six years before getting married. They raised her child from a previous marriage together until the girl was 16 years old. My client and his stepdaughter had a very close relationship, and the girl even called him Dad. When the couple broke up, the wife was so bitter that she would not even let him say goodbye to the child. It was heartbreaking. The stepfather just wanted to get in the same room with the child and tell her what was going on and that he loved her, but the mother said no. It was awful.*

Bottom line: A stepparent could spend years co-parenting a child, taking her to soccer games, nursing her through illness, dropping her off at school every day, and then be denied any say in important decisions about her life because he or she is not the birth parent. Unless you adopt the child as your own, you have no rights to your ex's offspring, even if you were married.

## Financial Support for the Children

True or False?

**Q. Living together or married: Both parents are responsible for financially supporting their biological children.**

Answer: True. This means that even if the father is not living with the mother, he is still on the hook for the child's welfare until that child reaches emancipation. Same goes for the ladies.

Jacqueline: *There is another twist to this. In New York, a child born to the marriage is presumed to be the child of the husband. Even if the child is not the biological offspring of the father but the child thinks he is, because the father has acted like one, raised the child, and gave the impression he is, then he can be financially responsible for the child. The court doesn't want bastard children, so this is how they protect them. It can be overcome with a paternity test, but if the true father is not found, then the known father can be on the financial hook. I had a case where the husband thought he knew who the real father was (an ex-boyfriend of his wife), but there was nothing he could do about it because he was not able to demand a paternity test from the ex-boyfriend.*

Bottom line: I know, this point sounds contradictory to the one above about stepparents not having access to their ex's children, but it's not. In that case, it is known that the children came from a previous relationship. Jacqueline's main point is that a child born to the marriage is presumed to be the child of the husband. If you suspect otherwise, get a paternity test. Otherwise, the child can be considered your responsibility.

As the saying goes: "Wrap it in latex, or there go your paychecks."

### Guardians

True or False?

**Q. Living together or married: Either parent can appoint a guardian, such as the new stepparent, to act on their death and assume parental responsibility for the child(ren).**

Jacqueline: *False. If one person dies, the surviving biological parent (typically) is automatically the custodial parent. If both parents die, then the will can dictate who the children go to.*

Yvonne: *But if the surviving biological parent is shown to be unfit (very hard to do), a guardian may serve in place of the surviving biological parent.*

Bottom Line: You may wish to adopt your stepchildren as your own in the event your partner dies and you wish to keep custody.

**Death and Taxes**

True or False?

**Q. Living together: If an unmarried partner dies without a will, the surviving partner will have to go to court to claim proceeds from the estate.**

Answer: False.

Yvonne: *There are no estate rights for unmarried surviving partners. This is why having a will is so important in these situations! But again there may be gray areas, such as states that recognize common-law marriages or if there is a cohabitation agreement.*

**Q. Married: A spouse can cut out another spouse from the will.**

Answer: False.

Jacqueline: *Unlike television, you can't leave everything to your cat and nothing to your spouse. There is something called the elective share, which allows the surviving spouse to claim 1/3 of the estate. The other 2/3 would go as probably dictated in the will. So Fluffy gets a chunk but not the whole thing.*

Yvonne: *Just to be clear, the estate refers to the assets that exist in the sole name of the deceased. There is a very complex statute that determines what the actual 1/3 is that the survivor gets.*

**Q. Living together: If one of you inherits money or property from the other partner, you will have to pay inheritance tax. Only married couples are exempt.**

Answer: False.

Yvonne: *It depends on what the estate planning document says, but it is correct that there is no equivalent of a "marital deduction" for non-married couples. However, there are no federal taxes for assets not above $5,430,000 unless some of that amount was gifted during life.*

**Q. Married couples: As far as married partners go, if one of you dies without leaving a will, then the other inherits all or some of the estate, automatically.**

Answer: False.

Yvonne: *Depends on the state's intestacy statute. It's all if no kids, and half if kids.*

**Q. Married couples: Under federal tax laws in the United States, you can leave any amount of money to a spouse without generating estate tax.**

Answer: Generally true, if the spouse is a U.S. citizen.

Bottom line: Do not die without a will, as this is extremely unpleasant for the surviving partner. There might also be some slim pickings once the ex and family members have had their share.

## Debts

This is a complicated topic, but in general, any debts you had prior to your marriage are yours alone to keep, provided they are in your name only. Same goes for unmarried couples.

Example: If I owned some property prior to marrying Tex, and Tex uses his income to help pay expenses on that asset (such as condo fees or property tax) before we marry, then he can't expect a credit back if we split up. If he helped me out during our marriage, then he can expect to be compensated.

Jacqueline: *If you have premarital debts and divorce, you keep these debts. If you use marital funds to pay premarital debts, you can expect to, but may not be compensated if you later divorce. However, if you use premarital money to pay the debts on premarital assets, your spouse can't expect to be compensated.*

Bottom line: If you are living together and not married, you should have a written agreement documenting any monies borrowed by your partner, if you would like to be paid back if you split up.

## Domestic Violence

True or False?

**Q. Living together or married: If a man sexually abuses his girlfriend, it's illegal; but if a man sexually abuses his wife, it's not illegal.**

Answer: Legal rights are the same whether you're married or not: if a man rapes his partner, he can be convicted. If a partner is violent to you or the children, the court can intervene. No one has a right to abuse you.

## Ending a Relationship

True or False?

**Q. Living together: Unmarried couples can dissolve their relationship and separate without going to court, even if there are children involved.**

Answer: Mostly true, but if children are involved, it is recommended that you seek legal counsel, as children significantly affect the way a common-law relationship is viewed in the eyes of the law. The court has the power to intervene as to their care.

Sophie: *In Alberta, Canada, where I am from, common-law regulations state that while you can leave the relationship at any time, you must be separated for at least a year to have your common-law marriage declared legally over, get into another "adult interdependent" relationship or get married.*[17]

**Q. Married couples: Require a court appearance to get divorced.**

Answer: False. The couple can do a separation agreement and uncontested divorce and not see the inside of a courtroom. Don't be fooled, though – you will still need a lawyer, and there is still legal paperwork required. If children are involved, it gets a lot more complicated.

## Fiscal Responsibility

True or False?

**Q. Unmarried couples have no legal obligation to support each other, and verbal agreements may be difficult to enforce.**

Answer: Mostly true, for most of the United States and Canada. In certain Canadian provinces where common-law marriage is recognized, spousal support may be possible but only when one partner seems entitled to it. For example, if one person had to give up their career to care for a child.

**Q. Married couples only have a legal obligation to support one another for as long as the couple is still living together or when there is a legal agreement or court order to continue to support the other after the marriage has ended.**

Answer: False. There can still be an obligation for support even if you aren't living together.

## Housing

True or False?

**Q. Living together: Unmarried partners cannot stay in a dwelling if the landlord asks one of the individuals to leave and they are not listed as joint tenants.**

Answer: Probably true. Check local laws and lease agreements. If you are unmarried, not a tenant and need to stay in the home, you will need to consult a lawyer. A court may be able to transfer tenancy or allow you to stay on a short-term basis. If your partner dies and they were listed as the sole tenant, you will have to request an amendment to the lease.

Bottom line: Your rights depend on your tenancy status. Make sure you are listed as joint tenants if you're in a deeply committed relationship.

**Q. Married: Both partners in a marriage have the right to stay living in the matrimonial home.**

Answer: If there is a divorce, you can decide who will stay in the dwelling. At the time of the divorce, you can make appropriate changes to the title.

**Q. Married: Premarital property remains the property of the original owner.**

Answer: True, except in certain circumstances. Discuss this topic with a lawyer.

## Joint Property

True or False?

**Q. Living together: If you are the sole owner of the property, the home is yours and you have the right to reside there and to ask the other partner to leave.**

Jacqueline: *There isn't an easy answer for this one. Technically, yes, except that if there is a marital component to the property or if there are children involved, it's not that clear-cut.*

You will need to hire a lawyer if you wish to pursue the path of claiming "beneficial interest". If you both own the property jointly, then you both have equal rights to stay in the home. If there are children, it may be possible to have the court transfer the property into your name for the "best interests" of the children until they reach adulthood.

**Q. Living together: Your partner may be able to claim a "cut" of the property, so to speak, if they can prove to a court that they made contributions towards the home that increased the value of the home. An example of this would be renovating a condominium that was purchased prior to living together.**

Answer: True. A written agreement beforehand, outlining how much each party contributes and can expect to profit from the sale of a home, will protect you. Also, you will need to prove that any renovations done had a significant impact on the sale price and that the condominium didn't simply increase in value due to market influences.

**Q. Married: Both partners have a right to remain in the home, regardless of who owns it.**

Answer: If you divorce, the long-term right to ownership can be decided when you go through divorce proceedings. The courts will give priority to making sure the children have a secure home.

## Next of Kin

True or False?

**Q. Living together: Hospitals and other institutions will generally accept the name of an unmarried partner as someone to contact in the event of an emergency or if medical treatment is required and the partner is unconscious or unable to give their consent.**

Answer: False. A physician friend of mine had the following to say: "In Canada and Australia (and probably the United States), if you are not married and your partner is unconscious, then you won't be able to make any decisions on behalf of the unconscious partner (unless the partner previously gave written, legal consent for you to do that)."

**Q. Married: Your spouse is considered next of kin by default when it comes to hospitals, wills and insurance documents.**

Answer: True.

## Money and Possessions

True or False?

**Q. Living together: Property you acquire together during cohabitation will be both of yours, especially that which is acquired from a joint bank account.**

Answer: True, as long as you are both on the mortgage.

**Q. Married: Anything you own prior to marriage is yours to keep.**

Answer: This can be true of land, savings or investments. However, if you divorce, then any marital property credits can be taken into account by the court when it comes to a financial settlement. There can also be issues about commingling of separate property that can transmute separate property into marital property.

Jacqueline: *For example, assume you have a premarital apartment, then you get married, renovate it, and it appreciates a lot. Some of the appreciation can be due to the other party and can become a marital credit if you get divorced.*

Bottom line: You want to document your personal assets going into a relationship and split any joint investments on the way out.

## Last Names

True or False?

**Q. Living together: Just like marrieds, you can change your name as you wish and there is no legal requirement to do so.**

Answer: True.

**Q. Living together: Once you take your partner's name, you are not legally required to change it back after you break up.**

Answer: True.

**Q. Married: If you become widowed or divorced, you can change your name back or keep it.**

Answer: True.

**Q. Married: Once you take your partner's name, you are not legally required to change it back after you divorce.**

Answer: True.

Jacqueline: *There are plenty of people who remarry and want their ex to stop using their last name but can't do anything about it.*

Bottom line: You can legally call yourself Batman if you want. Your name is your right to keep or change at any time.

### Taxes

True or False?

**Q. Living together: Couples who live together don't enjoy the same tax write-offs as married couples.**

Answer: True, but this is a complicated topic and I recommend a tax accountant because if you take the right steps, you can enjoy certain write-offs. Take the wrong steps, and you can be severely penalized.

**Q. Married: You get more tax breaks when you're married.**

Answer: True, for the most part. From Intuit, the tax software people: "Marriage can help reduce the tax burden for married couples who file jointly. Depending on the incomes, so-called marriage 'penalties' can be avoided. If the taxpaying spouses have substantially different salaries, the lower one can pull the higher one down into a lower bracket, reducing their overall taxes." There are other benefits as well, but that's something to explore with your accountant.

Yvonne: *If both spouses have substantial incomes, there is a substantial penalty for marrying. In general, more tax will be paid once married and filing jointly than they paid filing as single. Married filing separately is the worst penalty of all!*

**Q. Married: You can be held responsible for any errors or fudges your spouse makes in filing a joint tax return during the time you are married.**

Answer: True, but if you claim "innocence" and can prove it, you may be off the hook.

Bottom line: Marry for love, not money; and refer to a tax accountant, not a relationship book, when it comes to your money.

Yvonne: *Get a pre-nup!*

## Divorce

True or False?

**Q. Men have it rougher in a divorce than women.**

Answer: Depends!

Jacqueline: *Statistically, women do not typically fare as well financially and men do not do as well emotionally. In many of my cases, this does not as often apply to the women I represent because many of the women I represent are professionals with high net worth.*

## Same-sex Couples

True or False?

**Q. Same-sex, unmarried couples could be prevented from enjoying the same legal rights as marrieds, depending on their country of residence.**

Answer: True. As of January 3, 2017, less than two dozen countries around the world recognize same-sex marriage. Except for Israel and South Africa, no country in Asia or Africa recognizes it. This means that if one partner dies, the other may not be able to take bereavement leave from work, or file wrongful death claims, or automatically inherit property. They can be denied social security and insurance claim benefits from their deceased partner.

Bottom line: There are a lot of rights denied to same-sex couples, but the list is too long to go into here. Personally, I think this is a travesty of justice. Why shouldn't two hard-working, tax-paying people who are in love and committed to one another, not be able to get married in order to enjoy the same rights and freedoms as heterosexual married couples? I am convinced that in the not-too-distant future, we will look back upon this time and consider it incomprehensible.

## Pre-nups

True or False?

**Q. It is better to have no pre-nup than a bad pre-nup.**

Answer: False. Jacqueline advises that a bad pre-nup can still be better than no pre-nup in locations that don't recognize common-law marriages, because at least you have some rights instead of living together and having no rights. (Like many states in the U.S., New York doesn't recognize common-law marriage.)

*PEARLY WISDOM: Pre-nuptials are done when people are getting married, and cohabitation agreements are typically for people who are not getting married. People typically seek a pre-nuptial agreement if there are children, assets, a business, or family money that needs to be protected. You should have attorneys for any legal contracts.*

## Chapter Summary

If you see yourself spending the rest of your life with someone, make sure you get something in writing. You can skip the wedding ceremony, but you should never skip the paperwork that will protect your legal rights. It's not romantic, but it is practical: Couples break up, have children, get ill, and die. Without a cohabitation agreement, you have very few legal protections.

You can make your own binding agreement by Googling "cohabitation agreement template" and modifying it to suit your needs. Make sure it is signed by both parties, and witnessed. You can have a notary public witness it at City Hall or a UPS store if you wish to keep your agreement private from friends and family. To be safe, you should have your document reviewed by a lawyer once you've completed it, to ensure it complies with the laws in effect where you live.

To recap this chapter, here are some important things to keep in mind if you are living together and not married.

* * *

## HOUSEKEEPING: 10 Things to Keep in Mind if You Live Together

Here are 10 things to keep in mind about the legal consequences of living together, especially if you aren't married. If you've never discussed any of this before, chances are it's going to feel a little awkward, maybe even threatening, to bring it up. But here's the thing – if you're afraid of rocking the boat, you're already in choppy water. Time to do some relationship housekeeping!

**Task 1: Complete a cohabitation agreement.**

If you can afford it, hire a lawyer to review your cohabitation agreement. (Think that's expensive? Try splitting up after a few years.) If you see yourself marrying this person, you can also consider a pre-nup.

**Task 2: Beware of what you sign.**

Ensure that both names are on joint purchases, such as the mortgage, and that single names are only on titles for things paid for by one person, such as a vehicle.

**Task 3: Keep your own bank account and finances separate.**

In the event the relationship terminates, you want to have a good credit score.

**Task 4: Keep accurate records.**

Keep note of any financial and sweat equity contributions you make to any property held by your partner, and of any loans that you give them. This includes time you spend renovating any property they own.

**Task 5: Write "gift" or "loan" on receipts or checks written to your partner.**

This negates any suggestion that you have been supporting him or her. This is especially important if there are children involved, bringing the potential for a post-breakup "palimony" lawsuit.

**Task 6: Remember that an unmarried parent has the same child support obligations as a divorced parent.**

No deadbeat parents allowed.

**Task 7: Remember that verbal agreements don't mean jack.**

Ever watch "Judge Judy"? 'Nuff said.

**Task 8: Protect yourself.**

Refuse to guarantee any debts for your partner, unless you can afford them on your own and are willing to pay them if you break up.

**Task 9. Try to maintain some financial independence and job marketability.**

This is so you can support yourself in the future if you split up. If you are unable to do so, then make sure you have a written agreement that your partner is legally obligated to support you if the relationship ends.

**Task 10. Revisit your living arrangement in a year.**

It's a good idea to negotiate the terms of your agreement as needed. If you've been winging things with your relationship, now might be the time to write some stuff down so there are no assumptions. You would be surprised at how many assumptions there are when people don't bother to talk about things and just go on autopilot.

# Chapter 11: Sex and Desire - The Science of Falling in Love

*These violent delights have violent ends.*

— William Shakespeare, *Romeo and Juliet*

When you first fell in love, you probably felt a lot of passion for one another. You could make out for hours, and a day didn't go by where you didn't want to jump each other's bones. After about six months of living together, you probably experienced a cooling-off period. That insane need for sex all the time just sort of faded away and you moved into a comfortable period where cuddling became the norm and sex less frequent. Here's why.

## My Chemical Romance

What if love is really a chemical addiction between two people? It doesn't sound very romantic, but that's what scientists are discovering. According to researchers, the chemicals responsible for love, lust and bonding are driven by testosterone, estrogen, oxytocin, serotonin, and dopamine. When one of these chemicals hijacks your brain, you are putty in its hands. Romeo and Juliet are the perfect example of this.

The tragic story of Romeo and Juliet takes place over five short days. Romeo and Juliet first meet at a party on Sunday night. They marry Monday. On Tuesday, Juliet drinks the potion. On

Wednesday, they discover Juliet's body. On Thursday, Romeo and Juliet die. Sounds ridiculous, doesn't it? And yet, this is considered one of the greatest love stories of all time.

In the next few pages I argue that Romeo and Juliet is not really a story about love, but lust. They have so completely lost their minds for each other – are so drunk on love chemicals – that they fail to think through their actions or come up with much of a plan for their relationship; the consequences are disastrous. Would they have even made it through the first five years of marriage? My guess is, probably not. The hotter a fire burns, the faster it burns out, and these two lovebirds went up like an inferno.

As ridiculous as their story is, we still have our share of modern day hopeless romantics: these Romeos and Juliets who rush into marriage while they are still in the lust phase of their relationship, mistake their lust for love. (Drive thru wedding chapels in Vegas, much?) If couples had to wait a year to get married, most of them would sober up within six months and call it quits; it's science.

## Stage 1 – Lust

**Ever experience "love at first sight"? Well, guess what? That's lust at work. (The love comes after, if you're lucky.)** When my grandpa was a young man working as a cook in a restaurant, he saw a lovely woman slip into a booth with her friend. That woman turned out to be my grandmother, a girl of 18 who was about to go into the convent. Right then, my grandpa turned to his mother and said, "I'm going to marry that girl," and three weeks later, they were engaged. The story sounds impossibly romantic, but since he didn't know a thing about my grandmother beyond his attraction, their whirlwind romance had a lot more to do with lust than love at that point. In fact, when we talk about those couples who "just knew", I think we are living under a beautiful delusion. What likely happened was that there was the initial attraction and they later discovered they were very compatible. These are the lucky ones. There are plenty of people who become smitten and think they've found "the one", date, and then break up because they learn they are actually incompatible. They then tell themselves that person wasn't "the one" after all. Their stories don't turn into fairy tales, because that's how it goes when you're dating.

The chemicals responsible for lust are the sex hormones testosterone and estrogen. It's testosterone that is responsible for the male mating effort, but females are also affected since testosterone spikes the libido in both sexes.

**If you have low testosterone or low estrogen, it will be difficult to "fall in lust" or feel frisky.** Pay attention to this fact, because it's not uncommon for mature couples to struggle with issues of lust in their relationship. These struggles may have little to do with issues of compatibility and "growing apart" and everything to do with fading chemistry and hormonal imbalances. More on this later.

## Stage 2 – Love

What we have come to associate with love is essentially three main neurotransmitters: adrenaline, dopamine and serotonin.

Adrenaline makes your heart race when you see the object of your affection.

Dopamine is euphoric, and it's what keeps you awake at night. Helen Fisher, a professor at Rutgers University, has studied romantic interpersonal attraction for over 30 years. She suggests that dopamine is akin to cocaine. New couples show signs of surging dopamine through increased energy, decreased appetite, and sleeplessness.

Low serotonin keeps you obsessing about your sweetheart. If you can't stop thinking about him or her, it's because love lowers serotonin levels.

In stage 2, you are basically drunk on a lethal combination of adrenaline, dopamine, and serotonin. You are a fool in love, and you can't help but magnify your partner's virtues and boast about him to all your friends. You ignore red flags and incompatibilities and minimize your sweetheart's flaws. You think your relationship is somehow more special than anyone else's, and you feel "madly in love". Madly is the word for it, because you really are experiencing something akin to mental illness, something called obsessive-compulsive disorder. In an interesting study, Dr. Marazitti, a psychiatrist at the University of Pisa, analyzed blood samples from lovers who had been together less than six months. She discovered that "serotonin levels of new lovers were equivalent to the low serotonin levels of Obsessive-Compulsive Disorder patients."[18]

**This heady, love-struck phase usually lasts no more than six months.** In fact, when researchers tested these same couples a year later, they found that serotonin levels had returned to normal and they were no longer obsessed with their partner.

This drop in adrenaline, dopamine and levelling off of serotonin may explain why so many relationships don't make it past six months: once the love chemicals normalize (and the rose-colored glasses come off), the relationship breaks down. Would Romeo and Juliet have been able to go the distance? We will never know.

For the love junkie addicted to the heady rush of being in love, the next stage – attachment – is simply boring. Love junkies will terminate one relationship as soon as it becomes "boring", and start another one, repeating the process over and over again.

*PEARLY WISDOM: Don't get married until you've had at least a year of run time together. You're blinded by lust and your brain is swimming in potent chemicals for the first six months of a relationship. This is when you're prone to making unwise decisions, like eloping to Vegas. If you really are meant to be together, you don't need to rush it.*

## Stage 3 – Attachment

The final stage of falling in love is the attachment stage. The other chemicals start to stabilize and oxytocin and vasopressin take over your brain. These two chemicals promote fidelity and attachment. Oxytocin is called the cuddling hormone for a reason: when you hug, you get a pleasurable hit of oxytocin. Mature couples will sometimes prefer cuddling over sex for this reason.

Oxytocin is also referred to as the "love hormone". It reduces fear and increases trust and belonging. Women get a dose of oxytocin when we cuddle or have sex, and it allows us to pair-bond with our partner. In men, vasopressin serves the same purpose. It activates the bonding centers in the brain, producing feelings of attachment and protectiveness. Vasopressin makes men want to stick around after sex and cuddle. New genetic research seems to indicate that men with low vasopressin – the "cuddling hormone" – are less likely to pair bond. In a 2008 study by scientists at Stockholm's Karolinska Institute, men with a certain gene coding for one type of vasopressin receptor, aren't as cuddly and affectionate as their mate would like them to be. In fact, they are less likely to commit and twice as likely to report relationship problems.[19]

*PEARLY WISDOM: Genetics could explain why some men are unable to commit, and it has nothing to do with you! If a man says he doesn't want to get married, believe him. Sometimes, it's just the way a man is wired. It's not always about you. As I say in The Cha Cha Club Dating Man-ifesto: Next!*

So, now that you're an expert in the science of love, what do you do when love and lust start to fade?

You bring the chemistry back.

# Chapter 12: Sex and Desire - The Science of Staying in Love

*Give me my sin again.*

— William Shakespeare, *Romeo and Juliet*

Do couples grow apart because sexual chemistry fades? Or does sexual chemistry fade because couples grow apart?

In 2012, scientists discovered that a nasal spray containing oxytocin made couples more pleasant towards one another during an argument: the female subjects became friendlier, calmer, and less anxious, while the male subjects became more sensitive and positive. Oxytocin is sometimes called the "love hormone", the "cuddle drug" or the "monogamy hormone". It is released during an orgasm and naturally occurs in the body. It is one of the hormones involved in sex and sexual attraction, and it promotes trust, relaxation, bonding, and confidence".[20]

We often look for cause and effect, and simple binary solutions to our problems, and it's possible that many couples drift apart for a variety of reasons, but if taking oxytocin can heal relationships and reduce arguments, there is no doubt that chemistry has a role in bringing back loving feelings. If so, what can we do to stimulate more oxytocin and increase the love juice in our relationship, naturally?

We can change our behavior.

## How Your Behavior Can Change Chemistry

Here's an example of how behavior can change chemistry. Have you ever known couples who sleep separately because one works night shifts or snores? I know a few, and they're not having much sex. And if they're not having much sex, they're missing out on the potent alchemy of love.

Cara's husband slept in a separate room so he could have a better night's sleep. Eventually, he stopped wanting to have sex with her. She tried everything she could to coax him into having more sex: she bought sexy lingerie, went to therapy, and even tried to make him jealous. Nothing worked. She was very unhappy in her relationship and felt rejected. (This is more common for women in their forties than people realize.) To me, it looked like the end of their marriage. A year or so later, I noticed she seemed a lot happier in her marriage: there were Facebook photos of the two of them enjoying romantic dates and holidays. I asked her what had happened. She said it was really simple: she had insisted he sleep with her in the same bed each night. She didn't ask for more sex; she just asked for him to sleep in the same bed. Well, the physical closeness led to more nookie. A simple change in routine changed everything.

In another example of how behavior can affect chemistry, there was a large study done in the Philippines on 600 men. Testosterone samples were taken one year apart: before these men had children, and after. Researchers discovered that testosterone levels had dropped. Not only that, but the more time these men spent caring for their children – changing diapers, and so forth – the more it dropped. The study suggests that men's behavior and daily habits can affect their hormones in a significant way.[21]

Note: I am not advocating that men should stop taking care of children if they want to keep their testosterone levels high; in fact, it seems that nature wants it this way, as low testosterone prevents men from straying and increases the marital bond. Having a man around also ensures the survival of their offspring, from an evolutionary perspective. No, I'm all for equal parenting. However, if you're a new father and you're feeling the symptoms of low testosterone – erectile dysfunction, low libido, depression, and moodiness – it's worth making some lifestyle changes to increase your testosterone.

*PEARLY WISDOM: Weightlifting – especially large compound exercises like dead lifts, squats, and bench presses – is especially helpful for increasing testosterone, as is ensuring that adequate levels of healthy fats and zinc, which enables the male body to produce testosterone, are consumed each day.*

> **Guideline #26: If you want to enjoy your sex life, take responsibility for your behavior and your hormones.**

## What to Do if You're Low on Love Juice

What differentiates couples from being "just friends" is sex. Without healthy levels of serotonin and dopamine, oxytocin and vasopressin, couples start to uncouple and function more as roommates. Less touching and sex produces less juicy chemicals in the brain, and – less sex. It's a self-perpetuating downward spiral.

So, stop waiting for your partner to get you in the mood, and realize that sex, like love, is a choice you can make every day.

Want to feel less anxious and more relaxed? Have more sex. Want to feel loved and cared for? Have more sex.

Want to feel connected to your partner? Have more sex.

More sex means a healthier heart, better sleep, better skin and hair, a better immune system, less depression and fewer colds... and a more deeply connected and powerful relationship. **Regular sex means living together without growing apart.**

What's that you say? You're not in the mood?

I'll admit: Making yourself have sex can be a problem if you're the lower-libido partner. It's especially hard on individuals who feel they must be emotionally connected to their partner before they can be physically intimate. Negative emotions like resentment, anger or depression can prevent partners from enjoying a healthy sex life.

If this is the case, I offer two pieces of advice.

### 1. Advice for Higher-libido Partners

It's vital for the higher-libido partner to realize that intimacy must exist outside the bedroom. Helping out with household chores; demonstrating thoughtful gestures; hugs; appreciative texts; love notes; and kisses are all ways to stimulate oxytocin and vasopressin in a partner and reduce resentment. Do this several times a day, and you increase the bond and trust between you. Also, consider the hours leading up to sex as opportunities for foreplay.

*PEARLY WISDOM: Silently gazing into your partner's eyes for a couple minutes can be very powerful and magnetic. It establishes intimacy and connection like nothing else. Give it a try: it may feel strange at first, but it becomes quite beautiful with practice.*

## Guideline #27: Foreplay begins outside the bedroom.

Men experience sexual arousal and desire a bit differently from women. For men, arousal and desire are interchangeable. Men can see something sexy and feel instantly aroused enough to have sex, while women usually need to de-stress before they can feel frisky. If you've ever laughed at the "Porn for Women: Men Cleaning the House" books, you understand the seductive power of a bunch of hunky men doing household chores. Want to get your woman in the mood? Do some chores around the house. Seeing Tex in a fitted t-shirt and jeans, vacuuming the house turns me on. Every. Time.

Also, hugging your partner for at least six seconds, six times a day, has also been shown to increase oxytocin.[22] In their book, *How To Improve Your Marriage Without Talking About It,* Patricia Love, Ed.D., and Steven Stosny, Ph.D., say that hugs are the first to go when a relationship is on the rocks. They also say that the less often couples embrace, the more resentful they become. If you want more physical and emotional intimacy, make sure you hug each other outside of the bedroom. Often.

Men need longer, more-full body hugs. This may be due to the fact that men experience less touching in general. In a research study of sexual behavior in couples who had been together for more than 25 years, sociologists at the Kinsey Institute of Indiana University found that "Men who said kissing and cuddling were a regular part of their relationship were on average three times happier than those who did not." Over 1,000 couples in five countries were surveyed.[23]

Never underestimate the power of a hug.

## 2. Advice for Lower-libido Partners

If you're on the fence about sex, just do it! There are so many health and relationship benefits to having sex. Don't deprive yourself of something that is really good for you and will help your relationship. You are an equal participant in your sex life. Want to be a better lover? Learn! Practice! Very few of us are taught how to be good lovers; some of us are more intuitive in that regard, or more experienced, and have been lucky enough to have had help along the way, but really, most of us are just fumbling in the dark at it.

Mastering anything requires practice. Consider taking a couples' massage course, or attending Tantra classes, or pole dancing, to put you in touch with your body and become a more sensual person. You may also find that simply having sex makes you want to have more sex. It's up to you to flip that switch.

> *Masturbation helps a lot. The more you do it, the more in the mood you feel on a regular basis. I think this is why guys tend to have a higher sex drive than women – because they do a lot more... um... practicing than women tend to. They constantly remind themselves of how good an orgasm feels. Plus you learn your body faster, and you know what feels good and what doesn't.*
>
> — Donna

*PEARLY WISDOM: If you don't feel like sex, it's very possible that you are suffering from a deficit of pleasure in your life. By seizing opportunities to enjoy more pleasurable experiences in and out of the bedroom, you can decrease stress and increase joy and sensuality in your life. Pleasure and delight are not luxuries, they are essential to our well-being!*

Communicate with your partner in a loving way. If you don't like being touched a certain way, let your partner know and ask to be touched a different way instead. Most men are really accommodating if you bring things up in a way that doesn't make them feel attacked or as if they're doing something wrong. They want to hear you scream with pleasure!

Asking for what you want is how you live together without growing apart. The point is to understand what pleases you and to make sure that you get what you need to feel fulfilled.

### Just Do It

Tex has a higher libido than I do, and I have learned over time that if I have sex with him when I don't really feel like it, it can actually increase my appetite for sex so that I end up initiating the next time. It's as though my "off" switch suddenly switches to "on". So, I don't always wait to be in the mood to have sex. I know that it will feel good, and that it will do us both a world of good.

We also need the bonding that comes from having oxytocin and vasopressin flood our bodies during sex. If you'll recall, oxytocin is essential to bonding, and it brings that sense of peace and calm you feel when you're with "the one". Knowing this, I'm not surprised that if a week goes by without sex, I can start feeling a slight emotional disconnect from Tex. A quick roll in the sack restores that loving feeling, and we'll be sneaking kisses and acting more playful for hours after.

> **Guideline #28: Sex is like exercise: you almost never regret doing it. So, "Just do it."**

Sex is like exercise. Sometimes, you just don't want to work out, but you talk yourself into it and feel great after, and wonder why you had to talk yourself into it in the first place.

We all get into ruts. The trick is to recognize a rut and get out of it. Action is more powerful than words.

> *One of the most common hormone problems I see in my practice, among men and women, is that we are not having enough fun; we're not having enough pleasure. We are low in oxytocin, that yummy hormone of love and bonding. So, when you don't have enough oxytocin in your life, the glass feels half full.*[24]
>
> — Sara Gottfried, http://sexybacksummit.com

Low oxytocin may make you want to stay home instead of going out, or not want to have sex, but it's activities like cuddling, having dinner out, spending time with friends and shopping (for women) that raise oxytocin.

*PEARLY WISDOM: Sometimes, the things we resist the most are the best things for us.*

## Your Hormones

If you don't feel like having sex, it's highly possible your hormones are to blame. If you recall, sex drive and lust are triggered by testosterone in both men and women.

Women's sex drive can also be affected by estrogen. Estrogen levels fall dramatically in women when they go through menopause, usually between the ages of 40 and 55. Symptoms of menopause include mood swings, vaginal dryness and loss of libido, or sex drive.

Too much estrogen is as bad as too little. Too much estrogen is called estrogen dominance. Women aged 35–45 typically present with estrogen dominance. This means that you can experience PMS symptoms and your sex drive can drop. If you're a man and you have estrogen dominance, you're going to get man boobs and love handles, and lack sex drive. When testosterone drops, men prefer to cuddle rather than have sex. They lose ambition and drive. They get fussy, and their personality can change. The man-opause is real.

Testosterone and estrogen are linked to everything from low libido to cardiovascular disease and depression. According to Dr. Sara Gottfried, Harvard-trained M.D. and gynecologist and author of *The Hormone Cure*, hormone problems account for 75% of low sex drive.

*PEARLY WISDOM: While a drop in testosterone is associated with age, it's not the main reason for it. Lifestyle, diet, genetics, and lack of exercise are the biggest contributors.*

Growing older doesn't have to mean your hormones tank and your sex life is over. You can manage your hormones through medication, diet, sleep, exercise, and lifestyle changes. In fact, men and women with healthy hormone levels can enjoy some of the best sex of their lives after the age of 40.

So, how do you know whether your hormones are okay? You can ask your doctor to check them. If you want to save yourself the trip, you can also go to mymedlab.com and order a test there. For around $99 U.S., you can order the Hormone Bank panel, which includes five of the most valuable hormone numbers – estrogen, progesterone, testosterone, cortisol and thyroid. (High cortisol or low thyroid can diminish sex drive, decrease energy and cause weight gain, among other issues.)

The panel is available at over 2,000 locations nationwide across the United States without the cost or inconvenience of a doctor's visit just to have your blood drawn. You can view your results within 48 hours. If your hormones are low or flagged for alert, you can print your results and take them to your doctor for discussion, or discuss them with one of their experts. I've personally used MyMedLab twice, along with one of their thyroid experts. It was a great experience, since my regular doctor lacked knowledge in this area.

A prescription for bio-identical or synthetic hormones may fix some of the symptoms, but it will not address the root cause. Lifestyle, diet, and exercise can hugely impact your hormones and, in some cases, reverse a disease or put it into remission. **The greatest health (physical and mental) transformations occur when we address the root cause of our problems, not just the symptoms.**

## Fix Your Hormones, Naturally

Please note that although I have had a physician review this chapter, you should discuss any health concerns with your own doctor.

While some people will need to be on medication for life (I am one of them, as I have to take thyroid hormone every day), there are some lifestyle tweaks that can regulate your hormones and improve your quality of life. Think of each of these items as a leg in a four-legged table. Remove one leg, and you're going to have a problem.

### 1. Exercise and move every day.

The more muscles you use and the greater the intensity of your workout, the greater the increase in your circulating testosterone. Weightlifting, especially squats and dead lifts, increases human growth hormone and testosterone in men and women. However, too much exercise can tank your hormones. If you are spending more than a couple of hours a day exercising intensely, you could be setting yourself up for trouble.

**2. Get your vitamins and micronutrients.**

To decrease the likelihood of developing a vitamin deficiency, you need to consume 6–8 servings of fruits and vegetables per day. It's also important to "eat the rainbow", to ensure a variety of nutrients for your body. For example, yellow bananas are high in potassium, and red strawberries are high in vitamin C. It's a challenge to meet the minimum recommended daily allowances, even for the nutritionally minded who consume 6–8 servings of fruits and vegetables a day. Most people are deficient in things like vitamin D, omega-3s, potassium and zinc on a daily basis, and could benefit from quality supplements including a good-quality fish oil. Did you know that male prostate tissue requires 10 times more zinc than other cells in the body? Zinc is very important for men but also for women: low zinc in women can increase the risk of breast cancer. Zinc is pretty cheap as far as supplements go. However, popping vitamins won't do much to make up for a rotten diet. Try to get some natural vitamins and fiber in by eating more fruit and veg and whole grains.

Did you know that the average American gets less than 5 grams of fiber a day? At the time of this writing, the recommended daily average is about 25 grams a day (still too low, in my opinion). One large salad, one veg at dinner and one to two pieces of fruit a day, along with some whole grains, should meet the basic requirements but can still leave a void as far as vitamins are concerned. If you want to track your vitamin and fiber intake out of curiosity, use an app like MyFitnessPal to record everything you eat for a couple of weeks. You'll probably be shocked to find yourself falling short on vitamins and minerals. The app is free.

*PEARLY WISDOM: Foods high in zinc are seafood and oysters, then dark meats like beef and lamb, then toasted wheat germ and spinach, pumpkin seeds, and cashew nuts, followed by chocolate, pork and chicken, beans, and mushrooms. How many of these do you eat on a regular basis? Are you getting enough? In general, animal foods are better sources of zinc than plant foods. As an example, 3 oz. cooked oysters provide about 450% of your recommended daily allowance (RDA), whereas 1 cup cooked spinach only has 9% (RDA of 15 g zinc per day). If you take a multivitamin to fill in nutritional gaps, check how much zinc it has. A lot of multivitamins/multi-minerals market themselves by including a bunch of vitamins and minerals in a pill, but give you only trace amounts of each. Read the labels. Since supplements and vitamins can negatively impact medication, or have side effects if taken in too large a dose, be sure to discuss them with your doctor or dietician.*

**3. Get adequate sleep.**

Sleep is essential for proper hormone production. Sleep allows you to rebuild and repair. Insufficient sleep results in impaired mood, decreased cognitive ability, decreased testosterone and insulin function, higher cortisol, a taxed immune system, increased risk of diabetes, increased hunger and cravings, and weight gain. Sleep deprivation fries your hormones!

**4. Eat healthy.**

What you put in your mouth has a profound effect on your hormones. Eat high-quality protein, and healthy fats from nuts, olive oil, fish oil and coconut oil. Fats stabilize hormonal levels, and a low-fat diet can tank your blood sugar and sex drive. Cut the sugar and try to get your sweets from whole, fresh fruits and berries. When it comes down to it, sugary drinks – even fruit juice –

are no competition for whole foods and Mother Nature's "candy" – fruit!

Watching your blood sugar? Add water and fiber to your meals to reduce the glycemic index in a food item. For example, you can have a smoothie instead of a juice, since the increased fiber slows down the rate of absorption and slowly releases sugar and micronutrients into your bloodstream. You can also eat a handful of nuts or a piece of cheese with your fruit. Adding fats and fiber to meals will help keep blood sugar levels in check and prevent energy crashes and mood swings.

Fiber is important because it keeps you feeling fuller for longer, and reduces the odds of developing conditions like heart disease and diabetes. One good rule of thumb is to consume things that have a low carbohydrate to fiber ratio. According to the Harvard School of Public Health, the ideal ratio is 10:1 or lower: the lower the first number, the more fiber an item has. For example, if an item's Nutrition Facts label indicates 22 grams of carbs and only 2 grams of fiber, the carb to fiber ratio is 11:1 and not ideal. (You simply divide the amount of carbs by the amount of fiber listed on the label.)

*PEARLY WISDOM: While some people will tell you to stay away from white potatoes, bananas, and watermelon because they have a high glycemic index, the reality is that a high glycemic index is no indication of a high glycemic load. Case in point: Watermelon has a whopping GI of 72 (higher than a Coke at 68) but a load of only 4. Why? Because the absolute amount of carbohydrates in a serving is low. Google "glycemic index", and you will see some things that may shock you. For example, boiled white potatoes have a lower load than sweet potatoes.*[25]

## Bonus Points:

### 5. Have more sex!

Getting busy between the sheets means flooding your system with pleasurable chemicals that enhance mood, decrease stress, and increase bonding. If sex is painful due to vaginal dryness (associated with menopause), use a lubricant. Also note that having sex regularly can naturally increase lubrication.

Both partners are equally responsible for a healthy sex life. If you're the lower-libido partner, take care of your body, get your hormones checked, find some pleasure in life and recognize that you may not have fallen out of love with your partner, just lust. This can be fixed! You may be only a tweak away from feeling frisky again. Have a look at the points above – exercise, vitamins, sleep, and diet – and pick *one* you can improve on right away. Once that's addressed, move on to the next item.

It's quite amazing what can happen when we stop pointing the finger and take charge of our own well-being.

Kass says lack of sleep kills her mood:

> *I don't have kids, But working nights, I struggle with lack of sleep sometimes. It actually alters your personality and you can't think straight or ideas overtake your mind and you can't deal with things rationally anymore. If I'm overtired, I get extremely emotional and moody and my coping skills fly out the window. The last thing I feel is sexy.*
>
> — Kass

## Asexuals

Asexuality is the lack of sexual attraction to anyone, and true asexuals make up less than 2% of the population. Sometimes, asexuals will marry and have sex to satisfy their more desirous partner, but they really have no interest in sexual activity. For them, a relationship is more about comfort and compatibility than passion and chemistry. Such an arrangement can be very difficult for mixed-libido couples, especially if the higher-libido partner has been duped into marriage by an asexual partner.

How do you fix this asymmetry? I would recommend you draw up your own Love Agreement – and do it with professional help, someone you both feel comfortable talking to. Some couples will negotiate an "open marriage" so the higher-libido partner can have his or her needs met and the no-libido partner is free of the burden of sexual responsibility. I am not advocating this solution, as your relationship is unique to you, but I do think that if one of you actually dislikes sex, your situation is complex and you need to look for help beyond this book.

*PEARLY WISDOM: Chances are, if your relationship started off hot, neither of you is asexual. A declining sex drive is worth addressing: you have a right to sex in your relationship and all the joy it brings.*

You are born asexual, you do not become so. However, you can become low-interest over time. There are several reasons for this: resentment in a relationship, emotional disconnection, depression, boredom, fatigue, and hormones. New mothers are a great example of this, as hormones and lack of sleep are huge issues for them

*PEARLY WISDOM: So how much sex is good for a relationship? Well, it depends. If both of you have a high sex drive, you may want it every day. But if you are both low in sex drive, then once a month could be sufficient for you. It's only a problem if it's a problem for one of you.*

## My Hormones Are Fine, but I Just Don't Feel Like Sex

If your hormones are tested and they are normal, you eat well and exercise regularly, and your relationship is A-okay in all other respects, your sex life could be suffering from any of the following:

- Stress
- Depression
- Health issues and disease
- Poor body image
- Low sense of self-worth
- Previous sexual trauma
- Lack of sleep
- Not making time for sex
- Medications that lower libido
- Seasonal affective disorder
- Lack of excitement in the relationship

**Guideline #29: If we're stressed out, we are in survival mode, not reproductive mode.**

All of these things can suppress the libido. For example, when my father died, there was about a month where I really didn't feel like having sex. I was sad and grieving; I wanted to be held and comforted, but nookie was not my thing. The same thing happened when my mother was diagnosed with Alzheimer's at the age of 65. I'm also on thyroid medication, and there were several months when my prescription was being adjusted and I was on too low a dose. My sex drive really tanked then. Lastly, my weight has a huge impact on my libido. If I feel fat, I stop feeling sexy and my social confidence goes down. I hate to admit it, but it's the truth. When I can slip on my size 8 jeans, I feel much sexier. Yeah, I know that my cha cha shouldn't flex with my dress size, but it does, and I think this is true for a lot of women, despite the inspirational Facebook memes and commercials.

*PEARLY WISDOM: When your body is healthy, vibrant, and strong, your confidence and relationships flourish.*

**Guideline #30: Feeling sexy and confident = more and better sex.**

Poor Tex. He can do everything right, but if things are not going well for me, it's going to affect our sex life. It is up to me to take some responsibility for the sizzle in our relationship by taking care of my own physical and mental well-being. And it's his job, as my loving partner, to patiently support me as I work through these challenges.

He has. He does. And I would do the same for him in a heartbeat.

*PEARLY WISDOM: It's okay to not be in the mood sometimes, too. It's when you start to reject your partner (or vice versa) more than you accept them that it becomes a problem. Sometimes you just need a night to curl up on the couch and watch Netflix. Your partner should respect that and either curl up beside you or take care of their own needs.*

## Being Overweight Impacts Desire

With the current trend towards "curvy" and "plus size", I know this won't be a popular chapter. But bear with me, because being overweight can mean a much less satisfactory sex life. This isn't "fat shaming"; it's science.

In a podcast interview, "Exercise & Sex: The Good, The Bad, The Ugly", Brett Klika says that body image is a huge influencer on sexual desire. If you don't feel sexy, it's hard to feel sexual. A lot of this has to do with confidence. The comedienne Amy Schumer gave a no-holds-barred acceptance speech about what it's like to be a woman in show biz, and one of her lines was, "I'm 160 pounds and I can catch a dick whenever I want". Self-confidence trumps most things. If you have it, you're good no matter what. If you don't, take the steps to make it happen.

*PEARLY WISDOM: If you're very overweight, confidence may make you sexy, but it won't make you healthier.*

The truth is, being highly overweight (over 20% body fat in men, and over 30% body fat in women) can significantly contribute to a low libido. It can also contribute to sexual dysfunction. Being overweight can increase certain health risks, such as high blood pressure and diabetes, both of which can impair blood flow and cause erectile dysfunction and loss of stamina. You're much more likely to avoid sex if it feels like a lot of hard work or gives you performance anxiety. Which is a shame, because there are so many health and relationship benefits.

Being overweight also contributes to lower testosterone levels. One theory is that fat stores estrogen, so when you have an excess of fat, your testosterone-to-estrogen ratio gets messed up.

Interestingly enough, scientists have discovered that American men have lower testosterone than ever before. In fact, testosterone levels have dropped about 17.4% over a 20-year period, according to one large study presented in the *Journal of Clinical Endocrinology.*[26]

I find it interesting that men are more overweight than ever before, just as testosterone is tanking in the American male population. A decade ago, women carried more body fat than men. It's how nature designed us. Now, men's obesity rates have been climbing faster than women's and we are nearly the same.[27] Perhaps this is one reason why so many of my single-gal friends complain about men being too passive. Lack of male initiative is a problem for these ladies, at least in North America.

*PEARLY WISDOM: When women talk about men not having "balls", they're really talking about the psychological traits of confidence, risk-taking and aggression, which are scientifically linked to testosterone; 95% of testosterone is created in the testicles!*

## How to Sustain Desire

In the beginning, you probably didn't need much stimulation – visual or physical – to get turned on by your partner. Your relationship was new, and everything was exciting. Your hormones were going crazy and you couldn't keep your hands off each other. But the more comfortable you became in a relationship and the more secure you felt, the less exciting sex seemed to become. It's the paradox between the need to feel secure and the need to feel passion in a relationship. Your lifelong challenge, then, is to continually make your partner feel loved, while keeping sex fun and the passion alive.

**Guideline #31: Your lifelong challenge is to continually date each other.**

Make sure date nights are not just dinner at the local steak house – keep date nights sizzling by looking for new, fun things to do together. Every city has free magazines and newspapers listing events that are happening each month. Grab one from your local coffee shop and pick an activity.

Every week, Tex and I have a date night. Last week, we had read about the best place in D.C. for a grilled cheese sandwich, so we had to try it. Yup, it was pretty awesome. Afterwards, we went to "Perfect Liars Club", a monthly performance where four people get on stage and each of them tells a story. The audience has to guess which one is false. We were totally deceived, and had a good laugh over it. We love trying new things: it's not only fun and romantic; it makes us feel closer and more connected.

**Couples can also increase connection by taking time out from each other.** It may sound paradoxical, but if you do everything together, it's quite healthy to spend a weekend or evening away and give your partner the gift of missing you. This distance can bring back the mystery and allow your partner to admire you as unique and apart from them, just like when you first met.

## Five Ingredients for Good Sex

What do you think are the most important ingredients for good sex? Discuss with each other. My list is as follows:

- Confidence
- Novelty
- Imagination
- Playfulness
- Selflessness

If you add even just one of these ingredients to the mix, you're guaranteed to spice up your sex life. For example, you can touch your partner differently (novelty) and explore sexual fantasies together (imagination) or have sex in different environments (confidence). As an old teacher of mine used to say, "Variety is the spice of life, but monogamy brings home the bacon!" Don't forget to spice it up.

*PEARLY WISDOM: Ladies, the male ego is really tied to performance (which is why erectile dysfunction is so devastating for men). For most men, the sexiest thing you can do is joyfully surrender to his desire and enjoy his efforts. I'm not telling you to fake it: Just embrace it. We all love to please others and see them light up because of something we did. Joyful receptivity is a powerful thing, worth practicing in and out of the bedroom. It's how we live together without growing apart.*

* * *

## HOUSEKEEPING: Let's Talk about Sex

You won't always feel like sex. You won't always have good sex. But sex is one of the greatest privileges of an intimate relationship, and the wonderful thing is, it can get better over time.

**Task 1: Ask yourself...**

Which of the five ingredients do you need most in your sex life?

What could you do to make it easier for your partner to have sex with you?

What would make you feel more desirable and desirous?

**Task 2: Ask each other...**

What habits have crept in that are preventing intimacy?

**Task 3: Passion waxes and wanes in couples. You can bring it back by having intentional sex.**

Ask each other: How often should you be having sex each week? Can you make time for it? (Perhaps this is something to include in your Love Agreement.)

If you want to live together without growing apart, make sex part of your regular routine while finding ways to keep your love life exciting.

*PEARLY WISDOM: One of the reasons partners stray is that they aren't having their physical and emotional needs met. Is it wrong to cheat? Absolutely. But it is also unfair to expect a partner to remain monogamous while you withhold sex and physical intimacy for months and months. That's betraying the unwritten rules of a committed relationship. Ignoring the importance of sex is ignoring the needs of a monogamous relationship and a sure-fire way to destroy your love. As I said before, you have a right to physical intimacy in your relationship and all the joy it brings.*

**Guideline #32: A relationship without sex is simply friendship.**

## Desire Q & A

### Questions for Discussion:

What do you really, really desire in YOUR relationship? Is it something you've expressed to your significant other? If not, why not?

Clint wants trust:

> *Intimate trust is the base that everything else is built on. How can you touch, speak with, or even live with someone without deep intimate trust in, or the ability to forgive and unconditionally love, them and yourself? This is what I desire, look for, and work for.*

Nicole needs to be pushed:

> *I need someone who can push my boundaries and limitations and help me embrace all the possibilities that life has to offer. I want to be able to be completely open and want the same in return. Why? Experiencing someone who can make you comfortable stepping outside of your comfort zone would be, in my opinion, an amazing person. Life has enough limits to it, and someone that loves you enough to always want more or better for you is the definition of love to me.*

Breanna wants respect:

> *The thing I desire most is for my husband to stick up for me, which shows respect. It's something that is assumed when a couple gets married, but it isn't necessarily something that couples discuss, give or receive. I don't think my husband is actually capable of*

> *giving me what I want, because it's not in his nature. He avoids conflict as much as possible and doesn't like to antagonize people or stick up for himself let alone anyone else, me included. I've been married for over 20 years and my husband has only stuck up for me once in that time period and it was only because he received pressure from my (now former) sister-in-law who was going through something similar and wound up leaving her husband because of it. She tried to help my husband understand that it's an important part of a relationship and if a woman doesn't feel like a man can defend her, then she feels disrespected.*

Lisa loves kisses:

> *Someone recently asked me, "What are six things you can't live without?" Kisses (from my husband) was first on my list. If you'd asked me that same question before I started pole dancing (nine years ago!), I probably would've said, hugs from hubby. If I were being really honest I might have confessed that what I really wanted was to *feel* more desire. Because I thought I'd been born with a very low libido. The difference in our lust levels was the only kink in our marriage. Sensual movement unleashed my inner sexy siren. I learned how to turn myself on so my husband didn't have to.*
>
> *It turned out my body had been asleep. Not anymore. In addition to an insatiable desire for kisses, I discovered I adore and often initiate (something I never did before) Sunday morning sex with my smooth cheeked husband (no stubble for me). We've been married 25 years and have a loving, playful, passionate, lustful marriage. What do I really, really want? To be kissing him for at*

*least another *20,118 days* when I'll be 103 and he'll be 105. And we'll have celebrated 80 years of marriage!*

## Takeaways

I loved reading these shared stories. If you recall, I asked what men and women really desire in a relationship. To recap:

1. More than sex, people crave trust, openness, mental connection, and respect in a relationship.

2. The desire to make out with your partner doesn't fade after 25 years of marriage.

3. Low-libido partners may simply be "asleep". They can turn themselves on and raise their libido through sensual activities like pole dancing.

Now, what do you crave?

# Chapter 13: How to Feel Sexy and Sensual

*The curve is more powerful than the sword.*

— Mae West

## How to Become a More Sensual Person

Adam Gilard, author and dating advisor, tells people to "be erotically aware" if they want to fully embrace their sexuality. Being aware means to be awake to the pleasures of life, to feel alive and engaged in your senses and what is going on in the world. To become erotically aware, he suggests things like listening to the sound of leaves rustling in the wind, enjoying the sun's warmth on your cheek and feeling the softness of your clothing. Being aware means taking a moment to just be in your body and appreciate it.

In essence, becoming a more sensuous and sexy person means being more present and using all of your senses.

*PEARLY WISDOM: Note things that make you feel sexy, and include them more often in your life. If exercising with your partner makes you feel frisky, do more of that. If body care makes you feel more sensuous, make time for it each day. If you're an introvert, you may need to schedule alone time, because constantly being around others is a drain that sucks the sexy out. Self-awareness is critical to a healthy relationship.*

Have you ever noticed how easy it is to go on autopilot while driving to work or running errands? You stop noticing things. It's as if you're disengaged from your body. Now if you put yourself in a new environment, like a vacation, you can't help but appreciate new details. Your senses seem to come alive. This is why it's important to seek out new experiences with and without your partner.

Embrace your sensual side. Come alive.

Being sexy is about feeling healthy and vibrant, not how much lingerie you have. The key to feeling sexy is to put a little money in your sexy bank every day. Eat well, exercise and make time for yourself to recharge.

Everyone needs personal time (PT) to explore their sensual sides, so make sure you give each other PT in your relationship, even if you have to schedule this. (As I mentioned, Tex and I have agreed on 10 hours of PT a week.)

## What Makes You Feel Sexy?

For some people, feeling desirable makes them feel sexy. But what happens as you age, or become ill, and your body isn't as banging as it once was?

*Since I have a chronic illness, any day I don't feel like I am dying, I feel pretty sexy. I used to be super-model skinny with Farrah Fawcett hair. That ship has sailed; prednisone will do that. I have had to rely on my mind and sense of humor a lot more just to cope, and anyone will tell you: the sexiest part of the body is the brain. I can still feel cute physically, but I know if I have five minutes to talk to someone, they are mine.*

— Peggy

Teeth will go, skin will wrinkle, body parts will droop and hair will turn grey, but if you are with a person whose mind and attitude excite you, the attraction never gets old.

What makes you feel sexy and sensual and charismatic? For me, feeling good gives me cha cha, and there are a number of ways to get it.

### Twenty Things You Can Do to Feel Good Right Now

1. Plan a girls'/guys' night out.

2. Move! Dance, go for a run, do yoga. Feel your body mooooooove.

3. Laugh. Watch a comedy or go to a comedy club.

4. Wear something sexy.

5. Buy something soft to wear to bed.

6. Love the skin you're in. Massage it in the shower; exfoliate all over. Find a lotion you love.

7. Shop for a new scent.

8. Spend a little more time on your makeup.

9. Get a new haircut.

10. Ask your partner to give you a massage, or pay for one.

11. Light some candles.

12. Have a bubbly bubble bath.

13. Meditate.

14. Do something out of the ordinary.

15. Enhance your favorite facial feature – eyes, lips. Not sure how to do this? Book a free or nearly free makeover at a cosmetic store or aesthetic school and ask them to show you how.

16. Reconnect with someone you love, and acknowledge something you appreciate about them.

17. Turn off all electronic devices and distractions, lie on your back and breathe.

18. Indulge in a guilty pleasure, such as reading a book or sipping a frou-frou cocktail.

19. Sing along to a song you love.

20. Express yourself creatively. Bake. Scrapbook. Collage. Journal. Whatever puts you in the zone. Play some music while you do it.

In positive psychology, there is something known as flow, and in sports, this is sometimes referred to as finding your zone. It's a focused and energized mental state in which we are completely absorbed in an activity. We are living in the moment and enjoying every second of it.

Find your flow and feel good.

* * *

## HOUSEKEEPING: Get Sexy(er)

Alright, you sexy beasts. If you've been suffering from a deficit of pleasure in your life, it's time to change that. Start simple.

**Task 1: Engage your senses.**

The five senses are sight, hearing, taste, touch, and smell.

Can you think of ways to engage more of your senses and become more present? Can you listen to music more often (hearing), bring flowers into the home (scent) or buy something silky for yourself (touch)? Can you slow down and appreciate your food by plating it in a more visually attractive way? Can you take a moment to inhale the aroma of your dinner before digging in? Think of ways you can embrace your sensual side, on your own. Now think of ways you can invite your partner into the experience. You may want to jot some ideas down in a journal.

**Task 2: Fill in the blank.**

I feel sexy when ________________________________________.

Make it happen.

*As a classic nature-seeking introvert, I love to listen to silence. I have noticed, repeatedly, that when I am out wandering in the woods, I feel sexy. I notice myself walking around, getting more turned on. I am more attracted to men I've known when we are outside, even just friends! I guess it's several of the senses at play too, fresh air – smell, seeing green things, increased oxygen. For me, just standing in the forest for 10 minutes and breathing makes me feel more sensual.*

— Daniella

# Chapter 14: Trust

*To trust another person not only means that you will believe he will not hurt you intentionally, but that you feel he will take your interests as his own and so will avoid situations where he could hurt you unintentionally. To trust each other is to be vulnerable in the same way.*

— David Viscott, *How to Live with Another Person*

## Trust Increases Connection

How do you increase trust in a relationship? By being impeccable with your word. When you agree to do something, such as bringing in the car to get fixed or vacuuming the carpet, do it and do it in a timely fashion. If you let it slip, be the first to recognize it and apologize.

Being true to your word and apologizing sincerely when you screw up is how you build trust in a relationship.

I trust Tex more than anyone else in this world. I trusted him from the beginning, and over time, I've learned to trust him even more. I think trust is the foundation of our relationship. It's why I am so relaxed with him. It's why everything is just so easy. I feel safe. I feel protected, I feel loved. If he did something to betray this trust, I know things would never be the same between us.

I trust Tex because he has a lot of integrity. He always does what he says he'll do, and he honors my requests. He seems to take joy in doing things for me. I am a very lucky woman, because I didn't know just how wonderful he was until we lived together and I discovered that trying to please me was not just part of the courtship, but essential to who he is and how he loves. He is a "Quality Man":

> *A Quality Man is trustworthy. He will be honest and straightforward. He is respected by others. He does what he says. He doesn't leave you hanging. He has integrity. He will not lie. He will not cheat. He will not mooch. He is transparent. He is accountable for his actions. He is dependable and lives by a code. He apologizes if he has screwed up, because he wants your trust and respect. He is, as they say, "a great guy".*
>
> — Sophie Winters, *The Cha Cha Club Dating Man-ifesto*

I like to think I'm also a "Quality Woman".

## What Is Trust?

According to the Merriam-Webster Dictionary, trusting someone means you believe he or she is "reliable, good, honest, and effective".

In his extraordinary business book *The SPEED of Trust: The One Thing That Changes Everything*, author Stephen M.R. Covey says that there are 13 trust behaviors that establish trust (talk straight, demonstrate respect, create transparency, right wrongs, show loyalty, deliver results, get better, confront reality, clarify expectations, practice accountability, listen first, keep commitments, and extend trust). Covey's book walks you through each of these behaviors. More importantly, it shows you ways to check on your performance and to create plans for improvement.

Perhaps the biggest aha moment I had in the entire book was when Covey mentions how trust depends on two things: character and competence. We all know someone who is a great salesman (competent) but lacks integrity (character) and can't be trusted. Such a person might be very good at hitting monthly sales targets, but the way they do business may ultimately bring down a company's reputation. Similarly, we've all worked with someone who is really likeable and honest (character) but not very dependable (competence). We can't trust them to do quality work or to perform tasks on time.

When we trust someone, we can do so blindly or we can use smart judgement. This means withholding judgement, as a person's true colors are revealed in time through observation. Judgement usually comes with experience.

Although *The SPEED of Trust* is a business book, the same principle applies to couples. A partner may be of good character but unable to hold down a job or deliver as promised. He or she may not honor your Love Agreement or the rules of the relationship. When there are trust issues in a relationship, there are problems; nagging is one of them.

## Nagging Is a Sign of Trust Issues

If you're dealing with a nag, you're dealing with a woman (more often than not) who feels ignored, marginalized and disrespected. Nagging occurs when a person doesn't feel her requests are being heard or responded to in a timely fashion. Nagging is a sign of trust issues in a relationship. Zig Ziglar said, "If you treat your woman like a thoroughbred, you'll never end up with a nag."

I don't nag because I don't have to: I trust Tex to get stuff done. Experience has taught me that he's a quick responder and reliable and that he fulfills his commitments. If he doesn't get to something right away, I cut him some slack because I trust both his character and his competence.

We judge others by how fast they keep their commitments. One of the best way to restore trust is to make and keep commitments.

*PEARLY WISDOM: When we nag, it's because we don't trust our partner's character or competence, or both. And this is why we hate being nagged so much: deep down, we feel judged as lacking.*

## Nagging and Control Issues

Unfortunately, nagging can also result when we don't communicate our needs effectively, or when we have control issues. Whining and complaining about what you're not getting, rather than directly stating what you want, is going to make a man withdraw. When men feel they're being nagged, they become less responsive to their partner's requests, which further perpetuates the nagging and withdrawal cycle.

In Chapter 3 on Communication and Kindness, I referred to an article titled "I Wasn't Treating My Husband Fairly, and It Wasn't Fair."[28] Please go ahead and read that article. I link to it on my website. In it, MissFranJanSan talks about how her husband knows how to change the oil in the car, re-install a computer operating system, and fix thing around the house. He is not a stupid man, and making him feel small or stupid just because he does things differently than she would only makes him want to not do things for her. Since she had this revelation, she has stopped nagging so much and their relationship has improved.

Control issues also stem from fear and insecurity, but can be much more oppressive in a relationship than nagging. People with control issues fear chaos, and try to control their environment (and others) in order to have a more predictable outcome. Examples of a controlling person are: requiring their partner to promptly return all phone calls and getting angry when they don't; rigid and detailed planning of vacations or social events, white glove inspections on house cleaning; and specifying *exactly* how they want something done, or exactly how they want their partner to behave, without input from their partner. They may even rationalize their tyrannical behavior as serving the best interest of the family or relationship. When their partner falls short of their exacting standards, there is often hell to pay. Control issues can signal emotional abuse.

If you are dictating the terms and conditions of your relationship and keeping your partner on a "short leash" by telling them where to go and what to do, you have control issues.

## How to Stop Nagging

Women are much more verbal than men, but what we don't always realize is that **over-talking can lead to a partner under-listening.** Here's how the two of you can stop the nagging in your relationship. (Remember: It's Not You, It's Us).

1. Partner 1 (the nag): State your needs as simply and clearly as possible.

2. Partner 2 (the nagged): Fulfill commitments as quickly as possible.

That's it!

People hate being told what to do, when to do it and how to do it – so keep the requests simple, like: "Could you vacuum the carpet this weekend?" This gives your partner time to fulfill the request at their own speed and still maintain their dignity. No one should expect their partner to jump on their requests unless they are truly urgent.

I was watching a daytime news show the other day, and the hosts were interviewing the two authors of a book on how to appear smart. They said one of the key ingredients to appearing smart is to act confidently. They noted that women tend to talk faster and longer than men because of confidence issues and that, rightly or wrongly, this can make them seem less intelligent, especially in business situations. The key to appearing smart is **to slow down your speech and to stop once you've made your point**. We're more swayed by people who present their case with confidence than with actual subject matter expertise.

> **Guideline #33: State your needs as simply and clearly as possible.**

### Communicate Effectively to Build Trust

If you don't like the way your partner is doing something, then take a moment to clearly explain how you would like it done. Tex has a great analogy about this; he calls it "digging a hole": You don't just say you need a hole dug and then come back and check after the person has worked their butt off to dig a six-foot hole in a location you don't like. That's too late. You need to communicate your requirements and then check in on progress. Then praise the work. Just like you would for an employee.

Recognize that you don't need to be the boss all the time (control freaks struggle with this). Save the supervising for the stuff that really matters, and have the grace to accept that not everyone will do things exactly like you would. Micromanaging someone is a sure-fire way to cause resentment in a relationship.

At the same time, if something is important to you, say so! Never assume that your partner knows what is important to you.

Just remember, not everything needs to be urgent. The only thing that is really, truly important is your happiness as a couple.

**Guideline #34: When everything is urgent, nothing is urgent.**

A high-functioning couple is one where partners trust one another and fulfill all reasonable requests asked of them. The other partner shows appreciation when these requests are fulfilled. They use specific language to praise and acknowledge their partner's efforts. "Thank you so much for vacuuming this weekend", or "Great job vacuuming, the carpet looks great", goes a long way to fostering trust and good feelings. You may think you shouldn't have to thank your partner for fulfilling their half of the domestic responsibilities, but you do if you want to keep from growing apart.

*PEARLY WISDOM: Lack of appreciation and taking one another for granted is a disease in many relationships. It's why 80% of couples who divorce state "growing apart" as the primary reason for their divorce.*

Funny how easily we can praise a child or a friend but neglect to honor the most important person in our life.

**Guideline #35: Small, daily acts of kindness and specific words of appreciation keep a couple from growing apart.**

## Trust Makes You Feel Safe

When you feel safe, you let go of your need for control. When you let go of your need for control, you surrender to the present.

When you surrender to the present, you feel so much happier.

The trick is to:

1. Trust yourself.

2. Trust the person you're with.

3. Be with someone who makes you feel safe.

It is very difficult to trust someone if you don't trust yourself first. We tend to project a lot of crap on other people. For example, if you've ever cheated on someone, you're that much more likely to suspect your partner of cheating. This is why it is so important to live with integrity. The longest, most important relationship you will ever have is the one with yourself. If you let yourself down, you have to live with that for the rest of your life.

**You need to feel physically and emotionally safe with your partner to completely trust them.** If your partner has betrayed you in the past, it is very difficult to trust them going forward.

Trust credits are built up over time. A large betrayal such as an affair can bankrupt your relationship. Constantly failing to do what you'll say you'll do, will slowly drain your trust account.

**Guideline #36: Build trust, and you build security in your relationship.**

*PEARLY WISDOM: Be impeccable with your word, and your partner will be much more sympathetic when you are unable to do something you promised to do. Trust can be loaned if you have enough credit history. If you miss a payment, make sure you pay it back, with interest. Too many missed payments, and your account could be closed.*

How do you live together without growing apart? You keep building trust.

Partners who trust each other can share the most vulnerable parts of themselves and still feel loved.

If you can't trust your partner, then your relationship – in fact, your very happiness – is in peril. Anxiety, depression, addiction, resentment, anger, grief, and health issues (mental and physical) can all result from relationships where friction is high and trust is low.

## What to Do if Trust Is Broken

If you feel shame about something, chances are you have not lived up to your own relationship ideals, whether your partner is aware of this or not. **Where there is shame, there is an apology waiting in the wings.**

As I said previously, partners who trust each other can share the most vulnerable parts of themselves and still feel loved. They can apologize when they feel they have done something wrong, and expect forgiveness, in time.

When you have let down your relationship, you must find a way to fix the situation and begin the slow and painful process of rebuilding trust. Ask your partner what you can do to make things right, and know that it will take time to rebuild credit.

Since women are much more verbal, we are more likely to apologize in a flowery way, whereas men are much more likely to apologize through action. If you recall my story "It's Not about the Cup", Tex extended an olive branch by making me tea in his favorite cup.

Part of being in a relationship is clueing into the fact that your partner is different from you, and recognizing and appreciating your different love languages.

**Guideline #37: Where there is shame, there is an apology waiting in the wings.**

## Five Elements of an Apology

I highly recommend Gary Chapman's book *The Five Languages of Apology* for when you screw up in a relationship. He says that for an apology to be effective, there must be five elements:

1. *Expressing Regret – "I am sorry".*
2. *Accepting Responsibility – "I was wrong".*
3. *Making Restitution – "What can I do to make it right?"*
4. *Genuinely Repenting – "I'll try not to do that again".*
5. *Requesting Forgiveness – "Will you please forgive me?"*

Furthermore, amends are best made in the primary love language of the offended partner. For example, if your partner's love language is gifts, a verbal apology plus a thoughtful gift will go a long way to making them soften. If your partner's love language is acts of service, then doing something for them is a great way to apologize.

If you have been wronged in a relationship, you have every right to expect your partner to earn your trust again. You have every right to be disappointed or even angry. But at some point, you must forgive your partner for wrongdoing if you want to restore connection. Is there enough credit still in the bank for you to trust again?

**Trust is earned. Forgiveness is a choice.**

What's the wrong way to apologize? To say, "I'm sorry" and not follow up.

> *I dated this guy who was always saying, "I apologize", yet was totally clueless as to the real issue. He thought he was so damn awesome for apologizing and would even say, "I apologized; I don't know what else I can do."*
>
> — Daniella

*PEARLY WISDOM: An apology is a sign of strength, and mature people aren't afraid to give one. Keep in mind that "I apologize", sounds a lot less personal and sincere than "I'm sorry". Be vulnerable in your apology: lean into the discomfort and own your actions if you truly want to heal things. Bad mistakes require more than the words "I'm sorry"; they also require grand gestures. Keep that in mind when you really screw up. (Note: Control freaks and abusers have a hard time apologizing, and if they do, they will often deflect or blame someone or something else for their behavior, so what you get is an excuse, not an apology. This relates to the amount of shame they feel inside, and their difficulty in dealing with deep-rooted fears of inadequacy. I recommend professional help.)*

## Trust, Respect, and Intimacy

Lisa Bahar, a licensed marriage and family therapist who works with clients on relationship and intimacy issues, responds to my questions on trust, respect, and intimacy:

**Q: It seems to me that when people are upset or disappointed with each other, resentment builds up.**

Lisa: *Certainly. Unprocessed or unresolved resentments can affect intimacy and trust, which is the basis for intimacy.*

**Q: Would you agree that couples become less affectionate and may even stop being intimate together?**

Lisa: *This tends to be a normal progression, of protecting oneself from feeling more hurt and building bigger resentments.*

**Q: How do you return to intimacy once trust has been broken?**

Lisa: *Acknowledge the breakdown, be willing to communicate, invite a professional who both of you feel validated by and safe to share the experience with.*

* * *

## HOUSEKEEPING: Build up Trust Credits

Want to live together without growing apart? Fulfill all reasonable requests in a timely fashion. Act with integrity and be impeccable with your word. Show daily, specific appreciations for each other. Apologize and make appropriate amends when you screw up. Simple, isn't it?

**Task 1: Fill in the blanks:**

I trust my partner when ______________________________.
(This is how your partner can acquire more trust credits from you.)

I feel most loved when ______________________________.
(So your partner can learn how to "speak" your love language.)

# Chapter 15: Privacy and Personal Space

*No relationship can survive an overabundance of closeness.*

— David Viscott, *How to Live with Another Person*

## Privacy

Privacy means being free from observation or interruption by other people. It also means being free from attention and public exposure. We all need privacy to recharge and de-stress, but we need different degrees of it.

### Guideline #38: Sometimes we need space to just *be*.

Some people are very private, and others are less so. Some people share very personal details in social media, and others reveal very little. Some people share everything with their best friend, while others wouldn't dream of discussing their innermost thoughts and feelings with anyone. Respecting these different needs for privacy is vital to your relationship.

For example, Tex and I are not "friends" on Facebook. I brought it up once and we both had a bit of a chuckle, because it had been on our minds as kind of an odd thing about us; the fact is, we're happy with keeping this aspect of our lives separate. If I trusted him less, I would probably want to "friend" him to keep tabs on him, but I feel no such need to monitor his activity. I have my own life to live and so does he, and we share so much as it is that I enjoy having this little bit of personal space. If he were my friend on Facebook, I might censor my posts a little more or write things a little differently, because I would know I was being observed. I enjoy my social media privacy and a place to be just me with friends who knew me long before Tex was in my life.

> *It's ok to be your own person and have a life outside your partner's. Just because you're in a relationship, it doesn't mean you have to do EVERYTHING together and be involved in every aspect of the other person's life. They had a life before you fell in love with them which made them who they are. They should still be allowed to have some of that life and just tweak it so both of you fit into the picture.*
>
> — Donna

Privacy means giving each other the space to enjoy friendships outside of the home. It means **each person has a right to their own friends, and the friends don't have to be liked.** As children, we play games where friendships are concerned; as adults, however, we can disagree with our partner's choice of friends and still support their decision.

For example, Tex has a friend who becomes a different person when he drinks, and it's not a nice experience. I've been out with them a few times, and each time I felt awkward and uncomfortable with his buddy's behavior. I told Tex I didn't want to hang out with them in a bar anymore because of this. I didn't ask Tex to stop being friends with his buddy; he's a good guy when he's sober. Tex has a right to keep seeing his friend, regardless of how I feel about him. Similarly, Tex respects the fact that I'm not keen on his friend, so he doesn't force him on me by having him over for dinner. You don't have to like each other's friends, but you don't have to spend time with them, either.

The most loving, healthy relationships encourage their partners to have girl time and guy time, because they recognize that friends (especially same-sex friends) can provide things that each other can't. Good friends provide wise second opinions, laughter, and a boost to self-confidence. They help us through stress and illness and the loss of loved ones. They are there to celebrate life's moments and to provide encouragement and a kick in the ass. A diverse network of friends and acquaintances keeps us energized and emotionally healthy. As partners, we must encourage one another to continually develop and maintain friendships, especially ones that are healthy and bring out the best in us. After the age of 30, it seems to become harder to make new friends: we aren't in college anymore, and our social circles shrink, especially if we have children. It's important to pursue hobbies and activities outside the home, where we can form new friendships at all stages of life.

*PEARLY WISDOM: A wise friend once said to me that we have friends for a reason, friends for a season, and sometimes, if we're lucky, we have friends for a lifetime. It is normal to outgrow some friends and acquaintances as we age and change our opinions about the world, and pick up new hobbies and interests. Perhaps this is why falling in love with our best friend isn't enough. We need chemistry as well as compatibility if we are to go the distance.*

Privacy must be respected in a relationship. This means you don't have to share your mail, phone calls, texts and belongings. Nor does every thought or feeling have to be shared. If this is the case, your relationship needs healthier boundaries around trust and privacy.

Couples who respect each other's privacy do not snoop through each other's:

- texts
- email
- browsing history
- social media accounts
- phone calls
- mail

Protecting your partner's right to privacy also means respecting their need for a time out now and then, in order to think things through when life throws them a curveball. You may not like it when they withdraw, but a partner who doesn't want to talk may just need more time than you to work out their thoughts and feelings. Love and respect them enough to give them the space they need, and reassure them that you're on their team and trust they will figure it out.

### Guideline #39: A lack of privacy in a relationship signals boundary and trust issues.

When there is no privacy or personal space, no separateness or friendships outside of the home, the pressure to be each other's "everything" and to constantly fulfill all roles (best friend, lover, confidant and therapist, cheerleader, boss, mother/father, wife/husband) can be enormous. It's unhealthy, unrealistic, and ultimately unsustainable.

*PEARLY WISDOM: We cannot make our partners happy; all we can do is give them the love, support, and space to find their own happiness. In turn, our partners cannot make us happy, either; it's our responsibility.*

## Privacy Rules

We share so much in a relationship – our bodies, our minds, our money, a home, a bed, kids, pets, free time, and vacations – that we need healthy boundaries around privacy. Striking a balance between togetherness and separateness is tricky, and unique to every relationship. Some couples are glued at the hip, while others believe the secret to their success is long periods of time spent apart. Regardless, enjoying separate friendships, personal space, personal time, and privacy are critical.

The need for privacy is different from the need for secrecy. **Privacy becomes secrecy when there is a conscious motivation to hide something that might threaten the relationship**, such as an online love affair or gambling debts. If information is being consciously withheld or omitted out of fear or shame, then it needs to come out of hiding. Secrecy is the shadow side of privacy, and it can destroy a relationship.

> **Guideline #40: Privacy becomes secrecy when there is a conscious motivation to hide something.**

If you've done something to jeopardize the trust in your relationship, such as being unfaithful, you may have to give up some privacy for a time, until you earn your partner's trust again. Just know that such agreements need to have a time limit: if you need to consult on every decision, explain every thought process, and share every detail of all your comings and goings, your relationship will suffer over time. No relationship can survive that kind of constant scrutiny and suspicion.

*PEARLY WISDOM: High-trust relationships free from jealousy and fear are the ones that enjoy the most privacy and opportunity for personal growth.*

Without privacy, we feel bored and suffocated, and the romance wanes. Too much privacy, and we feel shut out from each other's lives; our relationship lacks warmth and connection.

It's possible that too much information kills chemistry while too little kills compatibility.

## Personal Space

Just like privacy, the need for personal space varies between individuals. How much ease and comfort you derive from a relationship can be directly affected by the amount of privacy and personal space you are given. For example, introverts need space, even from their loved ones, to recharge. I am an introvert, and I regain energy by withdrawing from the world. Tex is more of an ambivert, which is to say that he lies in the middle of the continuum between introversion and extroversion. He needs to fill more of his time with others so that he can recharge. I can actually see this in him: he becomes less buoyant if he spends too much time alone or in the house with me. He needs others to energize him. As an introvert, I become easily drained if I don't take time for myself. I can go out socially and enjoy it, but if I go out too often I feel depleted.

This means that Tex accepts more social invitations than I do, and fortunately he is fine with that. If he wasn't, it could be a source of friction in our relationship. He could easily feel rebuffed and rejected, and I would feel exhausted and misunderstood. I am so glad he doesn't have the kind of job that requires him to network and glad-hand a lot, like politicians do. I feel sorry for the introverted spouses of politicians. Their husbands/wives probably don't understand the toll it takes on them physically and mentally to just show up and smile.

It's not that we introverts are anti-social. We need people, and we value our friendships. It's just that being around others for too long drains our batteries. As introverts, we tend to prefer small gatherings and to cherish one-on-one time with friends, whether they're introverted or extroverted. I have a loud and extroverted friend I love to hang out with, but after a few hours, I start to shut down. She jokes about it now: "We just spent four hours together! You must be exhausted!" When her energy is quieter, or I am with quieter friends, I can spend more time.

Extroverts don't always appreciate our need for alone time. They may feel snubbed if we decline a social invitation or leave a party early because we're worn out from talking. Extroverts can be hurt if we don't immediately share our thoughts or support their opinion because we need a little more time to reflect on what has been said. An extroverted partner may feel hurt if we ask for personal time, or move to another room to read instead of sitting on the couch and watching television together. Perhaps explaining the differences helps:

Extroverts:

- Get energy by interacting with others.
- Make decisions by discussing and involving others in problem solving.
- Like to brainstorm ideas.
- Will talk about almost anything with others.
- Engage and initiate.

Introverts:

- Get energy by being alone.
- Make decisions through silent deliberation.
- Like to internalize thoughts before discussing their ideas with others.
- Dislike small talk and shallow discussions.
- Contrary to popular belief, introverts are not always shy (I am a confident introvert).

As an introvert, I have a great need for personal time. If I don't get enough of it, I can start to feel dull inside, restless, and slightly irritable. It feels like pressure builds up and I need an escape valve. Fortunately, Tex and I have built-in escape valves for our relationship. In our Love Agreement, we allocated 10 hours of personal time a week. Tex may be the funniest and most lovable man in the world, but **if I don't make time for myself, I feel less in love with him.** I think it's the same with him. I sense a prickliness if he doesn't get out and have some fun without me.

We know, in our hearts, that we can't be everything to each other, and cultivating friendships and experiences of our own will make our relationship juicier and give us fresh things to talk about. But we must be intentional about this: if we don't make time for personal time, it's unlikely to happen. So, when I see my beloved not taking enough time for himself, I will gently remind him to call up a friend and go out. And if I need some space, I will tell him. Because we've already discussed it, there are no hurt feelings. Personal time is respected.

**Guideline #41: Make time for personal time.**

## Personal Time Is Important.

Personal time reconnects me to my old self – the person I was, and am, without Tex. As much as I love sharing new experiences with him, I need pockets of time to do what I want, when I want. I need to explore things on my own, at my own pace. When I return to him, I feel more in love than ever.

> *The more one does and sees and feels, the more one is able to do, and the more genuine may be one's appreciation of fundamental things like home, and love, and understanding companionship.*
>
> — Amelia Earhart

I am happiest and most alive when I am exploring. I blame it on my genetics. A DNA test revealed that I have an "increased susceptibility to novelty seeking", possibly related to "less-efficient serotonin processing". I need the chemical hit that comes from sensation seeking.

Novelty seeking explains my adventurous side: I've owned two motorcycles and done a lot of solo traveling around the world. I've been to over 40 countries and all seven continents. I am an experience junkie, having dogsledded, winter camped, adventure raced and ice climbed. When I was 25, I shaved off all my long hair before a climbing trip. Friends think I'm fearless. I believe I'm just more curious and less risk-averse than your average Jane. As I accrued experience, I became more comfortable with risk and trying new things. I am officially addicted to living outside my comfort zone.

It's a trait that attracted Tex to me – my wildness and "worldliness", as he calls it. But this wildness scares me a little. I crave freedom and excitement: How can I find it in a marriage? How can I maintain the autonomy of my soul? I have always been afraid of having my freedom curtailed if I got married.

I remember sharing this concern with him on our third date. We were at a rooftop party, sitting on a lumpy couch and getting to know each other. We had just swapped travel stories, and I told him that no matter what relationship I was in, I would always need to travel, sometimes with my partner and sometimes alone. It was a warning, wrapped in a declaration: there would be times when I might be gone for a month or more. It didn't mean I didn't love him any less; I just had to travel and experience other cultures and ways of life, on my own. Of course, the subtext beneath this confession was: "Can you handle this free spirit of mine? Could you deal with me going away?" And so far, yes. So far, my novelty-seeking gene is still one of the reasons he's attracted to me.

I share this with you so you can understand that when your partner desires time alone, it probably has less to do with you and more to do with how they're wired. If you can appreciate that about them, you will have a more peaceful and enjoyable relationship – and a partner who feels very lucky to have you understand them so well. If you find it hard to give them this space, I can only recommend one option: get busy and focus on your own happiness. Ultimately, you'll both be happier and more fulfilled and have more passion in your relationship. If you cannot do this, you will both suffer.

## The Importance of Picking the Right Partner

Carl Jung, the founder of analytical psychology, said that dreams are a way of communicating with the unconscious and that they can reveal things about you, your relationships, and situations. Very early on in our relationship, I had an important dream as Tex slept next to me. I believe the dream was a strong message from my unconscious that he was the right partner for me.

In my dream, I was walking around grey city streets, living my life in a rather dull way, when someone told me that I was really an angel whose wings had been taken. Without my wings, I had forgotten that I could fly. Without my wings, I'd come to believe I was human, and stuck. With those words, I came to believe I really was an angel, and that's when I regained my wings. The dream ended with me flying over a crowd of people, spinning, and rolling and playing around in the air. People looked up and smiled and pointed. I was overflowing with joy and newfound freedom. It was an incredible feeling. When I woke up, I knew it was a sign that I was going to achieve my full potential soon. I turned to Tex and said, "I dreamt I was an angel who had forgotten to fly, and then I remembered I was an angel and I could fly". He drew me close and hugged me.

Ever since then, I tell Tex he gives me wings to fly. And that's all he has ever wanted: for me to be happy. His biggest fear about us is that I will stop being wild and free.

The relationship I'm in gives me a true sense of home and freedom at the same time. It's like having a nest I can fly away from while feeling secure in the knowledge it will be there when I return. Tex is home. His love gives me freedom to leave and come back. I was so worried that I would lose my freedom in a relationship, but I am actually freer. I am loved, and loved well by someone who understands me. My fear of marriage is gone. I have my wings.

## When Too Much Time Apart Is Bad

One thing is for sure – whenever Tex and I have time apart, we feel closer than ever. When he goes to visit his daughter, or spends a ski weekend with the guys, he gives me the gift of missing him. When I spend an evening by myself, he always seems to appreciate me a bit more when I come back. But too much time apart isn't a good thing, either. I learned this when I went to Ecuador for seven weeks, and Canada twice, for two and three months. We would be good for about a month and then start to disconnect. Fewer texts, less Skyping, not as many loving sentiments. I would start to feel anxious as he started to disconnect. It sucked, and I think that if we had been apart for six months our relationship would have entered the danger zone.

We need time away from each other, but too much time can be bad. Knowing this, I have a six-week travel rule. I don't want to be apart from him for any longer than six weeks now. It's enough time to have a little adventure but not too long to make it unbearable.

We all need some personal space, and time apart is healthy; but how much is too much, and how much is too little? Every couple needs to work that out for themselves. Some couples are happy doing everything together, while others function quite well living nearly separate lives. But if you don't strike a balance between closeness and separation, you can get caught up in pursuer–distancer roles.

## Pursuer–distancer Relationships

In a classic pursuer–distancer relationship, one person is unavailable for the relationship (the distancer), and the other goes into pursuit mode in an attempt to connect (the pursuer). During times of stress, couples can fall into this pattern of pursuer–distancer behavior, usually due to some emotional trigger.

For example, a parent dies. The grieving son withdraws and starts to work more, or spends time outside the house, in an attempt to distract himself from the emotional pain. His partner starts to feel neglected and pursues him, texting and demanding more of his time and attention. The shame he feels about his emotional unavailability causes him to withdraw further. (Note: This exact same dynamic can occur for women.)

It's vital to remember that distance doesn't always signal the decline of a relationship. Sometimes, we just need a little space to work through life's challenges, and if we're given it, we can return to intimacy that much faster. But if we aren't given the space we need to work things out, we will take it by emotionally shutting down or taking time away from the relationship. This can cause a lot of distress in our partner.

*PEARLY WISDOM: In general, it seems that women want to talk through things they feel powerless about, to either find a solution or receive emotional support, more than men do. Why is this? From my conversations with men about this, it seems that men don't like to discuss problems because, for one, men are afraid of being seen as weak and two, men often feel worse talking about a problem. It makes them relive feelings of powerlessness. They would prefer to figure things out on their own before they feel safe to discuss them. Sometimes, they may confide in a best friend, but for the most part, they keep their problems to themselves.*

## Advice for Pursuers: Drop the Rope

What do you do if you can't talk about your feelings without causing your partner to shut down further? You can reconnect by doing less.

That's right. Lean back. I know that it can be very difficult not to feel anxious and freaked out when your partner goes into distance mode. Just know that they are feeling overwhelmed in their own way and that this is how they're dealing with it.

It may sound counterintuitive to lean back and let go. In fact, everything in you may be screaming for more togetherness, but as the pursuer, the best thing you can do is to stop struggling against the situation. It's like a tug-of-war, and though you're struggling to pull them over to your side, the best thing you can do is drop the rope. When you drop the rope, you stop wasting so much energy and the tug-of-war is over.

When intensity is high, give your partner the gift of personal space and trust them to sort things out. Here are some further actions you can take to bridge the distance in your relationship:

### 10 Actions to Bring Intimacy Back

1. Continue to be warm and kind, and support your partner to the best of your ability.
2. Hug your partner.
3. Dial down the criticism and requests.
4. Resist the urge to call or text them during the day.
5. Acknowledge to them (in a kind voice) that there has been a change in the quality or tone of your relationship.
6. Assure your partner you still love them and want to figure things out.
7. Let them know that you want to give them the space they need to figure things out and that you'll be happy to talk about what's bothering them when they're ready.
8. Focus on yourself and what makes you happy.
9. Occasionally include them in activities, like a walk.
10. Resist the urge to "talk" about things until you feel connected again.

You can restore your connection more quickly by following these steps than by "talking" about the problem.

By focusing on yourselves for a while, you may find that your relationship ends up stronger than ever.

If you recall from my introduction, when I got back from Ecuador, I could sense Tex distancing himself from me. He no longer reached for me in bed. He no longer texted me during the day. He became prickly. I was left wondering, "Where is my sweet, adoring man?" This went on for two weeks.

I wanted to know what was wrong. We talked briefly and he told me he was questioning "us" and needed his own space and didn't know how to handle that. It made him feel guilty just thinking about it.

So, what did I do? I gave him space. I told him that I still loved him and that nothing was different between us except whatever it was he had going on in his head. (I was very firm here, and he told me later that he appreciated that confidence and felt reassured.) I told him I was going to give him the space he needed to figure things out. Then I dropped the rope.

The very next day, I went to a meet-up for people who wanted to practice conversational Spanish. There must have been 60 people. I spoke Spanish with a few people but spent most of the night chatting with Marcello, a nice middle-aged Ecuadorian guy. We split a seafood platter and danced the salsa. And it was FUN! I came back home glowing, and it made Tex happy to see his woman so full of cha cha again. I didn't cheat on Tex, and I didn't go looking for male company that night, but I did enjoy some male attention. In a way, it reminded me that I was still attractive, and I felt strong and sexy and confident again. (Ladies, don't ever kill that sexy part of yourself when you're in a relationship.)

After that night, I felt like everything was going to be fine, one way or another. I believe that letting go of the situation and focusing on my own happiness was what attracted Tex back to me. It freed him from responsibility and guilt and let him relax enough to deal with his own issues.

*PEARLY WISDOM: Feelings open up and love flows more freely when we aren't forced, guilted, or criticized by our partners to act a certain way.*

## A Word about Depression

If you live with someone who…

- Has little interest in himself or his appearance
- Doesn't participate in any social activities or hobbies
- Is withdrawn
- Never initiates contact with friends or family
- Blames others
- Has anger issues
- Undereats or overeats
- Can't sleep or sleeps too much
- Constantly overreacts
- Cries all the time
- Has unpredictable mood swings
- Has no sexual interest
- Is paranoid
- Is easily jealous
- Takes crazy risks
- Is always unsatisfied
- Is constantly anxious and fearful
- Is continually unhappy
- Is extremely negative
- Overspends

- Overindulges in alcohol or prescription drugs
- Never smiles
- Has no spark or light in their eyes

...he (or she) may be depressed. If this is the situation, we are not talking about a little tango in the pursuer–distancer dance. We are talking about mental illness, and it can have serious consequences for your relationship. According to the book, *How To Improve Your Marriage Without Talking About It* by Patricia Love, Ed.D., and Steven Stosny, Ph.D., **the divorce rate goes up nine times when one partner is depressed.** The authors also say that depression doesn't come from bad relationships so much as bad relationships come from untreated depression. The good news is, depression is highly treatable through behavioral and lifestyle changes, therapy, medication, diet, and exercise.

If you suspect that your partner is depressed and that their withdrawal and distance are not a temporary means to deal with stress, then you need to discuss the situation with them in a non-confrontational and loving way. You can still practice the steps in "Actions to Bring Intimacy Back", but I also urge you to seek professional help, even if it's just to get some advice on how to best handle the situation and take care of yourself.

It's not easy being in a relationship with a depressed person. In fact, it may be one of the hardest, loneliest, and most stressful things anyone can possibly bear. The person you care about most in this world is hurting, and you feel helpless to make them happy or bring them close. Home is no longer a place of comfort and peace, but a place of anxiety and painful emotions. When you live with a depressed person, it's as if you're always waiting for the axe to drop. It's enough to make *you* depressed. Self-care, friendships, and wise counsel are critical to getting you through this time.

* * *

## HOUSEKEEPING: Privacy and Personal Space

If you're the kind of person who needs personal space to sort things out and/or recharge, then ask for it instead of simply withdrawing and causing your partner to feel rejected and confused. **Asking for what you need is one of the most important relationship skills you can develop, and it is one of the best ways to ensure a long and happy union.**

**Task 1: Reflect on the following.**

Being introverted is different from being depressed. Introverts will bounce back after they've had some personal time to themselves. A depressed person is chronically unhappy or negative.

Are you taking enough personal time in your relationship to rejuvenate and get to know yourself better? It may be hard to ask for personal time, because it can feel like a selfish and unloving request, but if you're an introvert, you truly need more personal time than others do to recharge.

I talk more about personal time and how it relates to personal growth and the pursuit of happiness in the next chapter.

### Guideline #42: Alone time can enhance intimacy.

# Chapter 16: Personal Growth and the Pursuit of Happiness

*Our job in this life is not to shape ourselves into some ideal we imagine we ought to be, but to find out who we already are and become it.*

— Steven Pressfield

## Personal Growth

As I mentioned before, Tex and I operate on a Love Agreement. When the Love Agreement stops working for us, we change it. That's the beauty of a relationship; you can write your own rules.

Our Love Agreement reflects the things we need to thrive in our relationship, including our need for personal time to explore hobbies and friendships. By making time for ourselves, we honor the individuals we are. Many marriages end because people expect their partner to make them happy, but as I said in Chapter 1, no one can "make" you happy – that's your job in life. It is a noble calling, and we are each called to it in our own way. The challenge is to find someone who will support your journey.

Communicate with your partner; find out exactly how much personal time you each require to feel happy and fulfilled. At different times in your lives, one person may require more than another, in which case you may have to compromise a little.

Hopefully, you are compatible enough so that the compromise isn't too great. If it is, then ask yourself if one of you isn't using your relationship to avoid intimacy – or personal growth.

> *A relationship should be an extension of ourselves, where we can try to become the person we want to become. It should not be a dead end where we merely grow old or try to hide from reality.*
>
> — David Viscott, *How to Live with Another Person*

## Your Single Years Can Be Your Best Years for Personal Growth

People ask me why I was single for so long. To be honest, it's because I never met anyone I felt truly compatible with (or who felt compatible with me). I dated, and I had some relationships, but I was also content with my own life! I had plenty of personal time for travel, adventure, and personal growth. It was never about notches in the bedpost, it was about checking off items on my bucket list. I bought a condominium, my career took off, and I grew up. I travelled the world, had a lot of fun, wrote a book, and bought a motorcycle. I built excellent friendships and came into my femininity in my thirties. I consider that time to be really special, because I was able to focus on me. It was a time of tremendous personal growth and expansion. I don't ever want that to stop just because I'm in a relationship. If I had sensed that Tex would prevent me from growing and wandering, it would have been over before it started.

When you allow for personal time and pleasure, you're a better person to be around. You take better care of yourself and you feel stronger. You gain confidence by putting yourself into new situations, and you gain happiness and fulfillment by pursuing your dreams. You must take responsibility for your own happiness and identity, because no one else can do this for you.

## When Personal Growth Conflicts

There may be times in your relationship when your need for personal growth conflicts with the needs of the relationship. An example of this can be found in Livan Hernandez, the Cuban baseball player who defected from his country to play Major League Baseball in the United States. He had to leave his country and family to pursue his pro-baseball dreams. I don't think anyone could have anticipated his decision, least of all his wife.

This is an example of an irreconcilable difference, one where the fulfillment of a personal goal means the destruction of a relationship. These can arise in a relationship and are sometimes the cause of divorce. But what about situations that are not as catastrophic? Can you think of a situation that could arise (or has arisen) where one of you has a personal goal that conflicts with your relationship values?

I have one to share. My brother landed a dream job in Doha, Qatar, a tiny wealthy state of over two million people in the Arabian Peninsula. The job meant uprooting his wife and two daughters from Canada and living in incredible heat in a theocratic state under a very conservative Wahhabi form of sharia law. Women and men are expected to dress a certain way, not hold hands in public, not live together out of wedlock, and there are lashings for crimes such as drinking alcohol. The rights of women have not progressed much beyond the 19th century, and slavery exists in unofficial forms. In fact, Indonesia has banned domestic helpers from working in Qatar because of the number of human rights abuses, such as hiring workers and then taking away their passports and refusing to pay them.

Although foreigners (especially white ones) get treated differently, the girls will still have to dress modestly and I am sure it will not be easy for them living there. I can only hope that they will bloom where they've been transplanted.

What would you do? Is there something you desire that conflicts with your partner's happiness?

Say one of you is really into yoga. What if that person decides they want to spend six months in India deepening their yoga practice? Or one of you wants to take on a demanding job that requires a lot of overtime – one that pays less but is far more fulfilling? That decision is going to impact your lifestyle and disposable income as well as your family time. These are decisions that could potentially jeopardize your relationship and your future.

Life will throw curveballs, and you can expect some zingers the longer you're together. When that happens, you must remember that as much as you and your partner want to play your own game, you are still batting for the same team.

### When Giving Is Hard

If your partner wants something that is hard for you to give, it's important to:

1. Have faith in the future.

2. Communicate your hopes and fears about the situation.

3. See your partner's side and support them as much as possible.

4. Know that next time it could be you humbly asking for something that's going to be very hard for your partner to give.

It helps to adopt a curious mentality – to say, "Well, let's try it and see where it goes". You can always end your experiment if it's not working out for you.

A relationship is a give-and-take. If you're not willing to give, you might as well be single.

## The Biggest Challenge in a Relationship

**The biggest challenge in a relationship is to serve two masters: The Relationship and the Self.** If we sacrifice Self in service to the Relationship, we become a boring doormat. If we sacrifice our Relationship in service to the Self, we become selfish and distant. Neither is helpful when it comes to long-term happiness in a relationship.

> **Guideline #43: By making time for personal growth, we serve the Self. By making time for each other, we serve the Relationship.**

## Separate Vacations

Some couples swear by separate vacations. They feel that the break from one another rekindles their romance. Others take a whole summer away from each other to travel or focus on personal goals. Time spent on personal projects infuses fresh energy into the relationship.

Ironically, Tex is away on a skiing vacation with his daughter as I write this chapter. I'm happy to have the time to myself, sleeping in, and staying up late to write. I'm enjoying the solitude and the change of pace. I've had time to think about my priorities and do some goal-setting. I feel stronger somehow, more connected to myself. I'm also happy that he and his daughter are spending some daddy–daughter time together, because they need that. It's been a rejuvenating week for both of us.

Do you think it's healthy for couples to take weekend trips and/or vacations apart from each other?
I asked this same question on my Facebook page, and here are a few of the responses:

> *Kiley: Absolutely!! You are not just a partner; you are an individual who has your own interests & goals in life. A partner should support that. Also, sometimes you just need a guy or gal weekend.*

> *Peggy: Yes, within reason. If one or the other of you is gone all the time, maybe things aren't as fabulous as advertised.*

> *Rita: Yes, absolutely. Sometimes for galpal times, or as a break from kids. If you have different holiday interests, time apart is good for perspective as long as you have couple time too.*

Could separate vacations help your relationship? Why not try a weekend or week away and see what happens?

## Personal Happiness

I come from a mountain town called Canmore, where everyone's garages are chock full of adult toys: skis and snowboards, mountain bikes, road bikes, town bikes, kayaks, and stand-up paddleboards… the list goes on. Some people have even turned their garages into CrossFit and climbing gyms. The people of Canmore are a fit bunch: they eat triathlons for breakfast.

Canmore couples spend a lot of money on outdoor clothing and sports equipment. Being active and outdoorsy is what makes us happy. We do most of our socializing on the trails – biking, hiking or skiing. The challenge for some Canmore couples is finding the money for all the new toys and technical clothing, just as I imagine some power couples in Washington, DC, struggle to afford the designer clothes and plastic surgery that are an essential part of their lifestyle.

What do you spend money on? We all have that thing we think would make us happier. A Gucci handbag. A watch. A new pair of skis. What do you covet? Do you think it would make you happier?

Would it, really?

It seems to me that *things* rarely make us happy. Experiences do.

> *The business of life is the acquisition of memories. In the end, that's all there is.*
>
> — "Downton Abbey", Series 4, Episode 4

It may be an ego stroke to get a compliment on your handbag or to show off the latest technical skis, but what is the point of it? If you covet new skis, isn't it really about skiing and being outside with friends on the slopes on a bluebird day? There's a saying "It's not the ride; it's the rider". Basically, the gear isn't going to make you awesome; you are. The latest bike or skis won't do a lot for your performance, because you are 99% responsible for the experience you seek. Your skills, your courage, your attitude make or break your moments.

The fact is, you could save yourself a thousand dollars on the newest gear and settle for last year's model. Then you could spend that money to go on an awesome ski trip and make some great memories. Next year your skis will be last year's news, but your stories will last a lifetime.

The most interesting people in the world are the ones with lots of colorful stories to tell.

**Happiness is not about a thing; it's about experiences.** When we buy something, we hope to buy the experience of being happy: that's what the marketers would have us believe. But real happiness comes from having more fun in life.

> **Guideline #44: If you want to be happy, have more fun experiences, not more things.**

Don't let buying stuff prevent you from having more fun in life. Shared experiences connect us to other people better than material things.

* * *

## HOUSEKEEPING: Personal Growth and the Pursuit of Happiness

**Task 1: Take the next few days to reflect on the following, and possibly journal ideas.**

- You are responsible for your own happiness. Are you doing things that make you happy and fulfilled?
- How can you make time for personal growth?
- Understand that you have to serve the Self as well as the Relationship and that this requires communication and compromise with your partner.
- Consider separate vacations and time away from one another to pursue personal goals.
- Spend money on making memories.
- Have more fun in life.

# Chapter 17: Mental Health

*Happiness doesn't depend on outward conditions. It depends on inner conditions.*

— Dale Carnegie

I would like to speak a little about what it is like to grow up in a household where mental illness and addiction went unaddressed. There are so many couples where one or both partners struggle with these demons. Perhaps in sharing my story, it will help another. I will limit the scope of this chapter to the three things I dealt with in my own family: codependency, chemical addiction, and mental illness.

## Change Is Inevitable

When a couple has been together a long time, they will witness changes in their partner that they would never have foreseen. The younger they were when they got together, the greater the changes. This is because your identity and personality are still half-baked in your teens and twenties. This may be why **choosing a partner before you really know yourself often translates to higher divorce rates**. I know this is true of my parents, who dated at 15, married at 18, had me at 19 and my brother at 21, and divorced at 22. They then married other people, divorced, and remarried each other again later in life. Some may think it romantic that they got back together, as if it were "meant to be". Trust me: it wasn't a happy ending.

Statistically, the younger and less educated you are, the greater your chance of divorce. Teenagers who drop out of high school and marry at a young age soon suffer from not having the emotional maturity or income to cope with the challenges of marriage.[29] Adults who marry later in life are generally more self-aware and more established in their career and incomes, and this advantage means they are less likely to divorce.

Having said that, mental illness doesn't care about age or income.

## What Doesn't Grow, Dies

Growth equals change, and change is always threatening to a relationship; but change is essential to happiness. This may be one of the reasons partners in emotionally abusive and insecure relationships try to control how their spouses spend their time. They don't want them to change. They want their partners to always be available to them. They will even prevent their partner from spending time with friends. An emotionally abusive partner will make their spouse feel guilty for hanging out with other people or partaking in classes and activities that don't include them. This codependent type of relationship is the antithesis of personal growth because it prevents a person from living an independent and fulfilling life.

When you live your whole life denying parts of yourself, things eventually fly apart.

## Codependent Relationships

"Codependent" is a word that gets thrown around a lot and is often misused.

What does it mean to be in a codependent relationship? Let me describe my parents, and maybe it will help.

My father was slavishly devoted to my mother, and called it love. Sadly, I think this is what he understood love to be: sacrificing his happiness, health, and well-being in service to his partner. Unfortunately, **this love was ultimately destructive to their relationship, as there were no healthy boundaries**. My mother suffered from Munchausen's syndrome, a disorder where people feign illness or disease to draw attention and sympathy. It is also sometimes known as hospital addiction syndrome, thick chart syndrome or hospital hopper syndrome. My mother was a genius with a master's degree in psychology and would know exactly what symptoms to fake to get the medications she craved. (She studied medical journals and knew a lot about pharmaceuticals, so she would go to the doctor's office and tell him exactly what she "needed" for a prescription.) Over time, she became increasingly addicted to medications. She convinced my father she needed various pills and prescriptions like Fentanyl* patches to survive. Without them, she claimed she would be dead.

**Fentanyl is 50-100x more powerful than morphine.*

I believe my mother already had mental health issues, and the medications didn't help. She battled depression for decades, heard voices, talked about the fifth dimension, and believed her dead dog's spirit spoke to her. She was convinced she would die at the age of 42. It is hard to know if her delusions were caused by the meds or her fragile psyche. When she was lucid, she could be wonderful. She could be wise, and loving and unselfish. But she was also erratic and extremely sensitive to perceived slights; the way the neighbor looked at her, or how my tone of voice was, could set her into a tailspin. I remember her giving me a blouse for Christmas and then asking for it back the next day because I didn't seem excited enough about it. She took away the photos of me on the bookshelf when I disappointed her. She invited me and my boyfriend over for Thanksgiving and then left the house with my father for hours, leaving me instructions on how to cook everything. She would tell me stories about my childhood that never happened. She believed her own stories so completely, it was difficult to know what was real or not and I often second-guessed my reality.

When I was a child, I adored her. She was a “free spirit”. She would turn up the music and turn down the lights, and we would dance around, waving incense sticks in the air. She woke me up one night to watch *Gone with the Wind* with her. She sang and had a beautiful voice. She could say just the right things to comfort me, and she understood me better than anyone else. She took me on long walks and instilled in me an appreciation for nature... and blueberry pancakes. But as light as she could be, there was also darkness. She was often in bed with a “migraine”. We had to tiptoe around the house and close the cupboards very, very softly, or she would get mad. When I was 13, I went looking for coins in the mattress and found a suicide note. I felt ashamed, and slid it back and never said a word to anyone. But I remember the cold feeling of terrible fear: my mother didn’t love me enough to want to stay alive. I had to be good and make sure she was happy so she wouldn’t try to kill herself.

We all did.

As I grew older, and developed friendships and saw how other people’s parents were, I began to realize just how unstable she was. I recall spending my 23rd birthday with my best friend. My father drove downtown and intercepted us on the way to lunch. He got out of his car and yelled at me in the streets in front of my friend for being selfish because I didn’t make plans with my mother on my birthday. She was at home crying because of me. *How selfish.*

Being selfish was something I was accused a lot of, growing up. And for many years I thought I was, because that's what I was told. I realize now this was something called projection, where people deny something in themselves because it's unpleasant, and attribute it to others.

There was a lot of drama in my family. A lot of guilt, anger, shame, secrecy, and emotional blackmail. My mother created it, and my father enabled it.

My mother attempted to take her life several times. We never talked about it to other family members. It had to be hidden. My brother and I grew up alone, together, with a shroud of secrecy. It wasn't until we were in our thirties that we realized just how dysfunctional and twisted things were. My father couldn't see it. We think he had a kind of Stockholm Syndrome: he thought she just needed "more love". My parents had an incredible ability to deny the obvious: my mother was an addict and mentally ill, and her problems weren't limited to bouts of depression.

> *Stockholm syndrome, or capture-bonding, is a psychological phenomenon in which hostages express empathy and sympathy and have positive feelings toward their captors, sometimes to the point of defending and identifying with the captors.*
>
> — *Wikipedia*

After her fifth, possibly sixth, suicide attempt, it was clear to my brother and me that our mother needed professional help. We asked our father to commit her so she could be professionally assessed. He was angry at us for suggesting such a thing. The situation seemed hopeless.

About seven years went by before I saw my father again, and it was under tragic circumstances. He had suffered a massive stroke – a blockage in the basilar artery, which provides blood to the brain – followed by cardiac arrest in the hospital. He was unconscious and on life support and possibly already dead, since he was unresponsive to stimuli. Machines inflated his lungs and kept his heart beating. The doctors said the damage to his brain was catastrophic.

When I saw my father, I didn't feel any anger, just sorrow, and a sense of futility. I talked to him and told him I loved him. I held his hand and stroked his face. He looked like he had aged a lot in those seven years; his hair had turned snow white. I told him about my life. I introduced Tex. Sometimes my father's fingers would twitch and I worried he was conscious but locked in his body, unable to respond. The male nurse reassured me; it was a primal reflex and I should not be concerned. I wondered if my father could hear me and the nurse said no one knew for sure, but he thought it was good to talk in cases like this. So, I explained to my father what had happened to him and what was happening. Over the next 48 hours I also discussed the situation with the doctors and they showed me the brain scans: there was almost no chance of survival. My father would not come back from this, nor would he want to.

I recalled a conversation my parents had when I was a kid, when they talked about not wanting to be kept alive if they were a vegetable. It had always stuck in my mind.

I made the difficult decision to unplug him.

*He's gone.*

*I saw dad for the third and final time tonight. I spent an hour talking to him, then kissed him and said goodbye.*

*I waited with my boyfriend in the waiting room while they stopped his medication, stopped the machines, and removed the tubes. A nurse sat with him while his blood pressure dropped and his heart slowed to a stop. She sat with him until the end. She said it was very peaceful.*

The whole time my father was in the hospital, on life support, my mother refused to visit. She also declined the memorial service. All those years of devotion to her, and he died alone, with only his disowned daughter to arrange things. When the hospital gave me his wallet, I was shocked to find a laminated picture inside: a picture of me at 19. On the back, all those years ago, I had signed, "From your loving daughter. Xoxo"

My father loved me after all. He had just been trapped in an extremely codependent relationship.

## Characteristics of Codependent People

Because of my upbringing, I've bolded the characteristics of codependent people below that were a problem for me in my previous relationships, especially as they related to my parents. I see these characteristics so clearly now, but 20/20 vision wasn't possible until I did some deep soul searching. Back then, I held self-sacrifice in such high esteem that I may have even taken some of these characteristics as a point of pride!

The fact is, you don't inspire others by being a doormat. Cinderella is a terrible role model.[30]

Do you see yourself in any of the following characteristics of codependent people? I don't think one or two is much of an issue, but if you can identify with several of these points, you may want to look into this topic further.

From the © Copyright Mental Health America website, *Characteristics of Co-dependent People Are*[31]:

1. **An exaggerated sense of responsibility for the actions of others.**

2. A tendency to confuse love and pity, with the tendency to "love" people they can pity and rescue.

3. **A tendency to do more than their share, all of the time.**

4. A tendency to become hurt when people don't recognize their efforts.

5. **An unhealthy dependence on relationships. The co-dependent will do anything to hold on to a relationship and to avoid the feeling of abandonment.**

6. An extreme need for approval and recognition.

7. **A sense of guilt when asserting themselves.**

8. A compelling need to control others.

9. **Lack of trust in self and/or others.**

10. **Fear of being abandoned or alone.**

11. **Difficulty identifying feelings.**

12. Rigidity/difficulty adjusting to change.

**13. Problems with intimacy/boundaries.**

14. Chronic anger.

15. Lying/dishonesty.

16. Poor communication.

17. Difficulty making decisions.

## The Red Pill

When you're in a dysfunctional home, you can know something isn't right but find it hard to pinpoint what the problem is. It's a bit like being in a cult and brainwashed. Then, when you get out of the cult, you have to go through deprogramming. That takes time. If you've watched the movie *The Matrix*, it's like taking the red pill and waking up to a different reality. Only you don't wake up all at once, you wake up bit by bit and you question what really happened. I am grateful I have a brother so we can compare memories. Otherwise, I would probably question my own sanity.

Fortunately, codependency has not been a problem for me and Tex. This is because I've done so much work on myself. It's also because of Tex. He is consistent, he's loving, and he's an open book. That's what I need to thrive in a relationship.

If you were raised in a dysfunctional family as I was, and you didn't feel safe as a child, you may become quite anxious with a partner who is non-communicative, inconsistent, or moody. You can be enlightened all you want, but if you choose a partner who is abandoning or inconsistent, you will struggle with these demons.

> *"The most painful thing is losing yourself in the process of loving someone too much, and forgetting that you are special too".*
>
> — Ernest Hemingway, *Men Without Women*

Keep in mind that dysfunctional families do not acknowledge that a problem exits, and will even deny it when confronted. Family members repress emotions and as a result, disregard their own needs. They become numb emotionally, and develop behaviors that help them to avoid difficult emotions because feeling is painful.

The Mental Health America website has a great post on codependent relationships. Here is an excerpt:

> *The identity and emotional development of the members of a dysfunctional family are often inhibited….Attention and energy focus on the family member who is ill or addicted. The co-dependent person typically sacrifices his or her needs to take care of a person who is sick. When co-dependents place other people's health, welfare, and safety before their own, they can lose contact with their own needs, desires, and sense of self.*
>
> — Mental Health America[31]

In this case, my father placed the needs of his wife above his own health and the well-being of his children.

If you visit http://www.mentalhealthamerica.net/co-dependency you can take a questionnaire that will help you determine if you may be in such a relationship and what you can do about it.

For me, it took years to undo the damage set by my parents' example, but I am proof that you can enjoy a healthy and fulfilling relationship despite a troubled past. **You cannot control the past**

**or the family you were born into, but you can control how you wish to respond to those events.** I learned a lot from my parents, good and bad. I also learned what I didn't want in a relationship. Perhaps this is why I'm so passionate about helping others with their relationships.

*PEARLY WISDOM: In a happy, healthy relationship, partners don't cling to each other. There's no desperation, just a peaceful, easy feeling. If a relationship lacks drama or feels "wrong" or "boring", it may be because you were raised in a dysfunctional environment, and different, no matter how healthy and stable it is, feels bad. There are neurological reasons for this, too complicated to go into here, but just know that the discomfort is real. The good news is, we can rewire our brains – and make healthier choices – with time and conscious effort. Cognitive behavioral therapy has done wonders for some people.*

## Borderline Personality Disorder

We tend to look for relationships that mirror our childhood relationships. This means we can seek adult relationships with people who act like family members. If they don't, we may even go out of our way to provoke them to react in ways that are normal for us. This is especially true of people with borderline personality disorder (BPD); they may function well professionally, but they have unstable, intense personal relationships.

PEARLY WISDOM: *It's not romantic to be needy. The happiest couples in the world are ones where the partners don't hold each other hostage to their well-being and happiness.*

If your relationships are always filled with tension, worry and drama, the problem may be you. I say this in a loving way: get professional help. I am not suggesting you have BPD, but it is worth looking into. If you find it very difficult to manage your emotions, are prone to unstable, intense relationships, have fears of abandonment, tend to adopt the values, habits, and attitudes of the people you spend time with, are impulsive and prone to addiction, are emotionally unstable, feel empty inside or have suicidal thoughts and engage in self-harming behaviors like cutting, feel angry, and experience lapses in reality, then please seek help from a health care professional. There are effective treatments just for borderline personality disorder.

About 75% of people diagnosed with BPD are women. If you suspect that your mother (or the mother of your children) may have BPD, I highly recommend the book *Understanding the Borderline Mother: Helping Her Children Transcend the Intense, Unpredictable, and Volatile Relationship* by Christine Lawson. It helped me understand my own mother and the role that each family member played as I grew up. Reading it was like getting a huge hug from someone who understood. I recommended it to a friend who is now divorced. He said the book was "terrifying and yet is the only thing that has brought me understanding".

## Reflections

When we talk about mental illness, we are almost always focused on the person who has it. However, mental illness affects the whole family. My mother was the focus, and my brother, my father and I spent a lot of our lives trying to appease her and make her happy. We neglected ourselves and each other in the process. Had we learned to detach a little, and take care of ourselves, we would have been much better off and she might have been forced to take more responsibility for herself.

In a way, I am grateful that my parents stopped talking to us when we finally laid down some boundaries: my brother and I were finally able to focus on our own lives.

I always felt hurt that my father chose my mother over me. But now that I write this, and think of the laminated photo that my father carried around in his wallet, it occurs to me: *there was no photo of my mother in the wallet.*

Maybe my father sacrificed more than I realized.

*PEARLY WISDOM: You are not on this earth to take care of someone to the detriment of your own well-being.*

Codependency and mental illness take their toll on a relationship and stunt personal growth and happiness. If you are attracted to people who need to be fixed or rescued, that is codependency. If you constantly find yourself in unstable relationships, the problem may be you. You're getting some benefit from your poor choices even if that something isn't very good for you. Perhaps it distracts you from your own unresolved issues? If you can relate to any of this, I recommend looking for professional help outside this book.

I wish you much love and strength on your journey.

## Afterword

There is a somewhat happy(er) ending to this tale. My mother ended up in the hospital again after my father died – she herself called 911. She was admitted to a psychiatric unit for six months, where she was stabilized and evaluated. During this time, she was also weaned off all medications. Her cognitive functions declined rapidly (or perhaps they became more evident). Prognosis? Alzheimer's at the age of 65. She is now in an assisted-care facility. She is clean, and her personality is completely different.

By all reports, she is friendly, passive, and social. Her mother, brother and sisters take her out and visit all the time. She doesn't complain about her health at all, and she is nice to be around. Everyone is quite shocked and awed by the difference.

She asks about me and my brother but accepts that we can't visit because we live in other countries now. My uncle tells me she probably wouldn't remember the visit, anyway.

I did not expect this turn of events – that of all things, it would be Alzheimer's that would save her. My grandmother – the one who was destined for the convent before she met my grandfather – believes that God answered her prayers.

I believe that not having my dad around to enable her with his misplaced sense of love and duty is what saved her. She finally got the professional care she needed.

> **Guideline #45: Be there for others, but never at the expense of your own happiness and well-being.**

* * *

## HOUSEKEEPING: Mental Health Check-in

If any of this resonated with you, then I suggest speaking to a mental health professional. Sometimes, just one session can help put things into perspective, and your therapist can give you some activities to try. Don't think you'll have to see a therapist for years and years – although that's how it's often portrayed in the movies. If this proves to be true, then your counsellor probably isn't doing their job and you've just developed another codependent relationship.

You can look for a therapist on Yelp or ask some trusted friends. And in case you're wondering what the difference is between a psychologist and a psychiatrist, the loose answer is this: A psychologist has 6–10 years of university education (master's or Ph.D.) and is concerned with how individuals think, feel, and behave. They will use different techniques and treatments to help people overcome or manage their problems. A psychiatrist has a degree in medicine, can prescribe drugs, and often uses medication to help treat mental illness. Both psychologists and psychiatrists are accountable to regulatory bodies. They are similar in that they are trying to help people master their problems and make positive behavioral changes.

# Chapter 18: Heal Your Wounds. Claim Your Power. Get More Love.

*What is to give light must endure burning.*

— Viktor E. Frankl

Everyone's got some kind of painful memory or experience. The older we get, the more we see that tragedy is a part of life. We have the power to allow a tragedy to shape us into wiser, more compassionate beings, or to diminish us. As Tony Robbins says, your past only equals your future if you continue to live there.

Some people stay stuck in the past. They'll say, "I'm a survivor", with a certain pride. It's how they self-identify. Their pain becomes a badge of honor. But surviving isn't thriving.

When people get stuck in a personal narrative, they stop moving forward in life. Maybe they had an alcoholic parent. Were sexually molested. Experienced addiction issues. Bankruptcy. Cancer. Divorce. Some people like to share their stories of pain with other people because it's a way to connect. (Women especially.) The ugly side of this story-telling is when people use it to gain sympathy or to justify bad behavior. ("I can't help it. I have to control things in my relationship because things were so out of control growing up".) These are the scab pickers, who refuse to let a wound heal. For these people, healthy and happy relationships will be a struggle.

### Guideline #46: Surviving isn't thriving.

On the flip side, there are people who are in tremendous pain and don't even realize it. They don't talk about the people or events that have wounded them in the past. They can't or won't acknowledge the shame or hurt or anger they carry around. These buried secrets can lead inward to self-destructive behaviors such as eating disorders and addictions, or outward to bullying and abuse and ongoing relationship problems. Repressing painful emotions can even lead to health problems, including fatal strokes like the one my father had.

## Heal Your Wounds

The fact is, these hurts must be given voice in a relationship – sometimes with a therapist – or they have the potential to be a very destructive force.

**Unaddressed pain is like having an invisible roommate who never leaves.** And when you share a house with someone, your partner will feel the haunting presence of that roommate. You can't hide pain.

*PEARLY WISDOM: Your pain doesn't excuse you from acting like an asshole. You are not special because of your pain; you're just someone who refuses to acknowledge his issues and battle his own demons. P.S. Women can be assholes too.*

Living with someone can bring out the best and the worst in us. The best is love and selflessness; the worst is cruelty and rejection. When you want to have sex and your partner rejects you, or you argue about money or quarrel about petty things, your pain can be triggered.

How do you communicate in times of stress? Do you lash out or shut down?

Do you automatically think the worst of your partner when they screw up?

Do you gripe about your relationship a lot?

That's pain.

That's unmet needs. Where there is anger, insecurity and resentment, there is unaddressed pain.

Your ability to recognize the pain you're in is the only way to make it go away because what you resist, persists.

*PEARLY WISDOM: The first step to overcoming any kind of pain is to acknowledge the hurt. The second is to provide self-care. The third is to address the root cause.*

## Post Traumatic Stress Disorder (PTSD)

Nick Carpenter is recovering from significant trauma. He found a way to provide self-care through rock climbing:

> *After returning from Afghanistan, I started going through what would be a two-year divorce. I left the IC (Intelligence Community), moved back down to Chattanooga, and barely kept my sanity. "PTSD" as they call it.*

*.... My friend, Justin Norcia, pushed me to climb. Even on days I didn't want to leave the house, he would show up anyways, and by the end of the day, I always felt better. Rock climbing became my sanctuary.*

*I have a very active mind. It's a blessing and a curse. It served me well in the military, but in the civilian world, people see me as being paranoid.... When I climb, though, everything goes quiet.*[32]

— Nick Carpenter, *"Rock Climbing Saved My Life: A Veteran's Struggle with PTSD"*

After reading Nick's article in Rock and Ice magazine*, I reached out to him personally. I wanted to learn more about PTSD, how he was coping, and to see if he had some wisdom to share with others. What began as an interview turned into a rather personal conversation between the two of us about healing from trauma. I summarize the conversation below but retained as many of Nick's words as I could.

**I link to the full article here - www.itsnotyouitsus.com/chapterlinks.*

**Me: Could you talk a little about what it's like to have PTSD?**

Nick: *For me it becomes a screen of how I see the world. I was never a violent person growing up. I was always an athletic, mellow person. But after everything I did and after coming back from my deployment and processing out of the military, my fuse was a lot shorter than most people's. It doesn't take as much to get me to that angry place. Controlling my emotions, especially aggression, is hard. The same physical aggression used in a combat zone – that kind of mentality – isn't socially acceptable in the civilian world.*

*I am easily overstimulated. For example, soon after leaving the military, I moved to Washington, DC. Just the cars moving by spooked me. You're prepared for all kinds of threatening scenarios in combat, and you're still prepared for that in civilian life. You've also seen the worst of humanity and what people can do, and there isn't really an off switch to that. You feel like you never quite belong or fit.*

Me: I can relate a little to your point about being on high alert much of the time, and looking for threats. For many years, I would enter a room and look for the safest place to sit. I would look for an exit and sit with my back to a wall. I would quickly size people up to determine if they were a threat. I think this relates to growing up in such a turbulent house. I would watch my mother and try to determine what kind of a mood she was in. It was like waiting for the axe to drop. That went on for years. Now I don't do this, and I think there are a few reasons. One, I've done a lot of work on myself. Two, my mother is no longer in my life. And three, I have Tex. I feel quite safe when I'm with him. Maybe it's because I see all the ways he protects me: like when we walk along the sidewalk, he takes the side closest to the cars. And he often sits beside me in a restaurant and we hold hands. Being near him is so relaxing, I swear I can feel my cortisol drop. I think the right relationship can help you overcome a lot of trauma from your past.

Nick: *I can say right off the bat that my girlfriend Sara has been an absolute blessing, and she has the patience of a saint. We have been together four years now, shortly after I moved back to Chattanooga. She is very outgoing, loves the outdoors, but she has a calming presence and spirit. She has the ability to calm me down like no one else does. We also have an emotional support dog named Mountain Girl. She helps a lot too. They say the sheer act of petting a dog lowers cortisol levels.*

**Me: You find climbing to be a good way to escape from a noisy mind. I am wondering if the distraction helps (or helped) or just made it harder to deal with things later?**

Nick: *Rock climbing is kind of like maintenance for me now and calms down the mental processes. Climbing helps me live in that present moment, and whatever life problems I'm obsessing over can be filed away.*

Me: I understand that. I used to climb, years ago. I loved how it would bring me to the present. It was just the rock and me. I was purely in the moment and it was almost Zen-like. It was addictive. In a way though, I think it can be like a drug. Not as harmful as alcohol or drugs – much more healthy – but still a kind of escape.

Nick: *It can be like a drug, so it really helps to have a support system as well. I don't think climbing alone would have done it for me. I needed both the physical component from rock climbing as well as the emotional component from having a loving support system. Having the two let me fully deal with, and heal from, trauma. Rock climbing healed my mind while my family and girlfriend healed my heart. Without that balance, it might just be from one climbing high to another.*

**Me: Like climbing, getting high (on adrenaline), and then crashing back to reality when you have to go home?**

Nick: *Yes.*

Me: But maybe having a distraction for a little while helps us deal with the pain. I know some therapists would like to get into the past right away, and start digging up traumatic events and talking about them. They believe that's the only way to fully heal. But I think we must be careful about entering the darkness too soon. Sometimes we block out parts of our memory for a reason: we need time to deal with the traumatic events of our past. That's why self-care is so important.

Nick: *Your brain is very powerful, and I don't think we comprehend how powerful. We have self-defense mechanisms built in place for a reason because we can't handle the full experience all at once. Climbing lets me deal with those things on a not-so-overwhelming way. Being at home or at work is harder. Recently, I had to get up and walk out of a room and go outside because I had that overwhelming feeling.*

Me: I believe animals and nature can be easier than people when we are overwhelmed with feelings. We don't have to talk. Our dog won't judge us. The rock won't call us an asshole for leaving a room. The rock doesn't have any societal expectations of us.

**I also believe that every tragedy has its gift and its curse. Can you see the gift and curse in having PTSD?**

Nick: *I can see the curse. It can get so overwhelming, you shut down. But there could be a blessing in disguise. I feel a hyper sense of awareness, especially coming from the intelligence community. I am more able to read and react to situations.*

*For example, about three months ago, friends and I were bouldering in Chattanooga, in Little Rock City. We were climbing there and a friend's wife took a serious fall onto a tree stump. She ended up with 16 pins and almost lost her foot. When it happened, I saw all the panic in everyone and I immediately stepped up and took charge. I packed clothes around her leg to keep it stable and kept her calm before mountain rescue could get there. That situation didn't overwhelm me like it overwhelmed my friends. When things go bad, that intensity is a comfortable environment for me to be in. After it was over, my girlfriend and I rode back to the house and we didn't speak for about 10 minutes. It did send me back to that place a little, but I bounced back pretty quickly and I could talk about the event right away. My friends couldn't, even after a week.*

*I think I might volunteer in Search and Rescue because I'm good in those kinds of situations. So maybe that's the gift.*

**Me: Have you done any therapy?**

Nick: *I have had mixed results with my therapist at VA (Veteran Affairs). Honestly, a lot of my therapy has been done with talking with friends and family. Meditation is absolutely amazing. I do a lot of stretching. Getting into a flow state, especially a physical flow state, where your body is operating where you are not consciously giving it direction really helps. When I have an overwhelming feeling, I often get outside and go for a walk.*

**Me: I talk about healing your wounds so you can claim your power. Can you relate to any of that?**

Nick: *I can relate to this. When you have PTSD in any way, from combat or a life experience, it makes you feel incomplete. You feel like a part of you is missing, or like you've changed or part of you is buried. By healing and going through the process of accepting what happened is in the past, you can piece yourself back together. Climbing or exercise or having loved ones helps. You will never be back at that same place you were before the experience, but you start to feel more whole and like you can live a "normal" life again.*

*When you are in the deepest and darkest parts of PTSD, you feel like you are back at that moment, and you feel out of control. Claiming your power as you call it – rebuilding your life by living in the present, which you can control – makes you feel like you are more capable to handle other aspects of your life.*

Me: Have you heard of "Kintsugi" in Japan? In North America, we tend to throw things out that break, but the Japanese have a tradition of repairing broken pottery, like a vase. They use paste and gold to bond the pieces together. The vessel has the same form as before, but it's different after repair. The result is something stronger and possibly more beautiful than before. I like that the cracks aren't hidden. In fact, the cracks show the history of the object. Perhaps you are like that vessel.

Nick: *I like that.*

**Me: Is there anything else you would like to tell people who are struggling with PTSD or a traumatic event?**

Nick: *It does get better. Everybody says that, and it's exactly what your therapist and loved ones will say. Sometimes it has to get worse before it gets better but that part you feel you've lost touch with might just be buried even deeper. You have the ability to gain control of your life back. It doesn't have to be through climbing but I strongly encourage people to pick up some kind of hobby or task. I find doing repetitive tasks helps you to focus on being present. And that's what it comes down to – being able to live in the present and not in the past anymore.*

*Come to terms with the knowledge that you can't change the past. Once you learn to live in the present, and not in the past, you can start planning for the future. That is one of the hardest things to lose – the ability to plan for the future. The ability to look six months or a year in the future and say, "Let's go take a trip". When you get that back, you get back hope and the belief everything is going to be okay.*

Nick Carpenter has returned to college, where he plans to complete a business degree. He is proof that you can heal your wounds and find pleasure and purpose in life again.

## Claim Your Power

To be aware that something is lacking in your life, whether it is peace of mind, or purpose, or warmth of connection — and to do nothing about it — is to continue to make yourself powerless.

To claim your power, you must decide what you are going to do about the root cause of your pain. How will you respond to it? Can you recognize the gift of that experience, and turn it into a source of power and wisdom?

For example, a troubled childhood can make a person tough and stoic, but it can also make them emotionally closed off. In this situation, the gift is grit; the curse is disconnection**. Every tragedy has the potential for illumination or darkness.** It is wonderful to have grit: Courage and resolve in the face of challenges are admirable. It is also wonderful to be able to enjoy warm, close relationships with others and to love and be loved. By recognizing both the good and bad, and taking action to overcome the bad, you claim your power.

It is not uncommon for people who work in the field of psychology and health care to come from dysfunctional family backgrounds. They may have grown up with an alcoholic or mentally ill parent and may have been caregivers their whole lives, so it's a natural fit for them to want to continue to help others. This is their strength. But if they don't help themselves and address their own trauma, they may experience ongoing issues such as depression, control, paranoia, addiction, and anxiety in their personal intimate relationships. This is their weakness.

> **Guideline #47: Embrace your greatest strength. Acknowledge your hidden hurts.**

Carl Jung said, "Knowing your own darkness is the best method for dealing with the darknesses of other people." Take care of yourself. Accept help from others. Talk and let your secrets out with someone you can trust. Getting help is not a sign of weakness; it's a sign of strength. What keeps you strong isn't holding onto hurt; it's letting go. You let go, to receive something greater.

## Get More Love

Carl Jung coined the term "wounded healer" based on the premise that a psychoanalyst is driven to treat patients because the analyst himself is wounded. Research seems to bear this out, as nearly three out of four counselors and therapists have experienced one or more "wounds" that led to their career choice.

As a dating and relationship guide, my greatest strength is being able to help people get more love in their life, starting with themselves. My childhood wounds led me to this. I've read a ton of relationship and psychology self-help books to learn all I could on this subject. Had I not done so much work on myself, my intimate relationships would have suffered. I would have continued to suffer.

My greatest wound? The feeling that I am ultimately unlovable. This is a childhood wound that stems from growing up in a dysfunctional family. I've worked hard to heal this wound and claim my power. I've worked hard to love myself. I now enjoy the healthiest relationship I've ever been in, and I can use my experience and knowledge to help others.

My greatest wound became my greatest gift.

**Your sacred wound is something in the past that caused emotional trauma and pain.** We all have experienced trauma, either self-inflicted or caused by life's circumstances. If we can treat our wounds with compassion, the pain decreases. As a result, we emerge more forgiving, innocent, playful, and wise. We have more to offer others. We can even heal others who are going through trauma of their own. If we ignore our wounds, they fester. We suffer and become negative, cynical and disconnected from people and pleasure.

Healing ourselves is an act of self-love.

> *"You can never love another person if you don't know how to love yourself". I can relate to this in so many ways it's scary. I'm still trying to learn to love myself but I can see the progress and my life is so much better for it. I think a lot of people may have the question "How do you love yourself? How do you learn to do that?" That was the question I had to ask and answer for myself, and I think it's different for everyone.*
>
> *I think that recognizing things that make you happy (not your partner, not you and your partner, just you) is a great first step.*
>
> — Kass

What does loving yourself look like? Maybe it's posting candid and imperfect photos of yourself on Facebook that show the real you. Maybe it's exercising each day. Maybe it's quitting a soul-sucking job. Maybe it's choosing to dump a toxic friend. **Loving yourself means recognizing things that are healthy, authentic, and good for you, and cutting out things – and people – that aren't.** It may sound cliché, but learning to love yourself means treating yourself like a best friend.

**Guideline #48: Healing our hurts is an act of self-love.**

You may be wondering what all this has to do with a relationship book, and I say, *everything*. The inability to address old hurts and heal old wounds will limit your happiness and affect your relationships. **As long as people are in pain, there will be more pain.**

## Seven Ways to Heal Your Wounds and Claim Your Power

1. Avoid blaming others for negative thinking or actions. Only you can control your thinking and actions. If you need to, distract yourself from focusing on the bad stuff.

2. Avoid blaming yourself for things that happened in the past. You were probably doing the best you could. If you feel shame, it's probably because you knew deep down you could do better. Acknowledge that, and tell yourself you'll do better next time. (There's almost always a second chance at things, so pay the lesson forward.)

3. Be aware of when you may be playing the victim role, and realize that this only keeps you from fulfilling your dreams. (Which is sometimes the reason we unconsciously stay stuck – if we say we can't do something then we don't have to risk failure.)

4. Determine what you want in life, and go for it. Don't wait for someone else to give it to you.

5. Be aware that you may not have a choice about what happens to you (or what happened to you as a child) but that you always have a choice about how to respond to a situation.

6. Be kind to yourself and others. When we are in pain, it's hard to be kind. Try. You need loving care and tenderness

more than ever, and the more you offer this, the more it will be reflected back.

7. If you feel stuck, consider professional help.

## You Have a Choice

If your response to something is way out of proportion to the actual event – rage, tears or going numb – you are triggering what I call "Big Pain". These are wounds in need of healing.

You have a choice. You can stay stuck in a stew of negative emotions, or you can choose the path that contributes to your highest growth. What will make you feel most alive and at peace with yourself? What action can you take to increase the love you have to give others, and yourself?

Heal your wounds. Claim your power. Get more love.

> **Guideline #49: Heal your pain, and you heal the world.**

* * *

## HOUSEKEEPING: Claim Your Power

I went to the bank the other day, and the teller was a young bearded guy with a forearm tattoo that said, "Fight your demons". It's unusual to see this kind of thing, especially at a bank, but it reminded me that **everyone struggles with something.** This chapter is about facing personal demons. If there is something you read in this chapter that struck a chord with you, here are some powerful actions you can take. Consider it spiritual housekeeping.

### Task 1: Read Viktor Frankl's book *Man's Search for Meaning.*

Sometimes it helps to read stories about people who have had it harder than you and triumphed through misfortune. One of the most inspiring books I've ever read is Viktor Frankl's *Man's Search for Meaning.* As a boy, Viktor survived unspeakable horrors in four different Nazi concentration camps. Despite immense suffering and family tragedies, he refused to see himself as a victim. Even with a gun to his head, Viktor believed in the power of free will: he could still choose how to meet death. Would he cry? Would he beg for mercy? Or would he keep his dignity and remain calm? He could still choose his attitude in those last few seconds.

> *We who lived in concentration camps can remember the men who walked through the huts comforting others, giving away their last piece of bread. They may have been few in number, but they offer sufficient proof that everything can be taken from a man but one thing: the last of the human freedoms – to choose one's attitude in any given set of circumstances, to choose one's own way.*
>
> — Viktor E. Frankl

Without belittling your pain, I highly recommend Viktor Frankl's book. It's a very inspiring and comforting read for many reasons.

### Task 2: Face Your fear.

Where there is fear, there is often unresolved pain. As Rhonda Britten, author of *Fearless Living* says, fear stops you from "living the life your soul intended".

Fear of rejection prevents us from falling in love. It stops us from being vulnerable and connecting to another. It stops us from going after our dreams.

What do you fear? That is what is keeping you from being fully alive.

**Task 3. Pay attention to teachers.**

When you're ready to acknowledge your pain and fears, and to take action, know that healers and guides can appear in many forms. You may find wisdom and healing through books, quiet reflection in nature, a life coach, tapping with EFT (emotional freedom technique), meditation or yoga, your local pastor, an elder or a psychologist. In fact, you may need a combination of some of these things, as I did. While your partner may play a supportive role, they are rarely equipped to deal with big issues and childhood trauma even if this is their field of study. This is because they are too close to the fire. If your partner plays therapist for you, you'll both get burned.

You can find recommended therapists on Yelp. You can ask friends. You can take online coaching programs. When you're ready, the teacher will come. And if you don't like the teacher, keep looking. I tried three different psychologists before finding one I liked. Trust your intuition, but understand that your first appointment with a therapist will probably be uncomfortable.

Growing hurts. Remember what it was like to be a child and have shin splints and new teeth growing in? Yeah, it hurts to grow.

# Chapter 19: Exes, In-laws, and Relatives a.k.a. "You Mess with One Bean, You Get the Whole Burrito"

*If a man's character is to be abused, say what you will, there's nobody like a relative to do the business.*

— William Makepeace Thackeray

It sounds obvious, but once you marry or move in together, you enter a relationship with more than one person. I'm not talking about your significant other. For better or worse, you're also part of their family and they are part of yours. If you've ever seen the movie *My Big Fat Greek Wedding*, you have an idea of how big a deal this can be.

**Guideline #50: When it comes to family, "You mess with one bean, you get the whole burrito".**

Fortunately for me, I get along well with Tex's Greek relatives. Tex has also met my extended family in Canada, so no issues there. They see that I'm happy, and that's enough for them.

Even so, for the health of our relationship, we have ground rules around who we see and how much time we spend with family members. We've even talked about how we may answer certain questions should they come up (see the chapter on "Spiritual

Matters" for more examples on this). I highly recommend you come up with your own operating procedures around relatives, because it will allow for smoother relations. If your in-laws drive you crazy or drive a wedge between you and your partner, you really need some rules. Here are ours.

### Rule 1. Be Loyal to Each Other Above All

Tex and I are loyal to each other first. If a relative complains about one of us, we stick up for each other and then discuss the situation in private later. This is why we never criticize each other in public and we try to make a point of praising one another to friends and family. This shows solidarity and respect, and it raises our status in the eyes of others. As an example, Tex's mother would like me to attend church. She has brought this up a few times. Tex has told her that he loves and respects me and accepts me as I am and doesn't feel that I need to go. Her attitude bothers and amuses me at the same time. I stand firm in my convictions, as does Tex, and that's what matters. I hope she will find peace one day with the fact that I am a non-believer, but that's her journey.

*Note on loyalty:* If you have a problem with your spouse, I recommend that you don't bring it up with your parents or siblings. They want to protect you, and if you constantly criticize or complain about your partner, you will put them in a tough situation, one where they feel helpless to make things better. You may also find them growing cold towards your mate because of your complaints. Criticism makes for uncomfortable visits and relations. Your parents (or siblings) don't know when you make up, and they don't see all the good stuff in your relationship. If you're going to vent, at least make sure they also hear about the good stuff.

## Rule 2. Respect Each Other's Wishes

Tex and I have boundaries around who and how we visit. For example, when we went to Colorado so I could meet his daughter for the first time, I insisted we get a hotel room instead of staying at the home of his ex-wife and her new husband. Although the three of them get along great and he stays with them when he visits their daughter, I needed the privacy. That important first visit was far less stressful because he respected my needs, and on our next visit we stayed with them.

*Note on fidelity:* if Tex's ex-wife had not remarried, I would not have been comfortable with him staying alone with her. We have a rule about not overnighting alone with someone of the opposite sex – even an old friend – unless both of us agree to it. Yes, we trust each other, but if one of us weren't comfortable with the idea, we probably wouldn't do it. Ironically, couples who think they have nothing to fear and who never discuss the potential for infidelity, often run into issues later. You bulletproof your relationship and prevent future drama when you discuss potential scenarios and how you want to deal with them. Always go with your gut and respect each other's wishes.

## Rule 3. Make Time for Family

We make time for family, but not at the expense of our own quality time together or our physical and emotional energy. I am not fond of just sitting around and making small talk for hours. Maybe it's an introvert thing, but I find it draining. Knowing we would be seeing his lovely Mom about once a week after we moved to Texas, we decided to plant a garden in her backyard. Caring for the garden gives us all an activity to share. We can talk and garden. Knowing what makes you happy and applying a little creativity can make family gatherings much richer.

*Note on family:* Sometimes, people make too much time for family and are excessively attached to a parent figure, when they should be more independent or invest more time in their relationship with their partner. A classic example of this is the mama's boy, who lets his mom clean and cook for him and exert control over his decision-making, even when there is another female in the household. Basically, mama's boys allow their mothers to be the alpha females. The female version of this is the daddy's girl, who lets her father be the alpha male and primary decision-maker in her life. (I have also seen this happen with ex-wives and ex-husbands who still exert control over their former partner, even if they have remarried.) This doesn't work in grown-up relationships: **our spouse should be the first person we turn to when we need help.**

## Rule 4. Prioritize Each Other

Tex and I prioritize our relationship and our personal time and we don't mind sharing this information with others. For example, Thursday nights are date nights. If Tex was invited to do something with a friend or one of his cousins on a date night, he would probably decline or at least check in with me first. If you think this is the old ball and chain going on, you're wrong. It's about honoring our precious time together. When we dated, we made time for each other, so why should that stop just because we live together? Also, his daughter has equal priority to me, which means she can call him anytime she needs to. If she calls while we're having dinner, he is going to answer. This is because he wants her to know he is always there for her even though he lives in another state. I accept this. Since the first date, he made his priorities clear when he interrupted our date to call his daughter and wish her goodnight, which he still does every night.

*Note on prioritizing:* Your new family – your spouse and children – should be the most important people in your life. If a friend or in-law has a problem with this, the person with the primary relationship needs to address it. For example, if the mother-in-law complains about not seeing enough of her son and grandchildren, the son needs to step in and lay down the law. Likewise, if the woman's parents have issues with the son-in-law, she needs to address them head-on.

If you let people know how important someone is to you and you apply your relationship rules on a consistent basis, others will accept them or at the very least respect them, in-laws included.

Your number one focus should be each other and your kids. Everyone – and everything else – gets a back seat. Your primary relationship will no longer be with your parents. Or your dog. Or your cat. Or your employer. It will be with your significant other. And the goal is happiness. You have chosen to share a life together. How committed are you?

## The Apple Doesn't Fall Far from the Tree – Or Does It?

If you've heard the expression "The apple doesn't fall far from the tree", you probably know that it means children grow up to be like their parents. How they handle stress, money and even communication and hygiene, is a product of their upbringing. And this is true in a lot of ways. However, the more self-aware you are and the more work you've done on yourself, the more consciously uncoupled you can become from the negative aspects of your parents. But if your significant other is not a very self-aware person, then just be forewarned: the apple really doesn't fall far from the tree.

*PEARLY WISDOM: Don't fall in love with someone's potential. It sounds cliché, but it's true. Many people date and become addicted to someone who isn't a good fit for them, because the chemistry is so good. They believe that with enough time and love and encouragement, the person will change for the better – or at least, into someone they would prefer to be with. It's a trap, one that usually leads to bitter breakups and deep resentments when reality hits.*

**Guideline #51: Your partner is not your project.**

## Skeletons in the Closet

Tex knows all about my family's history: the mental illness and addiction issues, and the codependency. I waited to tell him about the skeletons in my family's closet, not because I was hiding anything but because I wanted him to get to know me first, without the darkness and drama. Too much information too quickly might have scared him away or caused him to look at me differently. I figured I would wait about six months before sharing any details. That would give him enough time to get a real sense of who I was. Also, six months is usually a make-or-break time for most couples because it's when you move out of the infatuation phase and into something more serious and committed. No point in sharing something so deep if we weren't serious.

As fate would have it, the death of my father brought everything out into the open only three months into our relationship. Amazingly, Tex didn't run away and he didn't judge me for any of it. If anything, he fell more in love with my vulnerability. Right after my father's service, on the drive home, he asked me to move to the United States with him. I was amazed. This man had met all my relatives, and heard more stories than he should have in one week, and he still wanted to be with me!

If you have skeletons in the closet – and every family does – then I hope your partner can help bring any hidden shame out into the open and love you despite it all.

* * *

## HOUSEKEEPING: "United We Stand, Divided We Fall".

For the health of our relationship, Tex and I have ground rules around who we see and how much time we spend with other family members. We also adjust for different situations. How about you?

**Task 1: Set some ground rules around exes, in-laws, and relatives.**

What are some ground rules you can establish that will make your union more powerful and peaceful?

Can you bring up an incident in the past, and how you would like to deal with it should it come up again in the future?

Can you role-play some potential scenarios you might experience with other family members, exes, or in-laws and how you wish to respond to them?

You are becoming quite a team now.

# Chapter 20: Spiritual Matters

*Anyone who thinks sitting in church can make you a Christian must also think that sitting in a garage can make you a car.*

— Garrison Keillor

*My religion is very simple. My religion is kindness.*

— Dalai Lama XIV

## When You Have Different Beliefs

Did you know that 45% of marriages in the United States are comprised of people of different faiths? That almost 60% of non-religious people live with a religious spouse? Having different spiritual beliefs is not uncommon in a relationship, but it does add complexity to the dynamic. You may disagree on how to celebrate the holidays. If you have children, will they go to church? If so, whose? Do you pray at mealtime? And how do you handle judgmental relatives?

Since Tex identifies as Christian (Greek Orthodox) and I see myself as non-religious, our different beliefs are an issue that we've had to tackle from the beginning of our relationship. Fortunately, we began discussing the R word (religion) on our third date. By the end of that date, we had struck an agreement. I said, "As long as you respect my beliefs and don't try to change me, and I respect yours and don't try to change you, this could work". Tex agreed, and two years later, we're still honoring our agreement.

Not trying to change each other has worked out beautifully, except when it comes to extended family. Like many couples of mixed faiths, our greatest stress has come from family members who see their religion as right and all other beliefs – or even a lack of belief – as wrong.

Here are some of the challenges we have faced and how we have addressed them. What would you do? There are no right or wrong answers. These are things that couples must work out for themselves, according to their own convictions.

## Challenge Number 1: Judgmental and Fearful Relatives

Tex's 11-year-old daughter, Hope, is a sweet girl and a devout Christian. She is being raised by his ex-wife, an enthusiastic Christian. They go to church nearly every week, and the daughter attends Bible camp and a Christian private school, so she is heavily influenced by doctrine.

According to the mother, the daughter is concerned about my being a non-believer and is worried her dad may become less Christian due to my influence. Hope doesn't like us living together before marriage. It is hard for her to reconcile the idea that I don't believe in Christ, and she prays for my soul every night. I am uncertain how many of Hope's fears are hers, and how many are her mother's.

How would you address this issue?

For us, it's not a single conversation. Hope should see, in time, that I am a good person, and that I make her father happy, and that this is possibly more important than whether I believe in Jesus Christ or not. Tex also reminds her that we are all God's children – believers and non-believers, Muslims, Jews, and Christians. When she is older, he expects to have more philosophical conversations with her about God and religion, heaven and hell. In the meantime, he lets her know he still goes to church, since this allays her fears about him losing his religion.

As for living together before marriage, he has told her that it's not ideal but life is like that sometimes. Hope is 11-and-a-half years old, so he keeps things simple yet lets her know that she can talk to him about any fears she may have. I think that meeting me for the first time and doing something fun together like skiing made a lot of her fears vanish. The more fun we have and the better she gets to know me, the less I expect her to worry about my beliefs.

*Moral of the story:* When it comes to children, keep it simple. When it comes to stepchildren, be patient above all. Accepting you – the interloper, the person who could take their mommy or daddy away – could take years. When it comes to handling judgmental and fearful relatives, be a role model of good behavior and have fun together. This is how you connect with hearts and minds and get birthday cards every year.

## Challenge Number 2: What to Do at Grace

Tex and I discussed this scenario months before I met any of his relatives: how to handle grace when we dine with his relatives. I told him I didn't want to pray or say amen, but I was okay with bowing my head and wanted to know what he thought of this. Tex said he appreciated that I would do that instead of excusing myself from the table or doing something to draw attention, because that would be a deal breaker for him. Since we had discussed this in advance, it felt fine when it finally happened. We have not noticed if it bothers other members of the family that I don't say amen.

*Moral of the story:* Be curious and willing to compromise to make your partner happy, but don't let go of your personal beliefs when it is unsafe, unethical, or uncomfortable to do so. With that in mind, anything new will feel slightly uncomfortable at first; be willing to try if there is no real harm to you.

## Challenge Number 3: Managing Church Visits and Religious Holidays

Although she knows I'm not religious, Tex's mother wants me to go to church with them on important holidays. She is Greek Orthodox, and she would love me to convert. I encourage Tex to join her, but I won't go. Tex has told her he loves and accepts me just as I am and doesn't expect me to go to church, but this seems to have had little impact.

Tex has asked me to come to one service, just to make his mother happy and to share the experience at least once. I agreed to one visit with one caveat: he wouldn't pressure me to go a second time. I also reiterated that he needs to let his mother know that I encourage him to go to church, but that it is not for me and he is okay with that. He agreed. I'll try anything once, and if it makes him and his mother happy, great. If I like it, I might even go a second time. If I don't, we have an agreement on how to handle subsequent requests.

*Moral of the story:* Again, be curious and willing to compromise to make your partner happy, but don't let go of your personal beliefs when it is unsafe, unethical, or uncomfortable to do so.

## Challenge Number 4: Nosy Relatives and Friends

Texas is in the Bible belt, and religion is very important to many people who live there. As I meet more people from Tex's side, I expect to be asked about my faith. How does one handle these kinds of questions with diplomacy?

Tex and I discussed this scenario a few months into our relationship. He asked me what I would do if a relative asked if I accepted Jesus Christ as my lord and savior. I said I would tell them the truth: that I wasn't religious. He grimaced a little and then asked me to make sure I looked around the room first to see if there were any children present, and if there were, to then offer to discuss things at another time. I kind of growled and said that if they asked me in front of the children, they should be prepared for a straight answer, but then I simmered down and agreed to save such scandalous conversations for adult ears only. However, I wouldn't hide my beliefs.

This conversation was prophetic in a way, because something similar happened when I met his aunt for the first time. She's a tough old bird, and within 10 minutes she asked me what religion I followed – right in front of his mother, whom I was just getting to know! I replied with, "Nothing", and Tex nearly had a small heart attack. But I answered honestly and added, somewhat vaguely, "I believe there is something bigger than us, but I don't follow any particular faith. I am a spiritual person, but I'm not religious". His aunt nodded slowly and said, "That's okay. You answered honestly, and I like that. You are an honest person. You did not pretend".

*Moral of the story:* Be honest about your beliefs and true to your convictions, and don't be an asshole about them. Others may not like your beliefs, but they will respect your authenticity.

**Guideline #52: Good people will respect your beliefs; bad people will try to shame you for them.**

*PEARLY WISDOM: If you're worried about pressure or conflict from religious extended family members and if they distance themselves from you or your children for religious reasons, rest assured that conflict and tension only seems to happen in 10% of cases.*[33] *Isn't it nice to know that only 10% of the population can be real jerks about their beliefs?*

## Before You Tie the Knot

The most important piece of advice I can give couples of mixed belief systems before they tie the knot is to discuss these kinds of scenarios beforehand. Your beloved may say they respect your beliefs and won't try to change you, but it's an empty promise until you put good intentions to the test. You need to know if your beliefs will cause friction with family or with your community, and how you will handle these kinds of situations together beforehand. You should not expect your partner to change for you – that is not love. **Love is accepting the person they are, not withholding love and acceptance until they turn into the person you want them to be.** It's only by discussing and experiencing different scenarios that you test the depths of your convictions and your love for one another.

*PEARLY WISDOM: I don't think I could feel more loved than when Tex defended me to his friends and family. There is something about knowing that your partner is loyal in the face of opposition, even when they may not side with your beliefs, that makes you feel truly loved and accepted.*

At the end of the day, you may not always agree, but you need to be able to fight for each other's right to disagree. If you cannot reconcile your convictions with your partner's beliefs, you probably should not get married or live together. Mike shares his experience:

**Q: Has having different belief systems been tough on any of your relationships?**

Mike: *I've never been able to make it work. I grew up in the church and now do not attend or subscribe to any religion, but my experience was that Uber Faithful Christians don't see a relationship for what it is. What I am saying is that they often neglect caring for a relationship, and only care if the person they are dating is religious themselves. It's like saying that I want to eat an apple, but not checking to see if it is a rotten apple. It looks good from the outside, but it still is a rotten apple. For example, I dated a girl at church for a month or two, and within a short period of time she was saying that I was a "gift from God". She was looking at me, seeing my involvement in the church and decided to be with me based on my participation in church activities... not in the actual relationship that we had. The point is, I find that many Christians are blinded by something I call "Faith Eyes", and the females are desperate to find a Christian guy and will do anything to get him.*

*I have seen it so many times among my female Christian friends … where they have a list of what they are looking for in a man. It's basically:*

1. *A God-fearing man.*
2. *A man.*
3. *It would be nice if he has a good relationship with his mother.*

*I wish I could show you all the posts on social media that I see from them … they are not in the right headspace to find a partner!*

*I was blown away by my relationship with the girl who thought I was her gift from God. We had so little in common, and I was just the guy that goes to church and that was good enough for her.*

**Q: Are there any other ways in which having different belief systems was tough on your relationships?**

Mike: *Typically, when a person is religious, their family is too. This will put a strain on the relationship because the family may find it hard to accept a non-religious person or a person of another religion in the family. My experience is that every time I tell my family that I have met a girl, the first question they ask is, "Is she Christian?" I find that rather disheartening because they never ask about who she is and how we get along. In previous relationships, this was very hard to deal with, and I shied away from it. I almost hid my relationships from my family. I was caught between my family's religion and my partner's lack of a religion. And this wasn't fair to my partner, and it took years for me to build the confidence to defend the relationship to my family … and she, of course, dumped my ass because I took too damn long.* ***I think that many people would like to believe that they are accepting of other faiths and religions, but very few people truly are.*** *I would say that if someone holds strong beliefs, they cannot date someone who does not hold those same values. Think of religious faith as a sliding scale, and people can't date someone more than a couple notches up or down on the scale.*

**Q: But what about couples who are both Christian? Can it work then?**

Mike: *You can be of the same religion but have different beliefs; different levels of faith will not work.*

**Q: How do you overcome this challenge?**

Mike*: If you will date someone from another faith/belief, then you must be confident in the relationship and be prepared to defend it. It's hard to date someone when your family doesn't accept the person, and you have to be willing to be with the person no matter what. Most relationships will fail because they will see it as a choice between having their partner or their family. It also takes mutual respect and the desire to support each other even if you disagree with each other's faith. You have to remember that their faith is what makes them who they are, and if you love them, that belief is what you need to continue to nurture. If you are dating someone who is religious, and they feel that you are pulling them away from their faith – you will probably be the one to go, not their faith.*

**Q: What advice would you give others?**

Mike: *My advice is:*

1. *Don't date someone who doesn't share your beliefs.*

2. *If you do date someone from a different belief system, then be clear with them about what you need from them regarding your faith, and ask them what they need.*

3. *NEVER try to change someone – they will resent you. If you would like to date a religious woman, learn what they are looking for in a man.*

4. *Once you learn what they are looking for or what they need, be honest with yourself: can you be that partner?*

*I have now met a girl who is also not religious, or at least she subscribes to the same "church" as I do: the church of nature! So, we get along pretty well.*

## You Say To-ma-to, I Say To-mah-to

> *Dogma: a principle or set of principles laid down by an authority as incontrovertibly true.*
>
> — Wikipedia

As Mike notes, even couples of the same religion can experience conflict when it comes to worship. If one partner is more devout than the other and pressures their partner to attend church more often, there can be struggle. Or if one person has a different interpretation of scripture, there can be intense arguments.

If you are inflexible around scripture or doctrines (You say to-ma-to, I say to-mah-to: Let's call the whole thing off!), then yes, there will be problems in your relationship. Being inflexible about anything is problematic in a relationship. When you add children and extended family to the mix, and have different ideas on how they should be raised within the church, you have a recipe for disaster.

People can also experience a change of heart when it comes to faith-based matters. You can marry into the same faith only to find your partner leaving the church at some point. It is not uncommon for people to experience a de-conversion or to convert to a different faith later in life. I am not sure why, but I have seen this happen when people reach middle age: suddenly, they rediscover and embrace the religion of their childhood. They may leave the church they've shared with their spouse and become a devout Muslim or Catholic. Call it a mid-life religious crisis.

*PEARLY WISDOM: Jesus wasn't a Christian. Think about it. Back in his time, people started calling those who followed him "Christians", but the actual religion took time to take root. As of 2012, there are over 43,000 Christian denominations, according to the Center for the Study of Global Christianity at Gordon-Conwell Theological Seminary. What do you want to bet that each of these denominations considers themselves valid and "true", and their interpretation of Christianity as the only correct one? We are never going to completely agree with each other on doctrine, but maybe if we look to the core of Christ's teachings – kindness, tolerance, and love for our fellow man – we can find fellowship... whether we're Muslim, Hindu, Buddhist, atheist, agnostic or one of the many 43,000+ flavors of Christianity. It is man's dogma and arrogance that divides us. An "us versus them" mentality seems to be in our DNA. This tribalistic outlook is at war with our highest natures, Christ's message, and our highest good.*

To show just how far apart a couple's viewpoints can be, I asked Benebell Wen, a New Age writer and the author of *Holistic Tarot: An Integrative Approach to Using Tarot for Personal Growth*, about her spiritual beliefs and how they differ from her husband's. She is a pagan, and her husband is an atheist from China, so they are worlds apart in their belief systems. After 12 years together, they are proof that love, respect and openness are the solution to making mixed-faith marriages work.

**Q: Tell me about your relationship.**

Benebell: *My spiritual beliefs would be considered pagan: a synthesis of metaphysical energy work, Taoist ceremonial ritual, and what my husband James Zhang likes to call witchcraft. James, on the other hand, is an atheist. I grew up attending Christian churches while James grew up in Communist China during the Cultural Revolution where the primary "religion" was patriotism. Thus, any theist concept of believing in deity or gods confounds him to a certain degree. He and I have been together for 12 years and married for seven.*

**Q: Is having different belief systems tough on your relationship?**

Benebell: *It can be. I take my spiritual practice quite seriously, and so it can be frustrating when your husband walks in on a candle-lit, incense-burning ritual and points and laughs. What's interesting is over time we do balance and temper each other out. He is becoming more open-minded to what I do and will even accept as plausible some of the metaphysical energy work I practice. I, in turn, stay grounded, level-headed, and rational. Also, in spite of my metaphysical, New Agey practices, I am still heavily influenced by the Christianity I was raised with, and want our future children to grow up with the Christian faith (and let them decide later for themselves what works and doesn't work for them spiritually and ideologically). James, however, sees religion and faith as enemies of reason and wants to raise "rational skeptics" who "believe in science, facts, and empirical data."*

**Q: How do you overcome this challenge?**

Benebell: *This is going to sound cliché, but with love.* ***If you need another person to believe the same thing you believe in, you're being selfish.*** *When you're being unselfish and truly love and accept another for who they are, you don't need to shove your religion or your beliefs down their throats. Also, conviction helps. I believe very strongly in my religious beliefs and spiritual practices, so I'm not threatened or offended by counterpoints. Oh, but when you start talking about in-laws, well then the situation does get complicated. I have no idea how you might overcome the in-law challenge – i.e. when your side of the family holds different religious views from those of his side of the family – since we haven't figured it out yet. A lot of walking around on eggshells, that's how.*

**Q: What advice would you give others?**

Benebell: *Religion needs to be discussed well before marriage and before a relationship becomes serious. The two parties need to figure out whether the differences in their spiritual practices are obstacles they can overcome. If your religion is one where anyone from a different religion is headed for damnation, then marrying someone from a different religion is going to be problematic. If you're open to the idea that there are many paths leading to the same spiritually fulfilling destination, then you'll probably be able to make it work.*

## When Interfaith Mixes Don't Mix

As Benebell says: "If your religion is one where anyone from a different religion is headed for damnation, then marrying someone of a different religion is going to be problematic".

In Dale McGowan's book *In Faith and In Doubt: How Religious Believers and Nonbelievers Can Create Strong Marriages and Loving Families*, the author writes: "Not all denominations are good candidates for the secular/religious mix. Though individuals will vary, Mormons and Jehovah's Witnesses are among the religious identities that show the highest levels of tension and conflict in relationships with nonreligious partners. They are also among the least likely to believe that atheists are candidates for eternal life – at least not the good kind".

Peggy says growing up in an interfaith household sucked:

> *Speaking as a child that grew up in an interfaith household, it sucks. My mom is Latter Day Saints (Mormon); my dad was vaguely Christian. My dad always supported our church activity, but his family... not so much. My mom struggled a lot, even though she*

> *loves my dad more than anything. My dad did join the church eventually and under his own terms. My brother married a wonderful woman who is not part of our faith, and he's not an active member either; they have still gone through some serious struggles and will go through even harder ones when they have kids. I wouldn't say that you should never marry someone outside of your faith; just be prepared to have it 10x harder than those that do. Even if you can talk to each other and work together, when cultures collide it is very tough. Most people who have a true conviction in their faith are not going to be able to compromise for long.*

As Peggy points out, when cultures collide, things get rough. One example of this is conservative Islam. McGowan notes: "According to the formal mandates of Islam, Muslim men may marry Muslim, Jewish or Christian women, but Muslim women may marry only Muslim men". Nor is it possible for conservative Muslims to marry someone who is non-religious.

Conservative or fundamentalist religions of any type can make things rough for couples. This includes Orthodox Judaism, Jehovah's Witnesses, Mormonism and Evangelical Protestants, whose beliefs are too inflexible to welcome someone with very different ideas on gender roles, salvation, incarnation, creation, evolution, and the afterlife. According to McGowan, fundamentalist–secular marriages have "the highest levels of conflict and divorce", but fundamentalist marriages, period, have the highest levels of divorce, even amongst each other. The common denominator? The word "fundamentalist", which describes a strict adherence to a set of principles. Fundamentalist Christians (especially Protestants) believe that every word of the Bible is true and divinely inspired, while Islamic fundamentalism refers to strictly observing Islamic law and the teachings of the Koran.

It's a black-and-white world view of things, and thou shalt walk a very narrow path. I am certain this lack of permissiveness attracts people who want more structure and authority in their life. (In my experience, many born-again Christians have had wild pasts – a friend of mine's parents had belonged to a biker gang. It would seem that the more the pendulum swings one way, the more it swings the other way.)

According to Barna Group, an evangelical Christian polling firm that conducts surveys and does research to better understand what Christians believe and how they behave, **conservative Protestants get divorced more often than any other group, and atheists and agnostics divorce the least.** Personally, I find it ironic that the segment of the population that pushes for "the sanctity of marriage" and is the most vehemently opposed to gay marriage is the one with the highest rate of divorce. Perhaps this is why:

> *Faith has had a limited affect [sic] on people's behavior, whether related to moral convictions and practices, relational activities, lifestyle choices or economic practices.*
>
> — George Barna, Barna Group

Note that this quote comes from George Barna, head of Barna Group – the author of 48 books, a pastor and a popular speaker at ministry conferences around the world. Based in Ventura, California, the organization has worked with thousands of churches across the United States.

That line by George Barna is so important that it bears repeating: "Faith has had a limited affect [*sic*] on people's behavior, whether related to moral convictions and practices, relational activities, lifestyle choices or economic practices".

It would seem that character trumps faith when it comes to issues of morality.

## Focus on Shared Values

While some religious combinations are more likely to end in divorce than others, there is no more likelihood that a non-Christian and Christian will divorce than two Christians, according to author Naomi Schaefer Riley in her book *'Til Faith Do Us Part*.

Author Dale McGowan agrees. In his book *In Faith and In Doubt*, McGowan notes: "Several studies show that couples who differ substantially on key social and political issues are at greater risk of divorce from that difference than from almost any other risk factor". It would seem that **values matter more than beliefs.**

Since religious and non-religious beliefs usually fall somewhere on a continuum, it is very possible for a liberal Protestant who believes in gay rights, supports abortion, and believes that atheists can be saved, to settle down with a liberally minded non-religious partner who holds similar views. But **the more polarized the beliefs around social justice and core values, the more difficult, if not impossible, the union will be.**

> **Guideline #53: Focus on shared values, not religion, to make your union work.**

If you are religious and your partner isn't, you are already aware of what "godly" characteristics they may have. Are they brave, kind, compassionate, graceful, humble, loving, loyal and patient? While these may be considered Christian virtues or Muslim virtues, they are not exclusive to either religion. These qualities are indeed the hallmark of every good human being, regardless of whether they are Christian, Jewish, Muslim or atheist. This is what I refer to when I say focus on values, not religion.

*PEARLY WISDOM: When it comes to core values, you have to walk the walk, not just talk the talk.*

As an example, Tex once said to me that I was a godly woman. I asked him what he meant. He said I was a good woman, and I said (eyebrow arched), "I can be a good woman, but I don't have to be godly". He was faintly annoyed by this. We were using different language to describe the same thing: a virtuous human being. In his case, the language was couched in religious terms. In mine, it was humanistic. (You say to-ma-to, I say to-mah-to.) I let it go because I sensed the huge compliment underneath. For Tex, calling someone "godly" is a form of praise. I give this example because your partner will have ways of expressing things which may annoy you, but it's important to see past the phrasing and focus on the core message.

## Communicate to Find the Common Ground

If you want to make your union work, you need to find the common ground. This means discussing your belief system with your partner and withholding criticism and judgement. Only by exploring ideas with genuine curiosity and respect are you able to understand your partner better. Only by explaining your belief system to someone else are you able to deepen it and understand yourself a whole lot better. As Tex says: "'Why?' is the most important question a person can ask".

Through conversation and self-reflection, I have learned that Tex doesn't believe in a literal heaven or hell; he thinks that they exist here on Earth through our actions, which can be good or evil and which reap consequences that can make a personal heaven or hell of our lives. Therefore, he believes in following your conscience and doing good. Nor does Tex believe that the soul of a non-believer is damned for eternity. In fact, many Christians have those same thoughts, and believe that good deeds count a great deal in the eyes of God – so much so that even atheists can go to heaven. Pope Francis seems to agree:

> *You ask me if the God of the Christians forgives those who don't believe and who don't seek the faith. I start by saying – and this is the fundamental thing – that God's mercy has no limits if you go to him with a sincere and contrite heart. The issue for those who do not believe in God is to obey their conscience.*
>
> — Pope Francis

Tex identifies as Greek Orthodox, but very few of his ideas would be considered acceptable by the Orthodox Church, a conservative branch of Christianity. For example, he believes we are descended from apes and doesn't believe that Eve came from Adam's rib. Our belief systems are fluid and a lot closer than one would think if we were to define ourselves only with the Greek Orthodox/non-religious label. We are not alone in our fluid thinking: many people don't fully identify with the doctrine of their faith, and even the Pope has had radical ideas that border on heresy by promoting birth control and women in the priesthood.

*PEARLY WISDOM: For most people, religious and non-religious beliefs fall within a continuum. As an example, I just recently discovered that there is a very rich spectrum of non-belief. In reading Dale McGowan's book In Faith and in Doubt, I found myself identifying as a seeker-agnostic rather than an atheist. Seeker-agnostics see open-mindedness as a virtue, which may explain, in part, why Tex and I roll so well with the religion thing.*

Moral of the story? Find the common ground! Most married couples believe it's better to focus on values, not religion, to make a union work.

**Guideline #54: Deed before Creed.**

* * *

## HOUSEKEEPING: Find Common Ground in Spiritual Values

If you find yourself in a relationship where one of you is religious and one of you isn't, or you have different ideas about your faith, I recommend that you reread this chapter together and discuss the stories herein. Do you see yourself in any of these situations?

**Task 1: Further reading.**

If you would like more helpful resources, I recommend Dale McGowan's book *In Faith and In Doubt: How Religious Believers and Nonbelievers Can Create Strong Marriages and Loving Families.* He also has a blog called "Parenting Beyond Belief" at www.parentingbeyondbelief.com, where he explores raising children in a secular or mixed-faith home. He himself is an atheist, and his wife is a Protestant. They have three children.

# Chapter 21: Kids, Stepkids, and Furry Kids

*No man should bring children into the world who is unwilling to persevere to the end in their nature and education.*

— Plato

## How Children Affect a Relationship: Personal Stories

Children and stepkids will affect your relationship in ways you may not be prepared for. Six women and one man share their very personal stories and advice below. These stories and each person's words have been edited for brevity and clarity while still trying to maintain their original voice and message.

## Cheryl's Story

### Q: How has having a child affected your relationship?

Cheryl: *"Nothing will change; it doesn't have to". Over and over again, this was our answer to friends and co-workers who were telling us to enjoy our last months together before we had a child. What we didn't know was that life would change and our relationship would change. It would be different – in neither a worse nor a better way, just different. The number one relationship changer: our relationship became more strongly bonded because it was tied together by our shared and intense love for the human being that WE created. It is a connection that is hard to explain in words, and nothing can prepare you for it.*

**Q: What are some good ways in which having a child has affected your relationship?**

Cheryl:

1. *You are forced to communicate more than ever before if you ever want to succeed as a unit.*

2. *You appreciate the small things in life way more – it's about quality, not quantity.*

3. *A two-hour mini-date can seem like a week away together!*

**Q: What are some bad ways in which having a child has affected your relationship?**

Cheryl:

1. *You have to schedule life, every last morsel of it (sometimes this includes sex).*

2. *Spontaneous trips are way harder to handle.*

3. *Financial stress is heightened and can take its toll on a relationship.*

4. *As a mother, you are responsible for growing, feeding, caring and guiding a child every minute of every day. Sometimes at the end of the day, the last thing you want is your husband hugging, kissing and loving you. It can feel like suffocation. Sometimes you just need a cave with*

*some personal space. And this can be hard on any marriage or relationship.*

**Q: You said, "Sometimes at the end of the day, the last thing you want is your husband hugging, kissing and loving you. It can feel like suffocation". So, what do you do about that? Do you have rituals to get you in the mood, or does having some personal time put you back in the mood?**

Cheryl: *At times, we need to schedule intimate time. I know, I know. It sounds so un-sexy. But honestly it works. It's like scheduling time to go to the gym. Balance is also key. For me, I need to ensure I have had time to be active, time to work, time to connect with other people, and quiet time. I also NEED to ensure we make time to connect intellectually and emotionally through conversation. You can and will get so wrapped up in your kidlets, and rushing around, that you forget to talk about LIFE. And I don't mean about what you did all day but the REAL stuff: your dreams, your feelings, your desires, etc. Lastly, I often need to consciously remind myself that we were a WE before we were a WE + ONE.*

**Q: One other question. If you could go back in time, what advice would you give to your younger self about having kids?**

Cheryl: *Talk. Make time to put each other first: after all, you both came before children. Love hard. This question is a little harder because it's VERY personal to my situation. I waited to have kids later in life. I waited because I wanted and needed to be selfish – to explore my career, to travel, to move (like a gazillion times over). BUT, to be honest, I wish I had had children earlier. The grass is always greener, I guess. Time pressures make conceiving really difficult and stressful. It's too late for me to have a big(ger) family, and some days that makes me sad.*

*Secondly, I would tell my younger self to live every day in my 20s to the utmost. To go on more road trips, more plane rides, to drink more wine, go to that concert or that late night show. Not necessarily to party hard and to live it up but to just experience and enjoy the freedom. I am sooooo thankful that I experienced all that I did. And if I went back, I would do MORE.*

*Lastly, I would tell myself to be patient. Being patient NOW will help you with the tremendous amount of patience you'll need when you have children.*

## Peggy's Story

**Q: How has NOT having kids affected your marriage, in good or bad ways? If you could go back in time, what advice would you give to your younger self?**

Peggy: *My husband and I knew we wanted a family. We both come from very family-centered homes, and kids and a small ranch were definitely our American dream. Once we began talking about marriage, we talked about family and agreed that three to four kids was perfect for us. We have always been able to communicate very well. Flash forward 14 years. We physically can't have kids, and adoption isn't working out for us. It's not something you think about when you are dating, because usually you're worried about getting pregnant before you are ready. It has been hard, since it's something we both want, and it is actually harder for me to deal with my husband's feelings than my own disappointments. He's just a big softie and would be the perfect father. We've always been very supportive of each other, and we don't play the blame game. It's just hard to watch someone you really love missing out on something you know would be great for them. If I had any advice for couples who want to go the distance, it's this: Talk about everything, even the hard stuff. It's okay to ponder something in your heart until you are sure how you feel about it, but don't keep secrets.*

## Kathleen's Story

**Q: How has having a child affected your relationship, in good or bad ways?**

Kathleen: *I celebrated my 25th wedding anniversary last year with my husband, Bob, who is my third (and last) husband. We each brought our own children into the marriage. I had a teenage daughter, and he had two boys, 12 and 10, way back then. The boys came on weekends. The daughter was with us 24/7. I knew Bob had a gentle soul and he actually got along with my daughter better than I did back then.*

*When we moved to California years later, I hadn't counted on him putting out the call that the adult children could move in with us. I wrote a book about that adventure called The Crowded Nest Syndrome, after two out of three took him up on it, plus pets and grandchildren.*

*It definitely affected the relationship, and though they eventually all moved out, the grandchildren are here every weekend. You have to love a man who has a heart of gold, who accepts taking care of various generations, and worries about their welfare. However, I'm the one who has to do the foundation work: laundry, grocery shopping, fixing meals. He pretty much just coasts along listening to their stories and watching television with them at home, though he is also very involved in their various sports.*

**Q: One other question. If you could go back in time, what advice would you give to your younger self about having kids?**

Kathleen: *If I could go all the way back in time to talk to my younger self, I would tell her not to have children at all. I started writing stories as a little girl and wanted to be a hermit when I grew up. I wanted to live in a forest and write books. I was not maternally inclined growing up nor played with dolls much.*

*As a writer yourself you may empathize with the idea of alone time, something very precious to me. Writing and dreams were shoved into a drawer and locked away for many years when I was a single Mom.*

## Crystal's Story

**Q: How has having a child affected your relationship, in good or bad ways?**

Crystal: *I have two kids, ages 12 and 9. It took us a while to have kids, and, in hindsight, we were glad to have that time to travel, save money, be alone. Once you have kids, your needs are often second (or third or fourth) and that can take the focus off your relationship with your partner. It is tough, but worth it.*

**Q: If you could go back in time, what advice would you give to your younger self about having kids?**

Crystal: *I would tell my younger self that it was okay to just be married for a while before having kids. The challenge is that many couples wait until they are older to get married, so they can't wait too long, as fertility starts to decline around age 28 (a whole other subject!). But for younger couples, taking time to just be a couple can be so valuable.*

## Suzie's Story

**Q: How has having stepkids affected your relationship/marriage, in good or bad ways?**

Suzie: *I've been married for over 13 years to a man who has three children, and I have never had my own. I get along great with his two sons, but his daughter and I have had a horrible relationship. Even though she's in her twenties now, my husband and I still get into heated discussions when it comes to her.*

*Marrying a man with children was tough on our marriage at times. As a matter of fact, it really was the only thing we've ever fought about in 13 years. I was the "bad guy" in his eyes at first because I didn't treat her as special. I saw her for who she was, without the parent filter, and so I was always the one catching her doing things she shouldn't be doing, like wearing low-cut clothes under her "normal" school clothes, sneaking out to smoke, lying about things – she's actually pathological now. It took him years to see it, and he felt like I was being too hard on her. I was, in hindsight. But in all honesty, I thought I was helping by letting her know she was responsible for her choices and that she could not get away with lying. My husband would turn a blind eye because he only saw her on the weekends. Plus, as always, there was mama drama. Her mother is an alcoholic and let her run wild from a very early age. Her mother got her a tramp stamp when she was 14! We saw it one day and flipped out. I was ready to hunt down the illegal tattooer and make sure he never worked again. We kept running into issues like that. The mother and daughter would keep stuff hidden from us and lie about it, so when we found out things, it was too late for my husband to give his input, and even when he did, it usually fell on deaf ears. So when she would come to stay with us, it was a challenge to get her to understand she was not going to get away with what she did with her mom. That was hard on my husband. He always felt like he was caught in the middle.*

*Now add to that the fact that my stepdaughter has a mild brain injury from an auto accident when she was young, it's no wonder she has a hard time staying rooted in reality. Her mother kept her disempowered by telling her that because of her brain injury, she couldn't do things like ride a bike, do her homework, etc. We taught her how to ride a bike and she had no problem with it. We forced her to do her homework – she was more than capable of that and many other things "normal" kids did. Her mom also told her somewhere along the way that I caused their divorce. They were divorced for two and a half years before I even met my husband. So as you can see, there was a lot of confusion and crazy lying, and it was difficult trying to get her to see what a calm, sober life was like and to appreciate it, when it was much more fun for her to chase men and party with her mother.*

*She's now 22 and pregnant (our worst nightmare), has never worked in her life, dropped out of school, has had three live-in "boyfriends" in four months and many bad dudes before that, no car, no job, no place of her own, no plans to work, go to school or anything. She still hates me and blames me for her parents' divorce.*

**Q: If you could go back in time, what advice would you give to your younger self?**

Suzie: *I would tell myself, if I could do it over again, to just be her friend. Let her be who she wants to be and just reflect the positive in her, instead of trying to force her to be a certain way. Maybe that would have helped. I would also say be prepared for all your own "stuff" to come up and be willing to work hard to process through it. Kids still want their parents to be together even if they don't talk about it. So, you will always be dealing with jealousy and resentment.*

*Do your best to make friends with the ex-wife. I tried with my stepdaughter's mother, but because of her addiction problem, it was doomed from the start. But most exes aren't going to be impaired 24/7. And some of them can be pretty darn nice if you just treat them like humans. They're going to have their own sadness about the marriage being over, probably, and be concerned that you will be "replacing them" with their kids; so open the dialog, keep the conversation flowing, and alleviate any of those fears the best you can. Think of how you would feel in that awkward situation. What would you need? I get along great with the mom of one of my stepsons. She's wonderful. And we don't bond over picking on my husband (I see that a lot). We bond over a love and respect for both my stepson and his dad. It can happen.*

## Meredith's Story

**Q: How has having kids (your own and stepkids) affected your relationship/marriage, in good or bad ways? If you could go back in time, what advice would you give to your younger self about having kids?**

Meredith: *Fifteen years ago, I married my second husband, a widower with eight children. I had three. We merged our blended family and moved together into an adjoined army townhouse where my husband was stationed. Then we birthed two more between two combat deployments, my master's program, and a custody battle with my first husband. There are lessons I've learned that in hindsight I would never want to repeat.*

1. *If you have an ex-husband, reconsider remarrying. Blending a large family requires delicate maneuvers, lots of soothing of hurt feelings and a clearly defined custody/visitation arrangement with the ex.*

2. *Make sure that a new spouse understands that agreement and doesn't try to impose his wishes or ideas.*

3. *Set up a list of rules of engagement, expectations, and guidelines. Discuss every possible configuration or problem that could arise with the newly formed family and consider potential resolutions.*

4. *Make your new spouse the center, but make it clear that your children came first and you have a responsibility to finish the job you started.*

5. *Don't try to play replacement parent.*

6. *Do show caring, love and consideration for your stepchildren and for your own children. Merging a blended family can be painful for the children. And if possible, solicit the help of a qualified family therapist to map out positive communication methods.*

**Q. Can you tell me about the custody battle with your first husband?**

Meredith: *After I married my second husband in 2000 and moved to the U.S. Military Academy at West Point where my husband was assigned, I became enmeshed in a grueling custody battle. Though the forensic psychologist recommended my husband and me for custody, the judge awarded full custody to my ex-husband because my eldest son didn't want to live in a large extended family. My children at the time were 12, 10 and 6. In New York, the family court doesn't separate siblings, so all three went to live with my ex-husband. I had liberal visitation: summers, holidays, etc. My ex-husband moved without notice to another state for a job opportunity, so the visitations became less frequent. At the same time, I was raising six of my eight stepchildren, whose own mother had died of a brain tumor in 1997.*

**Q. Are you still married to your second husband? If so, what was it like to blend families?**

Meredith: *Yes, we are still married, but it's been exceedingly difficult at times. Most of our children are grown now. All but the last two are in college or finished with college. But there were many complications. First was the blending of a family with two different sets of values and visions. The second hurdle was dealing with egos: my husband's and those of my husband's children, who felt outrage that my biological children had gone to live with their father. They felt that my eldest son had betrayed me, and they couldn't rectify those feelings when their own mother had died. While I drew comfort from their support, I was also empathetic to the conflict my own children felt. They didn't want to leave me, but my eldest couldn't adjust.*

*The third hurdle occurred much later. As my stepchildren moved into adolescence and then into adulthood, they began to question their own identities relative to their deceased mother. The older children pulled away from me and began to reinvent a mother character based on what they thought their mother was and decided I wasn't that mother figure. The younger four children, I essentially raised and still have a strong bond with. When the eldest daughter had her own children, she began to settle down, and while our relationship has improved and she understands my role and its limitations, I am not her mother, I'm not exactly the grandmother, and we try to bridge that in the best way possible. The fourth hurdle had to do with definitions. My stepchildren – my husband, actually – had inflexible definitions of family. I had a more fluid, open view because my own parents had been divorced and remarried. I have an excellent relationship with my stepparents. But my stepchildren struggled with these inflexible definitions my husband had set up.*

*About my husband, we are at a very difficult crossroad now. We have two young children together – 12 and 9. My husband has PTSD, mental health issues and physical disabilities, and struggles with the day-to-day. Because I have my accomplishments, like my master's degree in writing and my teaching, it keeps me sane. I can continue to create and to contribute to the household. Having my own identity helps me stay afloat. Unfortunately, my husband – a career military man and a mathematician – has not figured out how to reinvent himself.*

Note: Shortly after we spoke, Meredith contacted me to say she had given her husband an ultimatum: "Get help, get a complete physical and psychological workup, or I'm divorcing you". The marriage has taken a 180-degree turn for the better, I'm happy to report. Sometimes, ultimatums are needed.

**Q: Did you receive any help raising the kids while your husband was away and when you were working on your master's? Were there family members or friends around to assist with child care and domestic responsibilities?**

Meredith: *That's an interesting question. In large families, the older siblings watch the younger ones, and I always had a teenager or two at home during the early years. I never, ever used a babysitter. In fact, when my daughter Mia (age 12) was an infant, the kids used to alternate staying home with her when my husband had chapel services to run, and there is plenty of family lore about who had it worse as the babysitter, especially if Mia cried the entire time we were gone.*

*I did use childcare intermittently when I had to work before the babies were old enough to attend preschool. I didn't have an extended family that helped with the kids. It's a bit of an imposition to say, "Hey Mom, can you come and watch seven kids?" Although my parents did have us over for occasional barbecues. All those kids, all that work, they just found it overwhelming. In saying that, remember that we were military. Military families tend to look after one another.*

**Q: I feel that you could provide some real inspiration to women who think that their dreams need to be put on hold once they have children.**

Meredith: *I can tell you that children need mothers who have their own interests and lives. It makes us more interesting and well-rounded people to our children, as they become aware of who we are. When my eldest son looks back, he admires me. But I also made a conscious decision after losing custody of my children. I wanted to roll over and die, and one day I looked in the bathroom mirror and realized I didn't want my children to feel sorry for me, to remember me with sadness. I wanted them to admire me, to be proud of me. So, I decided to work on me. When my kids think about quitting, when they hit a snag in their own lives, they think about me, how I managed alone and found the strength to continue.*

## James's Story

**Q: How has having kids (your own and stepkids) affected your relationship/marriage, in good or bad ways?**

James: *My stepchild destroyed my marriage, and I am currently divorcing.*

*My wife and I went into the marriage with her and her child having a bond (which is good). Still, I could never fully enter into their relationship, and she didn't fully enter into one with me. It always felt like "me vs. them" even though I tried very hard to be loving and take care of their financial needs.*

*For example, I would enact sensible discipline (like no homework = no video games) and she would undo it. It led to constant drama in the household because she refused to set boundaries with her child and undid anything I tried. It created a stressful, chaotic environment. I received no respect and felt alienated in my own household. When we had our own child, it didn't get much better. My daughter just got exposed to her daughter's drama and chaos.*

**Q: What constructive advice would you give your younger self about entering a relationship when there are stepkids involved?**

James: *I would advise my younger self to be very careful of a blended-family relationship. A good friend who had entered into one (and ran into similar issues, including eventual divorce) warned me, but I thought mine would be different. It wasn't.*

*I would recommend that a man or woman look carefully at how his or her future spouse parents the child. Do you share the same values? Would you parent in the same way? Are you made to feel like an interloper, or are you included? Be brutally honest and don't let being "in love" cloud your judgment.*

## Summary

Some of the stories I heard were nightmarish: having kids or stepkids destroyed their marriage, either because of extreme differences in parenting styles or because the stepkids and stepparent could not get along, or because couples failed to nurture their relationship and not just the child. Unfortunately, knowing what kind of parents you and your partner will be is something you can't figure out until you have kids. There is no return policy on children.

So, what do you do? You can babysit together. Or pet-sit. Or, if your relationship is well-established, you can adopt a pet. Observe how your partner interacts with children and animals, and go with your gut. Will they make a good parent? You can ask them directly whether they think they would make a good parent, but always go with your gut. As James says: "Be brutally honest and don't let being 'in love' cloud your judgment".

*PEARLY WISDOM: Carefully consider what kind of parent your partner will make before you bring kids into the picture.*

## Furry Kids

I recognize that parents will hate this analogy, but the closest I've come to parenthood was having a dog for 13 years, so bear with me as I attempt to relate. For this freedom-loving gal, it wasn't always easy. Having a dog is a privilege but also a big responsibility, one I'm not sure most owners are ready for when they hold that puppy for the first time. I know I wasn't.

Chloe was 10 weeks old when my ex-boyfriend and I brought her home. We raised her together and agreed on training, exercise, vet visits and even the kind of dog food she should eat. I am glad we were of the same mindset. Chloe was never fed table scraps, and we never allowed her to lie on the couch. We were consistent in our discipline and in our commands. There was never any arguing about one person doing things one way, and the other person doing it another way behind their partner's back. As a result, Chloe was a very relaxed, well-trained dog. She never begged dinner guests for food while they ate a meal (probably because she never knew how good human food tastes). She was a lovable, well-mannered dog, and people enjoyed being around her.

But raising a well-behaved dog is work: Chloe had to be trained, and exercised. She was walked a couple of times a day for *at least* 30 minutes at a time. I won't lie; it sucked walking her when it was dark and cold outside, which is about half the year in Canada. She needed her dog booties when the temperature dropped. Without them, Chloe's paws would freeze and she would start to pick up one paw and then the other and finally refuse to walk. Putting on her booties was only slightly easier than carrying home a 65-pound dog. Most of the time, I enjoyed walking Chloe, but there were times when it was a total pain in the butt. Like after work, for example.

For years, I had to rush home after work so Chloe could go pee. This often meant declining social invitations and after-dinner drinks from co-workers. Holidays were also difficult to manage, because if we couldn't take her with us, we had to ask friends to pet-sit. If we did take her on a trip, we couldn't leave her in the car in the heat, nor could we always tie her up outside a store. Often, one of us had to stay with her in the vehicle while the other person ran inside. Vacations and weekend trips were greatly affected by having a dog. Pet-friendly hotels were very rare back then. Had she been a human baby, travel would have been a lot easier.

Having a dog requires scheduling, sacrifice and communication. After my ex and I broke up, I had Chloe for another six years. I had a good support system with friends who could look after her in a pinch, but even then, I had to say no to social invitations and activities more often than I liked. She needed two walks a day, and as she got older and her bladder weaker, she needed to be taken out more frequently. I wanted to sell my home at one point, but held onto it knowing how difficult it would be to rent a place with a dog. When Chloe passed away, I was terribly sad. She had given me unconditional love and been a wonderful companion for 13 and a half years. I loved her with all my heart, but once the grief stage had passed, I began to blossom socially. It's only now, four years later, that I can even consider getting another dog.

Was it worth it? Yes. Was it wonderful? Yes. Would I do it again? I'm not sure. I love my freedom and I love to travel, so I might have to stick with loving other people's dogs for a while longer.

## Merging Households and Pets

If you are merging households and one of you already has a pet, consider how that is going to work. Will you share responsibility for dog walking, meals, grooming, picking up poop, and discipline, or will the original owner assume all of the work? Will you respect the rules they created when it comes to caring for that animal? What if you disagree on things, such as where the pet is allowed to sit or what kind of treats it can have?

Raising a dog is a lot more simple and straightforward than raising a human, but there are lessons here that still apply when it comes to blending families and raising children.

## Blended Families and Stepkids

While having children is tough, it seems that blending families and stepkids can be a lot tougher on a couple, especially when teenagers are involved. Why is this? Couples marry because they fall in love, not because they're looking to be a parent. Becoming an instant mom or instant dad brings with it incredible responsibility and the potential for drama with the ex and stepkids.

*PEARLY WISDOM: One of the reasons divorce is so high in second marriages is stepkids. The issues for stepfamilies are completely different from those for first families. Challenges include the ex, legal issues, child support payments, visitation, child-rearing concerns, debt entanglements, and others.*

This was certainly the case for the couples I spoke to. If the stepkids are young at the time of remarriage, there is time to develop history and emotional ties, but when the children are already teenagers, "blending" families is a lot more difficult. As Harriet Lerner advises in her book, *Marriage Rules: A Manual for the Married and the Coupled Up,* go slow and be patient. She says it usually takes three to five years for all family members to adjust.

## Children as a Distraction from Personal Growth

The opportunity to pursue personal goals while raising children is made much more difficult due to a lack of personal time. This is why start-up companies hire a lot of 20-somethings: single and unattached, they can give everything to their job, including 70-hour workweeks. But what if you want parenthood and a career? Or what if, like Meredith, you want to complete a master's degree while raising a family? You need patience. It took Meredith six years to complete her degree.

**Guideline #55: If you want peace, lower your expectations of what is possible for you in the first six years of your child's life.**

When the children are young, it may be necessary to put some goals on hold, at least until the kids are in school. I think this is the biggest frustration for many professional women who enjoyed working but had to step out of the career track in order to raise children. Yes, there are some superwomen and men who appear to do it all, but I think those women and men are rare, and their sacrifices are greater than we're led to believe. In fact, it seems that the ultra "successful" people we admire on television – CEOs and celebrities – are often failures when it comes to parenthood and their private lives. Success, in my mind, requires context.

What do you want your tombstone to say? "Loving father", or "Top-rated sales manager"?

> **Guideline #56: You can be successful at everything, just not everything at once.**

A friend of mine once said she chose to remain childless because "I could be a great mother or a great wife, but I couldn't be both". I suspect that what she was really talking about was the need to thrive in a particular role. She couldn't divide herself three ways, so she chose two: her husband and herself. If you're an artist, scientist, or someone with a passion, it is very difficult to find the time to pursue your calling when you're also a parent.

Interestingly enough, I enrolled in an advanced photography workshop this week. There are eight of us, ranging in age from our late twenties to late fifties, and none of us have children. Classes take place every Monday from 7 to 9 p.m., which might explain why: parents have much less free time and availability for hobbies.

## The Mommy Track

Tex says you need to be more than a mom:

> *After you have children, life comes to a screeching halt for about six years, and you don't have any personal time. After that, you start to get more personal time and more free time. A woman who says she wants to be a mom, and only a mom, had better watch out, because when the kids are gone in twenty years she will be middle-aged, with no marketable skills in the business world and no identity other than being a mom. It's a very risky position to put yourself in.*

If you've never really known what you wanted out of life, having children gives you a sense of purpose, a job to do each day, but it is a job that may only last twenty years. What happens when the kids grow up and no longer need you? If your whole identity is tied to being a mother, it will be very difficult for you to recreate yourself when the children leave the nest. This doesn't seem to be the case for most men – at least not for those of my father's generation, who derived a lot of their identity and self-worth from their careers. Consequently, they are less devastated by empty nest syndrome (and more devastated by retirement).

It's important to have a life outside of parenthood, because it lets you keep that piece of yourself that can go missing when you become a caretaker of others. What did you used to love to do, back when you were single? What did you leave behind when you got married? Who were you before you were a mother/wife? What is your identity outside of motherhood, and how can you nurture it? Parenthood can be a wonderful distraction from figuring this out.

As Steinem said: "Everybody with a womb doesn't have to have a child any more than everybody with vocal cords has to be an opera singer". However, everyone needs to find fulfillment and purpose in life to be happy. If being a mom fulfills you more than having a career, then that is fine. No judging. But **how many smart, talented women have had their flames burn less brightly because they were busy tending the flames of others? Do not let your light go out.**

## The Daddy Track

There are plenty of men who love being fathers and would like nothing more than to be stay-at-home dads, just as there are plenty of women who are more suited to using their skills and talents outside the home, doing battle each day in the corporate world.

Thankfully, we live in an age where we no longer have to accept certain roles based on our genitalia – at least in some countries.

## Co-parenting Tracks

Be willing to explore the possibility of taking turns raising children while you each pursue your careers and education. One of you could stay at home for the first few years, and then you could switch. Or you could work on a flex schedule so that each of you gets time outside the home, developing important skills that keep you current and fulfilled. Two up-to-date résumés in a tough economy are a great hedge against risk.

## Child-free Relationships

I have spoken to friends about parenthood. Some of them have said they don't regret having children BUT… and there always seems to be a but. Usually, they comment on not having enough personal time and feeling exhausted. "If I could just have one hour to sit alone in a coffee shop and read a book like I used to when I was single…" I can see the toll that parenting takes, on the weary faces of my friends. Mothers, especially, seem to bear the greatest burden when it comes to child-rearing. All I can think is, "One hour, really?" I can't imagine not having an hour a day to myself. The very thought makes me cringe.

I enjoy the freedom of being in a child-free relationship. If I want to spend a month in Italy (assuming I can afford it), I have my partner's blessing. If I want to write at any hour of the day or night, I can. If I want to skip making dinner, no problem. If I want to take myself to the movies, it's as simple as sending a text that I'm going to go to a movie. There are no babysitters to arrange, no feelings of guilt.

Some people call this selfish, but I am not "lacking consideration for others", which is the definition of selfish. To me, it's selfish to have children because:

1. You didn't want to use a condom.

2. You don't have a purpose in life, and hope that children will fill that void.

3. You're worried that if you don't have kids, you'll regret it later (fear of future regret).

Fear of future regret is where you operate from a place of fear and your choices reflect your anxieties. It is not a good decision-making model because it disempowers you. It is more important to consider whether you (or your partner) would make a good parent, whether you have the resources to care for children properly, and what kind of health issues you could be passing on.

Bringing life into this world and raising good human beings is the most important job in the world, and you had better be ready for it. I wish more people would consider the consequences. In my opinion, there are far too many people on this earth already, and far too many neglected children. The world would be better off if more people chose to adopt or remain childless.

Elizabeth Gilbert says there are three kinds of women in this world, and not every woman is destined for motherhood. I am paraphrasing but basically, she says there are women born to be mothers, women who are born to be aunties, and women who should never be allowed near a child. She also says it is very important to know which one you are because if you end up in the wrong category, much tragedy and sorrow result. I would say the same goes for fathers. There are far too many baby daddies in this world.

Much damage has been done to lives because there are too many children in this world whose mothers and fathers are absent from their lives, emotionally or physically.

## Child-free versus Childless

Let's differentiate between the terms child-free and childless. **Child-free people have made the explicit choice to not have children; childless couples have not.** It's important to not judge people for not having kids, because you don't know their story.

Child-free couples can experience a lot of push-back on their decision to not have kids. Many people think these couples dislike children and live sad and empty lives. They couldn't be more wrong. Here are five myths surrounding people who don't want to have kids.

## Five Myths about Child-Free People

**Myth 1.** Child-free people don't like children.

Fact: Many child-free people DO enjoy being around children and serve as pediatricians, teachers, counsellors, mentors, big brothers or sisters, or godparents.

**Myth 2.** Child-free people are selfish.

Fact: Studies have shown that child-free people volunteer more in their communities than parents.[34] (Probably due to more free time.)

**Myth 3.** Child-free couples miss out on a great deal of joy by choosing to not have kids.

Fact: Parenthood is not a path to fulfillment in life, and research bears this out. In fact, happiness and well-being research shows that childless couples are more satisfied in their relationship, and feel more valued by their partner, according to a large study of over 5000 men and women by Open University in the U.K.[35]

**Myth 4.** Women are biologically driven to have children.

Fact: About one in five American women end their reproductive years without having children, compared to one in 10 in the 1970s. Since birth control has allowed women the choice to remain child-free, more women are opting to pursue careers and finding paths to self-fulfillment beyond motherhood. Some researchers say that the "biological imperative" to reproduce may have more to do with cultural conditioning, social pressure, and a learned desire. It is certainly true that the strong desire to have children doesn't mean someone will be a "natural" or even "good" mother.

**Myth 5.** Elderly people without children are lonelier and more depressed.

Fact: Seniors without children are not more lonely or depressed (except in countries that do not have good elder-care services). A Norwegian survey of 5,500 individuals aged 40–80 showed no indication that childless adults have reduced well-being.[36] Another study also concludes: "The support networks of the childless are more diverse than those of parents, and characterized by stronger links".[34]

## No Regrets

In my twenties, I figured I would have a couple of kids and even adopt, eventually; but the man I was with didn't want children. We were together for eight years – my most fertile years. When we broke up, I was 34 years old. It took me a little while to get my groove back and start dating again. I used this time to reinvent myself. It was a period of great personal and professional development. I blossomed. I travelled the world. I bought a motorcycle. I started a business. I sold a business. I wrote a book. I built excellent friendships, and I came into my femininity. I consider that time to be really special because I was able to focus on me, to experience tremendous personal growth and expansion. Had I met Tex earlier, I am sure we would have had kids, because he is "dad material". I would have felt safe having children with him, and he tells me I would have made a great mother. But if I had had kids, I probably wouldn't have travelled the world. Or bought a motorcycle. Or sold a business. Or had so many adventures. Or blossomed into the fullness of my being in quite the same way.

Nor would I have been the woman Tex fell in love with.

The baby ship has sailed. If I'm totally honest, I'm a little relieved that things happened this way.

## Parent Tips for Emotional Well-being

First, I would like to briefly touch on the subject of postpartum depression because it's a bigger deal than most people realize, and is one of the most difficult things to deal with in a marriage. Beth Seitz describes her experience:

> *I remember coming home with my first son and feeling...so disconnected! Like I was no longer me and I'd never be me again. My home felt like a prison, and all I wanted to do was drive away by myself till I found me and my happiness again. I had this beautiful, happy baby boy, who was calm and patient with momma, and all I could do was look at him and cry. My coworkers wanted to come see me and our new bundle, and I would put them off, make excuses why they couldn't come. I didn't want them to see this new me. I would sit in the bathroom hurting and crying. Staring at my alien*

*image, milk spots from lactating and sunken eyes and HATE MYSELF! My poor husband was just a mess trying to take care of me and our son.*

*My mother suspected and wanted me to call and get help and medication, and I refused! I was independent and strong and I would get through this on my own.....and I tried. I tried so hard. I smiled and I did everything I thought moms did. But the smile would quickly break and I'd secretly berate myself. I despised this person and was angry at her and at my environment.*

*My mother talked to my husband, and they both stood there as I called my nurse. I'll never forget her words after I tried to give her the gist of how I felt in just a short couple of sentences, being too proud to go into too much detail. But she got it, immediately. Her words were "OH, HONEY! You waited too long!" And she got the medication I needed to BECOME the mom I needed to be. It got better, and I bonded with my baby the way I always wanted.*

*Never be afraid to ask for help. I've learned that the strongest women need a shoulder just like the rest of us. That baby doesn't care if you don't fit the mold of what a good mom is. All they want is their momma. And you do everything you can and more for your children. Today I have two boys that think I've always been the best mom, and I praise God for that.*

— Beth

It isn't easy to believe that help is possible when we are in the throes of a deep, dark depression, but it is. When Beth got help, she was able to become the mom she wanted to be, and to bond with her babies. As I said in Chapter 18, you must be willing to accept help if you are to heal yourself, claim your power, and get more love.

Even if postpartum depression is not a concern, here are some important things for partners to keep in mind if they have children:

**1. Give your partner personal time away from you and the kids.**

You may even have to insist on your partner taking time out from family: new mothers seem to have an especially hard time being away from their children. Part of the reason is chemical, and part of it is fear that Dad, or someone else, won't do as good a job of taking care of the baby or kids. Yes, they will do things differently. And Dad may not do things as well, but that's only because he's had less practice. Give him the gift of time alone with the children. He'll get better with practice, and the kids will benefit from Dad time. Everyone will benefit.

*PEARLY WISDOM: It's important for couples to give their partners time off from child-rearing, even to insist on it. And it's never more important than in the first six years of a child's life, when mothers have so very little precious time to themselves and emotional exhaustion is at an all-time high. It's no coincidence that most divorces occur after eight years of marriage.*

**2. Schedule stuff and negotiate what needs to be done – personal time, household chores, child care, etc.**

A fair division of labor will minimize resentment and prevent partners from becoming exhausted, unwilling to have sex, and emotionally disconnected. A fair division of labor means you both have time to relax. If you are feeling overwhelmed by domestic responsibilities, work, and parenting, consider a cleaning service.

**3. Go on dates together, even if it feels like work.**

Eventually, it won't. You need to make time for "love nights", where you dress up and go out *as a couple*. As Cheryl says, you want to "connect intellectually and emotionally through conversation. You can and will get so wrapped up in your kidlets and rushing around that you forget to talk about LIFE. And I don't mean about what you did all day but the REAL stuff. Your dreams, your feelings, your desires, etc." Yes, babysitters are expensive. So is divorce.

It's normal to have some separation anxiety when you're away from your baby or children. However, it's healthy for your baby and children to be taken care of by others. As human beings, it has been our tradition to care for each other's offspring since the dawn of mankind. This is how humans evolved. Placing a child in someone else's care allows the child to trust in others, deal with separation, and learn from others.

Money can be a big deal when trying to arrange date nights and babysitters, but this is essential to the health of your relationship. **You must find it in your budget to keep the romance alive.** Can you live without that new technology gadget? How about less stuff? The average American home has over 300,000 items in it, and 1 in 10 Americans rent off-site storage because they have so much stuff.[37] Can you buy the children second-hand toys? Or maybe less toys? After all, the average 10-year-old owns 238 toys but plays with just 12 daily.[37] Can you swap child care with another parent so you can enjoy a night out? If you don't invest in your relationship, you're jeopardizing it. People talk about how much fun they had before they got married; this is because many people start to neglect themselves and their relationship once they have kids. It doesn't have to be that way.

### Guideline #57: The couple that plays together, stays together.

## Advice from a Family Therapist

In wrapping up this chapter, I think it's best that I hand the microphone over to Crystal Clancy, M.A., L.M.F.T. Crystal is a mom and a licensed marriage therapist and is better positioned than I am to give advice on how kids affect relationships.

**Q: What advice would you give to couples about having kids?**

Crystal: *I would advise couples to have serious, in-depth conversations about having kids and parenting. Talk about how many kids would be ideal. Talk about work – do you want to stay home after you have kids? Do both of you want to work? Does dad want to stay home? And how are you going to afford that? Talk about how parenting was handled in each of your families. How did your parents discipline? Show emotion? Spend time? What did you like/not like about how you were parented?*

*Many couples go into having kids without talking about these things, thinking they will just work themselves out. Really, they don't. (And PS,* ***having a kid doesn't make your marriage better****, either!) Statistically, the first year postpartum is the most difficult in a marriage.*

*As far as blended families, the conversations will be similar, except you have to accept that there is a third/fourth parent in the situation – the ex(es). So when talking about how each one parents, what are the parenting arrangements? What type of relationship do they have with their ex? What kinds of conflicts do they deal with? Again, statistically, second marriages have a much higher divorce rate than first marriages, and many stressors that come with having kids contribute to that.*

**Q: Can you give some advice as to WHEN a couple should seek out a therapist like yourself, and how to identify a good one?**

Crystal: *If I were queen of the world, people would seek out therapy before getting married and before having children. Why? Because a therapist can help you have these difficult conversations that most couples don't have.*

*The reality is that most couples wait until they are very unhappy, considering divorce, and feeling very hurt, stuck, and resentful. Therapy tends to be more beneficial before couples are in a crisis, when they are both still feeling love towards their partner and are open to change. Short answer – don't wait too long! It's OK to go to therapy to get some help with conflict resolution, communication skills, and parenting advice.*

*How to find a good therapist? I feel the best way is by word of mouth. If you see someone individually, ask that therapist for a good couples' therapist. Ask your friend, sister, pastor at church. I may raise some hackles with this, but I lean towards Licensed Marriage and Family Therapists being the best trained to work with couples. And you can always call a couple of therapists and talk to them on the phone before coming in. I have several people who call and ask me certain questions about my specialty or approach, or experience. I am never offended by that.*

*Finding a therapist is like test-driving a car. If you see someone a couple of times and it doesn't feel like a good fit, move on to someone else. But don't give up!*

* * *

## HOUSEKEEPING: Kids and Stepkids

Kids are a game changer. The point of this chapter isn't to counsel you on how to raise them – there are whole books and industries on that – but to give you some of the highs and lows of how your relationship could be affected by having kids (even the furry kind) and merging families.

To recap this chapter: Consider having children in your thirties if possible. Also, consider a life without children: your life can be as rich, rewarding and personally fulfilling as you make it. Fear of regret is not a reason to have children, and not everyone is meant to have them. If you do have kids, know that things get harder before they get better, and that divorce peaks at year eight. Let your partner know she or he is valued. You both have responsibilities, and it never hurts to show your appreciation when your partner does what is expected of them. Once you have children, make time for romance and sex, even if you don't feel like it. Sex is a way back to intimacy.

**Task 1: Develop your support structure.**

Behind every working parent is a support structure. This could be a nanny, a grandparent, or an incredibly supportive spouse; it can even be the local community you live in. Who can help out? Call your local city hall and ask to speak with someone in community services. Your tax-paying dollars help fund different programs, and they may have some suggestions for you.

**Task 2. Budget for romance.**

How will you fund your ongoing romance with each other once you have kids?

**Task 3. Become more informed about blended families.**

If you're living with or are married to someone who has kids, you may want to consider a magazine like *Stepmom* at www.stepmommag.com. There are also many books on this subject which could help you understand your role as a stepparent.

Reread Crystal's advice and take it to heart.

# Chapter 22: Vulnerability

*The wound is the place where the Light enters you.*

— Rumi

## Vulnerability and Courage

There are two kinds of courage: One is physical courage, such as the valor portrayed by soldiers, firefighters, and police officers. This is typically a male domain, as testosterone has a big impact on the willingness to take physical risks. The other is emotional courage, such as the ability to open ourselves to another person and share our hopes, fears, and desires. This is typically a female domain, and there are hormonal reasons for this as well. Women tend to bond with others by sharing personal stories.

We fear the consequences of taking physical or emotional risks, because the consequences could be dire. These consequences could be physical – injury, pain, suffering or death – or they could be emotional – rejection, embarrassment, exile from the tribe.

Examples of physical courage:

- Battling cancer
- Defending someone from bullies
- Becoming the first female taxi driver in Afghanistan and being threatened every day

Examples of emotional courage:

- Admitting you're in love with your best friend
- Coming out and telling your family you're gay
- Leaving your church

Courage is the ability to do the thing that frightens us, especially when it seems impossible or difficult. To live a more authentic and meaningful life, we must face our fears.

**The price of courage is vulnerability.**

As I touched on in Chapter 18, "Heal Your Wounds, Claim Your Power, Get More Love", if children experience violence and abuse early in life, the world will feel unsafe and they will expect people to hurt them. This makes intimacy and connection much more difficult for them as adults. If, as an adult, we experience divorce or heartbreak, it can be very difficult to open up to someone again. And yet, **vulnerability is the only path to love.**

How does vulnerability play out in a long-term relationship? Defenses drop when we're vulnerable. When the armor comes off and we stand defenseless before our partner, it is possible to trigger their compassion. If our partner can accept and love us in our most vulnerable and imperfect moments, we have a keeper. **If our vulnerability triggers contempt, we are with the wrong person.**

> **Guideline #58: If your vulnerability triggers contempt, you are with the wrong person.**
>
> *Contempt, they have found, is the number one factor that tears couples apart. People who are focused on criticizing their partners miss a whopping 50 percent of positive things their partners are doing and they see*

> *negativity when it's not there. People who give their partner the cold shoulder – deliberately ignoring the partner or responding minimally – damage the relationship by making their partner feel worthless and invisible, as if they're not there, not valued. And people who treat their partners with contempt and criticize them not only kill the love in the relationship, but they also kill their partner's ability to fight off viruses and cancers. Being mean is the death knell of relationships.*
>
> — Emily Esfahani Smith, *"Masters of Love", The Atlantic*

## Vulnerability Is Sexy

What's so sexy about vulnerability? It's emotional nakedness. It's about being 100% real in your relationship so you can connect. Being vulnerable means risking emotional discomfort to admit the truth about something.

*PEARLY WISDOM: Men are generally more comfortable with anger; women, with tears. At the root of both is hurt.*

It means saying things like "I miss kissing you", or "Could I have a hug?" It also means saying things like "I know it's not your fault, but I feel annoyed that you're late. I need a few minutes to get in a better mood". It doesn't sweep things under the rug. It doesn't pretend. It doesn't attack. Being vulnerable means owning your stuff. If there's an elephant in the room, vulnerability will say, "There's an elephant in this room, and it makes me uncomfortable that we don't talk about it".

> **Guideline #59: Be real, but also be kind to one another to minimize shame.**

I asked Tex what courage and vulnerability in a relationship meant to him.

**Q: When we first got together, you said something about being willing to walk away from a relationship. Do you remember what that was?**

Tex: *During a relationship, a man may not push back, challenge or speak up to his significant other out of fear of losing her. When that happens, he loses his voice, which starts a spiral of diminishing confidence and self-esteem. The power dynamic starts to become lopsided. Suddenly, he has no say: events are playing out in front of him and he just has to roll with it. He might be spoken down to, or pushed around, all because he fears losing that person. But if you don't fear losing someone, then you'll have more confidence to raise your voice. If you raise your voice, it means there's communication. If there's communication, then the couple will better understand and respect each other, thus forming a better union. Or, the couple starts to realize they're not right for each other. But if you say nothing out of fear of losing someone, the communication dries up, it becomes stale, lopsided, and every day is further away from a harmonious, powerful union. This applies to women as well.*

**A healthy, powerful relationship takes emotional courage: it is only possible when you are 100% yourself.** Unhealthy relationships depend on one partner being submissive and never speaking their mind. These relationships tend to worsen over time.

Now, let's discuss the kind of relationship where huge emotional courage is required to overcome the fear of leaving. I am talking about domestic violence. "The Calgary Police Service spends more time responding to calls about domestic violence than any other crime",[38] and this is probably true of most police forces. It's time for more public awareness.

## Six Myths about Domestic Abuse

For this section of the book, I recruited an expert who has worked in the domestic violence sector both in Canada and internationally for the past 10 years. Since one in three women have been victims of violence, I think it's good for all of us to become better educated – for ourselves, and for the benefit of others. The expert (who prefers to remain unnamed) said, "Everyone has a right to live a life free from violence in their own community and home, and we all have a responsibility to help make this happen". Here are some common myths about domestic abuse, along with a Q & A at the end.

**Myth 1.** The occasional slap or punch is not abuse.

Fact: Domestic violence is something that escalates over time, and "The level of injury resulting from domestic violence is severe: of 218 women presenting at a metropolitan emergency department with injuries due to domestic violence, 28% required hospital admission, and 13% required major medical treatment. 40% had previously required medical care for abuse".[39]

Domestic abuse can also take other, non-physical forms: verbal, emotional, financial, spiritual, and sexual abuse, all of which are incredibly damaging and isolating.

**Myth 2.** Women are the victims of domestic violence.

Fact: In 2010, women aged 15 and older accounted for 81% of victims of all police-reported spousal violence in Canada,[40] but women can and do abuse their intimate partners. Often the abuse is very different and is of a more emotional nature. It should be acknowledged that abuse also happens in gay, lesbian, and transgendered relationships. It is wrong no matter what context it happens in.

**Myth 3.** Only certain types of women get abused: strong women would never let a man slap them.

Fact: Domestic violence is not about "letting" the violence happen; it's about the abuser's choice to be violent. There are no given personality traits that make someone more susceptible to being with an abuser. Domestic violence occurs across all socio-economic classes and all cultures.

**Myth 4.** The head of the house has the right to control their partner, since they are supporting everyone.

Fact: No one has the right to control their partner's life, including what they wear, who they see, where they can go and what they can spend.

**Myth 5.** If your friend or colleague wanted help, she would ask for help.

Fact: If you suspect something, don't wait for your friend to ask for help. Your friend may not feel comfortable confiding in you, because she may be ashamed or fear being judged. She may not feel ready to leave, or it may not be safe for her to leave. She may worry that by confiding in you, it could make things awkward between you and her partner. One simple thing you could ask is, "Do you feel safe at home?" and see where that leads.

**Myth 6.** "If I could just be a better ____________, the abuse would stop".

Fact: The abuse isn't about you. Abusers will always find a reason to abuse, no matter how "good" their partner is.

*PEARLY WISDOM: Even when they are "angry", abusers can control their behavior. A good example is the case of an abuser being "angry" and yelling until someone comes to the door, such as a pizza delivery guy. Suddenly, the abuser is perfectly capable of changing his/her behavior immediately and being "nice" to the pizza guy. They have total control over their behavior and "choose" to abuse their intimate partners. It is not an anger issue; similarly, it is not an alcohol issue. It is a violence issue.*

**Q: Do victims usually recognize when they are being abused?**

Answer: *Everyone is different and at different stages in their journey. Some will recognize that their partner is abusive, and others will not. Some may be in the early stages of dating, and others may have been with their partner for years and tried to leave in the past. Women will often recognize that they are being treated with disrespect. They might not label it "abuse" or "violence", but they know the behavior is wrong. They may minimize, rationalize, or make excuses for their partner's behavior, which indicates they know the behavior is wrong.*

**Q: What do you do if you're being abused but you're too afraid to get help or talk to anyone?**

Answer*: There are support lines and crisis lines you can call to get support around the abuse. These support lines will also help you plan for you and your children's safety, which is always paramount. If you don't wish to talk to someone, there are websites where you can read about safety planning. Most websites have a "quick exit" button to cover your tracks on the Internet. Alternatively, perhaps you can think about a family member or a friend you can reach out to for support.*

*If you are in immediate danger, call 911. If you need support, check for local services in your area.*

**Q: What can someone do if they suspect that their friend is being abused? How can they help?**

Answer: *Ensure that you are in a safe place to have the conversation. Talk to your friend and ask her what would be helpful for her. Perhaps it means keeping some important documents or a bag at your house in case she decides to leave; perhaps it's being a supportive and non-judgmental ear. Call a support line and get accurate information about services in your area so you can recommend them to your friend. Above all, ensure that you offer a non-judgmental approach, avoid saying things like: "Why don't you just leave", "You should just leave him", and do not minimize his behavior by saying things like: "It's not that bad", or "It only happens when he's drinking". Domestic violence is everybody's business, and we need to talk openly about it. This will help create a culture where it is no longer accepted in society.*

*PEARLY WISDOM: The time when a woman leaves her partner is the most dangerous. The majority of homicides happen after a woman has left. He may control the finances, and if she has children it may be very difficult to provide for the kids. It is very difficult to find housing; shelters are often full; and there is research pointing to discrimination towards women who are leaving a domestic violence situation, when it comes to landlords and housing. It may be difficult or unsafe to leave for many reasons.*

* * *

## HOUSEKEEPING: Exploring Vulnerability in Your Relationship

**Task 1: Fill in the blank.**

My partner is vulnerable when ______________________________.

Hint: When your partner wants to be spooned in bed, they are feeling vulnerable.

**Task 2: Ask your partner: "Was there something that happened this week that made you feel vulnerable?"**

Discuss.

**Task 3: Watch Brené Brown's TED talk "The Power of Vulnerability".**

Vulnerability deepens a relationship and builds trust and connection. Learn more about this in Brené Brown's 20-minute TED Talk. I link to it at www.itsnotyouitsus.com/chapterlinks.

> **Guideline #60: A healthy, powerful relationship requires emotional courage.**

# Chapter 23: Criticism and Defensiveness

*Criticism may not be agreeable, but it is necessary. It fulfils the same function as pain in the human body. It calls attention to an unhealthy state of things.*

— Winston Churchill

I have already talked about how no relationship can survive an excess of criticism and how toxic it can be, but criticism can also be good for a relationship if done right. There is no point in pretending everything is perfect when it's not. Sometimes, we need to shine a light on a partner's less than healthy behaviors.

How do you react to criticism? Is your immediate reaction to argue? Or do you believe there must be some truth to every piece of criticism, and immediately apologize? Neither is especially healthy.

The way we interpret criticism – and the world, really – has a big impact on how upsetting the world seems. **Our perceptions about an event, such as criticism from our boss or our partner, influence our reality.** When we experience an intense negative emotional reaction to something, we actually experience a physiological response to what we perceive as a harmful event. Individuals with higher levels of emotional reactivity are more prone to anxiety, defensiveness, and aggression. Criticism is a threat to the hypersensitive personality. When such individuals are in "survival mode" or "flight/fight" mode from a perceived threat, personal growth and self-actualization aren't possible.

When a person feels defensive, they shut down and are unwilling to listen to their partner, even if their partner's suggestions have merit. Habitual defensiveness becomes a barrier to effective communication.

> **Guideline #61: Where there is defensiveness, there is often insecurity.**

## Be Astute: Consider the Source as Well as the Content

Not all criticism is unfounded; some of it is fair and accurate.

Not all criticism is justified; some of it is based in jealousy, anger, or fear.

It's important to be as objective as possible when faced with criticism: consider the source as well as the content. Confident people do not crumble when they are criticized; they apply the parts that seem legitimate. Context is king.

> *As a highly reactive person in relationships, this is one of the hardest things for me. Criticism is incredibly difficult to take, and it makes me worry about things I don't need to worry about. I think it is, again, about the person you're with and their reasons for criticizing you. Is it actually to make you a better person, or to get you to do what they want?*
>
> — Kass

Criticism can be a very good thing: For companies, it makes their product stronger. For artists, it makes them look at their work differently. And for individuals, it helps them grow.

To accept and reflect on criticism with dignity and grace is a sign of maturity.

Being in a relationship means being on the pointy end of criticism once in a while. This is why relationships can be difficult and yet so rewarding: they help us grow.

> **Guideline #62: To accept and reflect on criticism with dignity and grace is a sign of maturity.**

## Taking the Path of Dignity

Criticism usually triggers feelings of disapproval and rejection, so most people get defensive about it. But this reaction takes you away from your power base.

There is another way. I call it the path of dignity.

The best way to handle criticism, especially criticism you're not sure you agree with, is to say something like, "I'm not sure I agree with that, but you might be right. Let me think about it".

The best way to handle unfair criticism is to have a detached response. By saying nothing, we give the criticism no energy. By remaining silent, we maintain our dignity and respect.

Practice a detached response to criticism. It is completely disarming.

If you decide there is some merit to the criticism, it helps to approach your partner at a later time and say, "You know, I thought about what you said, and I have to agree with…"

This is noble and powerful.

Even more powerful is to tell them how you plan to apply this newfound knowledge.

Imagine if you criticized your partner and they came back to tell you that you were right? Would you not feel so much more respect for them in that moment? **It takes humility to see our own flaws. It takes strength to admit to them. It takes courage to want to change them.**

Humility. Strength. Courage. How wonderful that a relationship can offer us these virtues.

We agree so often with praise and flattery, but rarely with criticism. And yet, criticism can be extremely helpful for our personal growth.

What do happy, committed couples do differently?

They encourage feedback and "own their shit" in order to improve themselves and their relationship. When they fall short of their standards and ideals, they call each other out on it.

In my experience, most mature people appreciate being called out on their bullshit. People may reject it or get angry at first, but if it's legitimate, they'll come around and they'll have more respect for you for speaking up. No one respects a doormat.

Insecure folks tend to take it personally. The thing to remember with criticism is this: criticize the behavior, not the character of a person. Calling someone "stupid" for something they said or did is a personal attack and is not constructive.

> **Guideline #63: Criticize the behavior, not the person.**

If your partner calls you out on something, especially if you've asked for their honest opinion, have the grace to consider it. They could be right. In fact, your partner may actually have done you a tremendous favor by keeping it real. (Yes, your butt looks bad in those jeans.)

*PEARLY WISDOM: The more confident you are, the more you can accept criticism. If you are self-aware and strong, one person's opinion isn't going to put you into a tailspin. Only people lacking in self-esteem are shattered by negative feedback. If you have trouble taking in criticism, consider that you may also have self-esteem issues. Think you're tough? Some of the "toughest-talking" people in the world (on the outside) are the most insecure (on the inside). It's called overcompensation.*

The other point with criticism is this: if you dish it out, you had better be able to take it in.

## Giving Constructive Criticism

When giving "negative feedback", it helps to keep these constructive tips in mind:

1. Focus on the behavior you would like changed.
2. Be specific in your example.
3. Explain how it affects you.
4. Request a change of behavior.

Some people find it easy to be critical: others do not. However, calling each other out on less than ideal behaviors is the job of both partners in a relationship. Nip bad behaviors in the bud so you can get back on track. I discuss how to resolve conflict in more detail in the next chapter.

* * *

## HOUSEKEEPING: Reacting to Criticism

Louise Hay says: "If you're going to clean a house, you have to see the dirt". It's a great metaphor for this chapter and the following housekeeping exercises.

**Task 1: Think about how you react to criticism.**

Do you get defensive? Aggressive? Or do you turtle? Would your partner agree with your answer?

**Task 2: Can you think of a time when your partner (or someone else) was right in criticizing you?**

Bonus points if you have the *cojones* to share this insight with your partner.

**Task 3: Do you feel that there is too much criticism in your relationship or that it could be handled better?**

Discuss.

# Chapter 24: Resolving Conflict

*Peace is not the absence of conflict but the presence of creative alternatives for responding to conflict – alternatives to passive or aggressive responses, alternatives to violence.*

— Dorothy Thompson

Conflict occurs when people disagree on something. Conflict is not unhealthy, nor does it have to lead to arguments. How you deal with conflict determines how healthy your relationship is, how confident you are and how skilled you are at communication.

When you disagree with someone, you've bumped into a different opinion, recollection, or mindset about something. That's all. Insecure and immature people will often go into fight, flight, freeze or submit mode. Fight mode is where they name-call, hurl insults, judge, condemn their partner's viewpoints and turn disagreements into arguments. Their ego depends on being right. Flight mode is when people's nervous systems get overloaded and they choose to leave the room or the house or distract themselves with other activities so they don't have to engage. Freeze mode is when a person clams up, stonewalls or refuses to discuss the problem. Other people will simply submit to their partner's opinion and deny their own thoughts and feelings, which can lead to passive–aggressive behavior and resentment later on.

All of this is toxic. People who thrive on drama and arguments in order to keep the passion alive in a relationship are not communicating. They may enjoy fierce arguments because it leads to passionate make-up sex, but "break up and make up" ages you really fast. It's also hard on the immune system.

Healthy, sustainable couples resolve conflict through collaborative discussions. They see disagreement as an opportunity to get to know each other better. The goal for these couples is long-term happiness and mutual satisfaction: they would rather know their partner's heart and mind and figure things out together than be right for a day.

What if you could just shift your thinking a little, and see conflict as the potential to open up new possibilities in your relationship?

*PEARLY WISDOM: A relationship is about relating. If you don't want to relate, you might as well be single.*

There is a wonderful talk by Zig Ziglar about being married and pointing out something to your partner when you feel taken for granted. With permission from his son, Tom Ziglar, I transcribe the following excerpt:

> *Well, the reality is, basically, human beings are self-centered and selfish. And so when they get married, they kinda have to give up some of that. And there's some people who give it up with great reluctance: they go kicking and screaming when you try to make those little changes. This is where communication gets to be so extremely important. Not with anger, not with disappointments or frustration, but simply with a calm demeanor.*

*We say, "You know, honey, one of the things I married you for and loved you was the fact that you were always kind and thoughtful and considerate. We seemed to be on the same page with our financial expenditures, and things that seemed to be ideal for an ideal marriage. But honey, let me share with you my feelings at this moment.... I feel like, that for whatever reason, I am no longer appreciated. It seems that I go out of my way to do things for you, and yet you don't seem to be concerned when you come in an hour late for dinner and everything is cold. It seems that you ask me to pick up the laundry and do those other things and I do them without complaint, but when I asked you to stop by to pick up two cans of tomatoes last night for the soup, you didn't like it at all. Now, honey, am I being unfair? Am I being unreasonable? Is this just one of those things, or is it something you just haven't thought about?"*

*Confront the individual in that way. Because sometimes, particularly us husbands, are not sensitive enough to what the wife is actually doing for us that she IS doing for us. One of the little things that has made our marriage so stable and happy, is: we make it a habit every day to do something for the other one that the other one is capable of doing for themselves.... It says, "Honey, you're very important to me – I love you very much."*[41]

A relationship provides a wonderful opportunity to be humbled, to become more tolerant and to see things in a different way. A relationship can make you a wiser and better human being.

When you disagree with your partner on something, you can choose either of the following:

1. To reject their thoughts and opinions.

2. To try to understand them.

In any given moment, you have the opportunity to say, "Tell me more – I want to understand why you think like that".

Isn't that a lot less confrontational?

How would you feel if your partner and you disagreed on something, and he or she said (kindly and with genuine curiosity), "Tell me more – I want to understand why you think like that", instead of shutting you down?

Would it not feel like a conversation instead of an argument?

And could it possibly lead to a deeper understanding of your own beliefs?

**Guideline #64: When arguing, check your ego. Choose to listen. Seek to understand. You may learn something.**

Treat your partner like the best friend they are, and soon you will find yourself collaborating on a resolution. Less bickering. Less ego. More love.

### Catch the Small Stuff

Couples who openly and immediately discuss things that bother them, and then resolve them, have less friction in their relationship. They also develop better communication skills through practice. If you *really* don't like the way they leave their clothes on the floor, say it. It is much better to bring things out in the open than to get huffy and irritable and let things explode in some dramatic fashion. Give your partner a chance to make things better! Here are three steps to settling conflict quickly:

1. Gently ask for what you want. (I want more sex.)
2. Explore the concerns. (I'm feeling rejected and unloved.)
3. Come up with a mutually agreeable solution. (Let's schedule sex twice a week.)

This requires vulnerability and courage – and a little flexibility. In asking for what you want and exploring the concerns together, you may find that the solution is not what you originally thought you wanted or needed. In the example above, you may discover it's not actually sex that you miss, but touching, kissing and intimate time together, which satisfies the need to feel loved and desired. Through discussion, you may find ways to achieve that and to get more than you could have imagined or hoped for.

This may be difficult for some people to hear, as they may take these requests as criticism. Their first reaction might be one of shame and defensiveness: I am not a good husband/lover/wife/provider/etc. This is ego talking. **Get over your ideas of how you have failed, and embrace the opportunity to provide your partner with exactly the thing they are requesting.** Next!

### Ask for What You Want

It is so much better to ask for what you want, clearly and simply, than to complain about things you don't want. Example: "I want more sex. I want to feel your hands on my body. I want to kiss you and look into your eyes", versus: "We never have sex. I feel like you aren't attracted to me anymore. You barely look at me".

Avoid extreme language like "never" and "always" because it condemns. Avoid assuming negative intentions behind your partner's actions.

When we don't ask for what we want out of fear that we won't get it, our frustration grows. We begin to resent our partners for not giving us what we need, and we become emotionally cold and distant. Our partners are not mind readers, but they will sense the disconnection even if they don't know why it's happening.

Have you ever entered a room and felt tension in it? This is how some people live – in a constant state of stress and disappointment because of unmet expectations. Their homes are not happy places.

It's not up to our partner to read our minds and make us happy; it's up to us to ask for what we want and to give them the opportunity to fulfill that request. By asking for what we want, we avoid focusing on the negative.

Janice says that women beat around the bush too much:

> *I've found that, in general, men are much better at asking for what they want. They're direct and concise with what would make them happy. Women tend to "beat around the bush" and ask for what they want in a non-direct manner, and then get upset because their partner can't figure out the clues. I've been that girl. It sucks not getting what you want. Flat-out asking makes me feel better every time, even if my needs aren't met exactly the way I wanted.*

## See Your Partner as Innocent

We are so good at giving children the benefit of the doubt, but what if we could also see our partner as innocent when they do things that annoy us? Rather than confronting them with an accusatory tone, is it not better to see them as unaware of the effect their actions have on us?

Worse is when we perpetuate a situation by saying and doing nothing about it.

Can you say, "Is there a reason you do X?" and can you say it gently? Tone is everything here. Say it with a smile. Say it playfully, and you may have a fun and revealing conversation.

Chances are, your partner is not out to get you. It's not personal. There are reasons behind their actions, and they make sense to them. Why not try to understand what they are?

Here's an example:

> *It's 7:20 pm and getting dusky outside. Tex should have been home an hour ago. He said he was going to work out, so I expected him home by now. I'm feeling perturbed and a little worried. Did he go out with friends? Did he get in a car accident? Boy, I'm glad I didn't bother to make dinner!*
>
> *I could take it personally, but I choose a different mindset. I decide to approach the situation with curiosity. There must be a good reason – this isn't like him. I text him.*
>
> *Me: What's up? Working late?*

*Tex: Having dinner at our after-work meeting.*

*Me: Ok.*

*Tex: Leaving soon.*

*Me: Honey, I don't mind if you go out after work. I'm busy writing. I just worry something has happened when you stray from the normal routine. Have fun. Enjoy. (You've got me trained to think you'll be home at 6:15.) :-)*

*Tex: I'm sorry, love. I mentioned the meeting yesterday but didn't update you on how long it will take. Thank you for caring about me.*

*Me: I love you. Thank you for taking that in.*

I had totally forgotten about his meeting. Silly me. I'm glad I texted him. Our conversation reaffirmed everything I love about him: he's hard-working, dependable, and gracious. And this connection was made possible by shifting my mindset and approaching the situation with curiosity instead of resentment.

## Praise, Don't Scold

Praise, don't scold, and you will encourage your partner to keep doing things that you like. We do this with pets when we train them. We do this with children when we teach them. We do this with employees when we reward them. People love praise. Praise reinforces good behavior and emphasizes gratitude. We all need more gratitude and praise in our relationships.

Tex praises my baking and loves a certain cookie that I make. Whenever I want to do something nice for him, I bake him these cookies. It's worth seeing his eyes light up after the first bite. The act of baking becomes an act of devotion.

The more you praise, the more you encourage your partner to keep doing things that make you happy. Although giving is its own reward, it's a wonderful feeling to be appreciated.

By showing gratitude, you remind yourself (and your partner) that you are right for each other.

**Want to be happy? Focus on the positive, and you will see your love expand. Want to be unhappy? Focus on the negative, and you will see your love contract. It's that simple.**

Acts of service are acts of love and devotion. Recognize them, and your relationship will bloom.

## The Best Thing You Can Do to Resolve Conflict

The best thing you can do to resolve a conflict quickly is to practice resolving conflict, quickly! Start with the little things that you would like changed. Ask for what you want. Explore the concerns. Come up with a creative solution together. Practice early, and practice often. This will build up goodwill and trust credits so that you can tackle the bigger issues that invariably arise in a relationship. With practice, you can anticipate a positive outcome. Your communication skills will improve, and you will become a high-functioning couple. In time, you will see that conflict is not a scary thing but an opportunity to fix issues in your relationship right away so that you can get back to enjoying life as a couple.

*PEARLY WISDOM: Immature couples avoid conflict because they see it as threatening to the relationship. Mature couples see it as an opportunity to improve.*

Don't be afraid of difficult conversations! If you treat each other with love, respect, and gratitude, keep a cool head and ask questions to better understand each other's position instead of trying to be right, your relationship will improve and your connection will deepen.

> **Guideline #65: Happy couples behave like good friends, and treat each other gently during conflict.**

## When You're Too Emotional to Talk

Sometimes, when you're too emotional to talk, it helps to acknowledge this out loud to your partner. In this situation, it's good to give each other space. I've had two fights with Tex where my response was to go into flight mode (Let's just say that old wounds were triggered, and that I'm human too.) Physically, I wanted to get away from him. I had an overwhelming need to leave the room. Fortunately, he was able to give me that space. I had a bath and calmed down, and we were able to talk again and make up. It was all over within an hour. Sure, there was the emotional hangover the next day, but no real damage was done. If anything, my overreaction made me realize that I still have some work to do on myself.

If you find yourself turning into the Hulk, it's good to give the beast a time out.

*PEARLY WISDOM: Recognizing when you are in fight or flight mode and acknowledging it out loud can help you get out of this state more quickly. For example: "I'm feeling overwhelmed and just need some space right now. We can talk later". Don't use this time to punish your partner, though. Use it to comfort yourself and soothe your sympathetic nervous system, which is in a stressed state. Go for a walk, do some yoga, or have a bath – whatever calms you.*

## Have a Safe Word

Some people have a safe word they'll pull out when things are getting heated and they need their partner to back off. Betsy and Warren Talbot, from the website *Married with Luggage*, are an example of this. As a couple who live, travel and work together 24/7, they have a lot of opportunity to argue. When the going gets tough, the tough blurt out "Orangutan"! They explain how this works:

**Q: Some people have safe words for sex. You have a safe word for arguments. Can you explain how your safe word works and why you chose it?**

Betsy and Warren: *Humor is our go-to method for defusing a fight. But using humor solely to de-escalate a fight is a bad use of the strategy. The purpose is to call out when a boundary has been crossed. It allows for a realization about what happened, a reaction to it, and a calm conversation about how to move forward. This method is used for awareness and correction of negative behavior that is detrimental to our relationship.*

*We are usually clear of the situation in under two minutes, moving forward in our day and our lives with a slight course correction instead of a full-blown storm.*

**Q: Can you describe a situation when you used it?**

Betsy and Warren: *Let's say that we were shopping at a quaint little Portuguese market, and Betsy was in charge of bagging the groceries. And let's suppose, just for fun, that Warren stopped paying attention to his job of monitoring the prices and paying for the groceries to tell Betsy exactly how to bag them.*

*In this imaginary scenario, Betsy would be frustrated, as she is fully capable of bagging groceries and Warren should have been doing his job of watching prices and paying. And let's just pretend for fun that Warren had done this routine many times before because he knows Betsy does not fully optimize the bag space as he would.*

*In the past, Betsy would have snapped, "You always do this to me! Knock it off. I know how to bag the damn groceries". And then Warren would have snapped back, "My way is better, and you're going to run out of room!"*

*The checkout clerk would realize, even through the language barrier, that we were a little bit insane (and that we eat a lot of cereal).*

*The conversation would have devolved from there, so that by the time we were outside the store we would be fighting about control issues in our entire relationship instead of getting the bags in the car and enjoying a beautiful drive through the tree-covered hills of Portugal on the way back to the farmhouse.*

*Thankfully, this little scenario never played out because Betsy unpacked the "orangutan". She looked up from bagging the groceries and quietly said "orangutan". Warren turned back to the clerk to do his job, and she kept bagging groceries.*

*The "orangutan" functions much like a "safe word" in sex. It's a way to let your partner know a boundary has been crossed and to immediately stop. In our case, it allows us to address minor annoyances with each other without having to fight about it every single time.*

**Q: Who uses this word the most, and why?**

Betsy and Warren: *We each have our boundary triggers, so we use it in different ways. Betsy gets aggravated when Warren tells her how to do something his way when her way works just fine. It's a recurring argument in our relationship. (Just like Warren hates it when Betsy tells him how to drive... there's always an orangutan in the car with us!)*

*A big argument over minor stuff is exhausting and unproductive, especially if you go off track and start fighting about other things.*

*"Orangutan" is a word we use to gently remind the other person that he or she is "doing it again", whatever "it" happens to be. It's a quick "in the moment" reminder that immediately stops the behavior in progress, which is the best way to train yourself to stop doing it. And it lets the offending party get the message without them whipping themselves into a frenzy.*

Betsy and Warren have found an intelligent and humorous way to deal with conflict in their relationship. How about you?

## Annoying Habits

Annoying habits. We all have them. If you think you don't have any, it's probably because your mate keeps silent. What a saint!

One of my annoying habits is that I will fill a water glass, drink half and leave it in a room. Then I will fill another one and leave it in a different area of the house. At the end of the day, there are three or four half-filled water glasses around the house. This amuses Tex more than it drives him nuts, so I know he's perfect for me. What annoying habits can you live with? Sometimes you don't know until you live together. It can take about a year of living together for the annoying behaviors to creep in. Things like:

- Talking to each other through the bathroom door when someone is on the toilet.
- Yelling from another room.
- Leaving socks and underwear on the floor.
- Eating in bed.
- Leaving the toilet seat up.

And the list goes on.

It can be a slippery slope, as we often start to mirror the bad behavior we see in our partner. As I said before, if you don't like something, speak up about it. But also have the humility to recognize that you may be just as guilty. If you're asking for a change of behavior, offer up one of your own. This is how you build up your relationship credits.

### Having Different Viewpoints

As a couple, you can hold different viewpoints and feel bonded because of your differences. I know it sounds strange, but let me give you an example. Tex and I both believe in same-sex marriage, but he thinks these unions should use a different word from marriage. He believes "marriage" should only be between a man and a woman. In exploring this issue further, I asked him, "So what word are they supposed to use? Union? 'We're getting unioned' doesn't have quite the same ring". He grinned and replied, "I don't know. Some other word". To which I told him, "Well, I don't share your opinion". To which he replied, "I know". We could hear the air crackling around us and kinda liked it. Disagreeing can be very sexy as long as the core values are the same. On the rare occasion when we disagree, it reminds us that we are two strong-minded individuals with our own views and personalities. We are together because we like those differences and find them intriguing!

## Love Without Words

In my opinion, nothing can replace clear communication when it comes to resolving conflict: ask for what you want, explore the concerns, and come up with a solution together. However, this is much more easily done if you have a positive connection. If you're feeling distant, distrustful and disheartened about your relationship, then **you may need to work on your emotional connection first in order to restore communication.**

How do you do this? According to the book *How To Improve Your Marriage Without Talking About It*, by Patricia Love, Ed.D., and Steven Stosny, Ph.D., if couples are to reconnect, they must talk less and do more. Sharing pleasurable activities will re-establish a bond and naturally lead to better communication and deeper intimacy. Activity, touch, and sex help couples reconnect in a loving, wordless way.

Go for a walk, have a bit of fun, pour a glass of wine and *then*...talk.

* * *

## HOUSEKEEPING: Resolving Conflict

Remember, the way we interpret the world has a big impact on how upsetting the world seems. Our perceptions about a situation, such as our partner coming home late, influence the way we feel about it. We can make ourselves miserable through the meaning we attach to things. We can, as the old folks say, "make mountains out of molehills".

**Task 1: Check yourself before you wreck yourself.**

The next time you feel hostile towards your partner, is it possible that you are misinterpreting things? Is it possible to perceive the situation differently?

There is something called the "Three Perspectives Technique" in couples therapy. In it, you try to see the situation three ways:

1. From your perspective.
2. From your partner's perspective.
3. From the perspective of a neutral third-party or outsider.

How does the situation look now?

# Chapter 25: Compromise

*Never ASSUME, because when you ASSUME, you make an ASS of U and ME.*

— Jerry Belson

## Mastering the 1–10 Scale for Decision-Making

I've already talked about how to resolve conflict: 1) ask for what you want, 2) explore the concerns, and 3) come to an agreement. The point is to resolve both of your concerns through conversation and come to a mutually satisfying compromise.

**One other strategy that you may find beneficial when negotiating a compromise is something I call the 1–10 scale.** Tex and I sometimes use it when we choose to go to a movie or do an activity together. For example, we'll ask: "On a scale of 1 to 10, how badly do you want to see this movie?" If one of us feels quite strongly about it, say a 7 or 8, and the other person is a 5, then the high score wins. Yes, we have even agreed on how we are going to agree! But the fact of the matter is, if something isn't a big deal to one person and it *is* a big deal to the other, why not go along to please your partner? You can always get your way next time. Of course, you shouldn't cheat the system by always claiming the high score so that you can have things your way. You'll quickly run out of credibility that way.

By checking in and quantifying our attachment to something, we know exactly where we stand. Sometimes we even surprise each other.

Here's an example. We were both feeling we should get out for the evening, but we were both dragging our asses about it. So, I finally asked Tex, "How badly do you want to go out?" He said, "Not really. Maybe a 5". I laughed and said, "I'm a 5, too". We decided to stay home and watch a movie instead. **Checking in on things, instead of assuming you know what your partner wants, always makes for better outcomes.**

You can use the 1–10 strategy for negotiating the important things, like a household budget, or the not-so-important things, like where you want to go on vacation. If there is potential for conflict, or if even one of you is feeling anxious about asking for something, state how important it is on a scale of 1 to 10 and get it off your chest. This is especially important for couples where one partner is more submissive or has a hard time speaking up for himself. Having someone constantly acquiesce to their partner's wishes may seem like a good deal for one of you, but it's ultimately destructive to love and self-respect. A healthy relationship is a balanced one, where the partners look out for and protect each other's best interests.

For example:

> *Me: "I really want to be a successful author-entrepreneur. This is important to me, like a 10 out of 10".*
>
> *(Fortunately, Tex wants this for me, too, so there is no disagreement, but let's pretend for a moment that he wants me to get a "normal" job instead.)*

*Tex: "But that's a long ways away. I really could use some help bringing money into the house right now".*

*Me: "On a scale of 1 to 10, how strongly do you feel about this?"*

*Tex: "I'm a 9 on this".*

*Me: "What are your concerns?"*

And then we work towards a compromise. Remember: **Ask. Explore. Agree.**

**Guideline #66: Master the 1–10 scale for decision-making.**

## Opinions Are Not Facts

The thing about opinions is that they are not based in facts. A fact can be proven. It can be measured and verified. (For example, it's a fact that mothers, not fathers, give birth.) Opinions can't be proven, because they are a person's thoughts. Opinions are judgements, beliefs, and feelings. (For example, dogs are better than cats.) People will often fight over their beliefs and opinions. Entire wars have been fought in the name of religion, which is really a belief system based on faith, not on facts. Does it make it less credible? Not to the believer. It does, however, make for strong differences of opinion on the matter.

If you hate to change your opinion on something, it's possible that you may be overly attached to a certain belief system. This may be because your identity or sense of self-worth is tied to an ideal or story you've been told or sold. If this is the case, changing your mind is scary and nearly impossible because you are emotionally invested in that belief.

*The greatest deception men suffer is from their own opinions.*

— Leonardo da Vinci

* * *

## HOUSEKEEPING: Resolving Differences

If you and your partner are polarized on an issue, there are some things you can do to resolve your differences of opinion.

**1. Recognize that you are each entitled to your opinions and beliefs.**

You may think that you're right and your partner is deluded, but realize that they are probably thinking the exact same thing! Treat each other's opinions with courtesy.

**2. Ask for some time to consider the issue.**

It is hard to think when you're hearing something threatening for the first time. By agreeing to reconvene at another (possibly less emotional) time, you may find that new ideas will come to light. With time and distance, you may come up with a creative resolution and find some middle ground.

(If it helps, think about how your beliefs have changed over the years. Certain opinions you would have ferociously defended at one time, probably make you shake your head now that you're older and wiser. Young and immature people tend to view the world in black and white. Wise people see the greys.)

**3. When you reconvene, try to see the problem objectively.**

Frame it as a mystery to be solved – almost as if it's someone else's problem that you're discussing. This takes some of the emotion out of it and may allow you to entertain ideas you wouldn't have otherwise.

**4. By taking time out, you may find the issue resolves itself!**

If you give the issue some space, you may find it's not as significant as first thought. You may also find the issue has a way of working itself out.

If you can't agree on an outcome, it may be due to one of you being unwilling or unable to compromise. This can happen out of sheer pig-headedness, but it can also happen when people run into an issue around boundaries. If this is the case, you may need to swallow your pride and hire a professional to mediate between you so that you can come to a mutually agreeable solution. An objective third party could provide new insights.

*PEARLY WISDOM: Sometimes you just have to agree to disagree! Some marriages function quite well even when partners have different views on religion or politics.*

# Chapter Bonus: The Art of Difficult Conversations

> *The single biggest problem in communication is the illusion that it has taken place.*
>
> — George Bernard Shaw

The following is from Chapter Nine of my first book, *The Cha Cha Club Dating Man-ifesto*. While it's a book on dating, written for women, a lot of the advice applies to both men and women, and to relationships. I think it's worth including here, since we are discussing conflict and how to resolve it.

## The Art of Difficult Conversations

We accept and sanction bad behavior by saying nothing. For example, if a man is constantly cancelling or not making plans because he's "too busy" (man-speak for not making you a priority) and you say nothing though it makes you feel bad, then you're basically signaling that you're okay with this kind of treatment. If you want things to change, you need to speak up. So how do you talk so that he'll listen? How do you ask for what you need without sounding like a nag?

### How to Have a Difficult Conversation

The art of having a difficult conversation is all about: a) remembering your audience, and b) having a goal in mind. Remember this principle, even if you don't remember all the "techniques" that follow, and it will get easier with practice.

## Set a Time to Talk with Your Man

Tell him you would like to chat about something important to you, and ask him when would be a good time. Just because you're feeling emotional and ready to burst doesn't mean he's ready to hear what you have to say. You wouldn't just barge into someone's office at work and start laying into them, so treat your man with the same courtesy and respect. No broadsiding when it's important, and definitely no heavy late-night discussions in bed. Set yourself up for success and ensure he's in the right headspace to listen and talk. This means choosing your time and your environment with care. (Hint: If your best talks are when you go for a walk together, suggest a walk.)

Example: "Steve, there's something I need to ask you about. Can we go for a walk and talk about it? When would be a good time?"

*PEARLY WISDOM: Difficult conversations fall apart when people go into combat mode and don't bring enough respect for the other party into the equation. Never make assumptions about the other person's intentions. Try to see them as "innocent" and the conversation as an opportunity to understand and improve the situation. When you treat the other person as innocent, they are less likely to feel judged and more likely to open up.*

## State the Reality

What is the current reality of what is happening right now, in observable terms?

"I understand you're very busy at work and we haven't been able to spend much time together".

You're not agreeing or disagreeing with whether he's actually busy or just using it as an excuse. You're simply restating the observable facts: he says he's busy, and you haven't been spending much time together. You're not attaching any meaning or intention to his words and behavior.

Still, you can expect him to get a little defensive. If he does, just listen and then –

**Tell Him How You Feel**

Keep it simple! I can't stress this enough. Try to sum it up in one sentence.

"To be honest, I'm feeling a little lonely… I miss you".

Notice that you're not attacking, or using your intellect? You're sticking to how you feel. This takes courage. There is a lot of power and strength in this kind of feminine vulnerability. Keep it real and you will melt his heart and knock away his defenses.

He will probably ask for more information. If not, just continue.

**Tell Him What You Want (not what you don't want)**

It's so much easier to fulfill. Remember, the art of having a difficult conversation is: a) remembering your audience, and b) having a goal in mind.

"I'd really like to spend more time together".

**Don't Bring Up the Past**

Do not talk about the last time he did this, or some other way he may have disappointed you. That will come off as blaming and nagging and cause him to shut down. Stay present and focused on the current issue.

**Make a Request, Not a Demand or an Ultimatum**

Make it specific, and actionable.

“Do you think we could take a road trip next weekend?”

**Stay Positive**

Let him know that fulfilling this request would affect you in a good way.

“It would be fun to get away for a whole weekend, just the two of us. I’d love that”.

**Listen**

Remember, this is a conversation, so ask him what he thinks. By asking him what he thinks, you’re gathering ideas and exploring solutions together. This moves the conversation into more friendly territory, and it cements the idea that you’re a couple, solving life’s problems and challenges together.

“What do you think?”

**Give it Time**

If his response is lukewarm, be patient. People can get a little grumpy when called out on their less than ideal behavior. Be open to the possibility that he’ll turn around.

**Stay Busy While He Figures it Out**

Keep living your own life and do things that make you happy. This will give you distance and perspective.

**Watch for Changes**

Remember: judge a man by what he does, not what he says.

> *As an instructor, you must be able to distinguish between poor performance caused by lack of ability or aptitude on the part of the student and poor performance caused by lack of effort. You should treat the first with patience and the latter with firmness. You must never apply sarcasm and ridicule.*
>
> – Bruce Lee

Bruce Lee's wisdom applies to your relationship. If your man isn't meeting your needs, ask yourself if the problem is aptitude or attitude, and respond accordingly.

Think of difficult conversations as an opportunity to grow and understand. It's a chance to improve the current relationship situation. **It's an act of love and faith not to give up on someone but to take the time to have a conversation that matters.**

Try these techniques, knowing it might feel unnatural at first; anything that matters is almost always a challenge. Rest assured that the art of difficult conversations is one of the hardest to master but one of the most rewarding. Professional coaches and therapists spend a lifetime honing these skills.

Be gentle with yourself whenever you're trying something new and remember –

**Guideline #39: Failure Is a Form of Progress.**

It means you are trying. All you need to be concerned with is forward momentum, not total perfection. That goes for losing weight, getting fit or trying to save a relationship.

> *Failure is simply the opportunity to begin again, this time more intelligently.*
>
> – Henry Ford

So what happens if you have a heartfelt discussion and there are no changes in behavior? Well, you need to ask yourself if his inability to fulfill your request is a deal breaker in your relationship. That's the hard truth of the matter.

In fact, coming to this realization is possibly harder than the actual conversation. Just knowing you could have a possible deal breaker on your hands if things don't work out may be the reason you wish to avoid having the conversation in the first place. Don't. Don't stay in a dead-end relationship because you're afraid to learn the truth.

You can't live in limbo land. If something is bothering you and affecting the quality of your relationship and your feelings for this guy, you need to talk. Bad feelings lead to resentment. Resentment leads to loss of connection. Loss of connection leads to loss of love and to breakups. You owe it to yourself and him to have an honest conversation and see if you can't fix things.

### Guideline #40: Be Fearless (but Kind).

It's important to be able to have fearless conversations if we want to improve our relationships. Just keep in mind that dating is give and take. Try not to make assumptions until you can really understand your man's perspective and position. Treat a man well, and you may turn him around for good. And if you can't, you can hold your head high and know you acted like a Quality Woman.

If you would like to read more, *The Cha Cha Club Dating Manifesto* is available at your favorite bookstore.

## Guy-to-guy with Tex

You learn more from your mistakes than from your successes. So, here's some man-to-man advice from Tex about staying happy in your marriage.

1. Don't play into the stereotype. Marriage is not the old ball and chain. You don't have to believe that you're only going to have sex once a month once you're married.

2. The woman wants you to take charge.

3. There are not two pilots on the plane, there's a pilot and a co-pilot. There are not two presidents, there's a president and a vice-president. They're both a big deal and they both have each other's backs, but each of them has different duties. In a relationship, one person can be president of the house, and one can be president of finances. You can even switch it up, but things work best when one person is in charge of their area.

4. The grass will always look greener. You might see a woman and think, "She's a little more this or a little more that", but then you get to the other side and it's no different.

5. Dance with your woman. Do couples dancing. It solidifies a bond you can't have with anyone else.

6. Defend your woman, but call her out when she's wrong. Never publicly humiliate her, though.

7. Keep yourself interesting.

8. Take care of yourself physically. Your wife will still love you with love handles, but she won't complain if they're not there.

9. Communicate, because no one is a mind reader.

10. Listen to country music. You can learn a lot from other people's mistakes.

## Gal-to-gal with Sophie

Ladies, I actually don't recommend listening to country music. You'll end up buying a pair of cowboy boots. Then a hat. It's just a slippery slope of chicken waffles and Daisy Duke shorts after that.

All kidding aside, here's another top 10 – it also applies to the guys.

1. Don't stop having fun or courting each other once you move in/get married.

2. Seek pleasure, often.

3. Your relationship, your rules.

4. Be there for others, but never at the expense of your own well-being.

5. Laugh with your man. Laugh at your man. Laugh at yourself. Just laugh.

6. Praise your man in public, but criticize him in private.

7. Keep yourself interesting.

8. Take care of yourself physically.

9. Communicate, and ask for what you want.

10. Above all, be kind to one another.

# Conclusion

As I write this final chapter in Canada, the sun is going down over the mountains. Tex is 3,000 kilometers away in Houston, taking part in some fun cycling thing called Critical Mass. He just texted me a video of it and said, "What's a pilot without a co-pilot?" (That's Tex-talk for "Wish you were here. I miss you".)

We've been apart for a month now. I am in Canada while we await approval on our Fiancée Visa. It will be another four months before I can return to the United States to marry my sweetheart. Then a new chapter will begin...

I am certain that, after 10 years of marriage, I will have a lot more to say on the subject of living together without growing apart, but for now, I think this is a good start. What do you think? I'd love to know.

We've talked about what it takes to be a happy couple. We've explored the topics of communication. Kindness. Love agreements. Fairness and respect. Hygiene. Money. Property and possessions. Commitment. Covering your ass(ets). Sex and desire and chemistry. How to feel sexy and sensual. Trust. Privacy and personal space. Personal growth and the pursuit of happiness. Mental health and codependency. Healing your wounds and reclaiming your power. Relatives, exes, in-laws. Religion and interfaith marriages. Kids, stepkids, and pets. Vulnerability. Criticism and defensiveness. Resolving conflict. Compromise. The art of difficult conversations.

We've covered a lot of ground. By now, it should be apparent that a relationship doesn't just happen without effort. Its failure or success is in proportion to your ability to master your communication skills as well as yourself.

Your relationship is in your hands now. You've got a road map.

Your destination? Joy. Intimacy. Respect.

Good luck on your journey.

## One Last Thing…

We independent authors live and die by word of mouth. If you believe this book is worth sharing, please take the time to tell your friends about it. Heck, why not gift them a copy? **A review would also make a big difference for other readers** who are trying to decide if this book could help them.

Thank you so much and please, feel free to email me at thechachaclub@gmail.com. I would love to hear from you.

# About the Author

Sophie Winters is the author of *The Cha Cha Club Dating Man-ifesto* and *It's Not You, It's Us: A Guide for Living Together Without Growing Apart.* Sophie's real name is Adele Frizzell. Seven months after publishing The Dating Man-ifesto, she met the man who would become her husband through an online dating site. Maybe that's because writing a dating and relationship book (and following her own advice) made it crystal clear what kind of man she wanted to date and let into her life. She and her husband currently live in Texas with their dog, Belle. Adele enjoys travel, hiking, yoga, and lifting heavy weights. She loves inspiring people to get more out of life.

Adele's third book, *Forty Daze*, is a light-hearted but practical look at mindfulness, behavior change, and the quest for self-improvement through a series of 40-day challenges. Both a book and a movement, you can sign up for her mailing list at www.fortydaze.com to get involved.

**Questions or Comments?**
Email thechachaclub@gmail.com

**Connect Online:**
www.thechachaclub.com

**Chapter Downloads:**
http://www.itsnotyouitsus.com/chapterlinks

## Acknowledgements

This guide would not have been possible without the support and advice of nearly 70 people. Thank you to all my beta-readers, editors, experts, and contributors of colorful content. Your stories inspired me, and your feedback helped to provide clarity and direction. Without your contribution, this guide would have fallen short of its potential. I would especially like to thank my friends Don, Jess, Katarina and Kristie for providing such generous support and valuable feedback on the manuscript.

Don and Kristie: your belief in me and your encouragement was more important than you could ever know.

Most of all, I want to thank Tex. This book would not exist at all without your love and generosity. *Thank you for giving me wings.*

## The Relationship Guidelines – Summarized

1. Guideline #1: When looking for a life partner, look for someone who is resilient in the face of adversity.

2. Guideline #2: If you're choosing to share your life with someone, give some thought as to *how* you're going to be happy together.

3. Guideline #3: One sure-fire way to spot a happy couple: they laugh together.

4. Guideline #4: You need to like each other in order to properly love each other.

5. Guideline #5: Long-term happiness and love is an inside job. It starts with YOU.

6. Guideline #6: The quality of your relationships is a direct reflection of how you feel about yourself.

7. Guideline #7: Good relationships help you become your best self.

8. Guideline #8: Check in with your partner whenever you perceive a mosquito in your relationship.

9. Guideline #9: Ask for what you want. No drama.

10. Guideline #10: The secret to a long and happy marriage is an abundance of kindness.

11. Guideline #11: It's HOW you love each other that matters. Love Agreements help you figure this out.

12. Guideline #12: No one should be doing certain tasks just because of their genitalia.

13. Guideline #13: The more polarized you are on things, the more tension there will be in your relationship.

14. Guideline #14: Don't mistake sharing *everything* for true intimacy.

15. Guideline #15: Your appearance matters to your partner.

16. Guideline #16: Being in a relationship means doing the little things to please your partner.

17. Guideline #17: Smelling nice. It's not just for first dates.

18. Guideline #18: Never stop courting each other.

19. Guideline #19: Treat your personal finances like a business; beware of bad investments.

20. Guideline #20: Money problems in a relationship are often communication problems in disguise.

21. Guideline #21: Men need man-caves, and women need lady-lairs.

22. Guideline #22: Everyone deserves something to call their own, even if it's just a favorite cup.

23. Guideline #23: Don't build a romantic relationship on convenience.

24. Guideline #24: Have hard limits and soft limits.

25. Guideline #25: Compatibility is more important than chemistry in a long-term relationship.

26. Guideline #26: If you want to enjoy your sex life, take responsibility for your behavior and your hormones.

27. Guideline #27: Foreplay begins outside the bedroom.

28. Guideline #28: Sex is like exercise: you almost never regret doing it. So, "Just do it."

29. Guideline #29: If we're stressed out, we are in survival mode, not reproductive mode.

30. Guideline #30: Feeling sexy and confident = more and better sex.

31. Guideline #31: Your lifelong challenge is to continually date each other.

32. Guideline #32: A relationship without sex is simply friendship.

33. Guideline #33: State your needs as simply and clearly as possible.

34. Guideline #34: When everything is urgent, nothing is urgent.

35. Guideline #35: Small, daily acts of kindness and specific words of appreciation keep a couple from growing apart.

36. Guideline #36: Build trust, and you build security in your relationship.

37. Guideline #37: Where there is shame, there is an apology waiting in the wings.

38. Guideline #38: Sometimes we need space to just *be.*

39. Guideline #39: A lack of privacy in a relationship signals boundary and trust issues.

40. Guideline #40: Privacy becomes secrecy when there is a conscious motivation to hide something.

41. Guideline #41: Make time for personal time.

42. Guideline #42: Alone time can enhance intimacy.

43. Guideline #43: By making time for personal growth, we serve the Self. By making time for each other, we serve the Relationship.

44. Guideline #44: If you want to be happy, have more fun experiences, not more things.

45. Guideline #45: Be there for others, but never at the expense of your own happiness and well-being.

46. Guideline #46: Surviving is not thriving.

47. Guideline #47: Embrace your greatest strength. Acknowledge your hidden hurts.

48. Guideline #48: Healing our hurts is an act of self-love.

49. Guideline #49: Heal your pain, and you heal the world.

50. Guideline #50: When it comes to family, "You mess with one bean, you get the whole burrito".

51. Guideline #51: Your partner is not your project.

52. Guideline #52: Good people will respect your beliefs; bad people will try to shame you for them.

53. Guideline #53: Focus on shared values, not religion, to make your union work.

54. Guideline #54: Deed before creed.

55. Guideline #55: If you want peace, lower your expectations of what is possible for you in the first six years of your child's life.

56. Guideline #56: You can be successful at everything, just not everything at once.

57. Guideline #57: The couple that plays together, stays together.

58. Guideline #58: If your vulnerability triggers contempt, you are with the wrong person.

59. Guideline #59: Be real, but also be kind to one another to minimize shame.

60. Guideline #60: A healthy, powerful relationship requires emotional courage.

61. Guideline #61: Where there is defensiveness, there is often insecurity.

62. Guideline #62: To accept and reflect on criticism with dignity and grace is a sign of maturity.

63. Guideline #63: Criticize the behavior, not the person.

64. Guideline #64: When arguing, check your ego. Choose to listen. Seek to understand. You may learn something.

65. Guideline #65: Happy couples behave like good friends, and treat each other gently during conflict.

66. Guideline #66: Master the 1–10 scale for decision making.

**Guidelines from *The Cha Cha Club Dating Man-ifesto*:**

1. Failure is a form of progress.

2. Be fearless (but kind).

# Selected Bibliography

## In Alphabetical Order by Author

Chapman, Gary. *The Five Love Languages.*

Chapman, Gary. *The Five Languages of Apology.*

Chapman, Gary. *Things I Wish I'd Known Before We Got Married.*

Covey, Stephen M.R. *The Speed of Trust: The One Thing That Changes Everything.*

Frankl, Viktor E. *Man's Search for Meaning.*

Gladwell, Malcom. *Outliers: The Story of Success.*

Lerner, Harriet. *Marriage Rules: A Manual for the Married and the Coupled Up.*

Love, Patricia, and Steven Stosny. *How to Improve Your Marriage Without Talking About It.*

McGowan, Dale. *In Faith and in Doubt: How Religious Believers and Nonbelievers Can Create Strong Marriages and Loving Families.*

Pressfield, Steven. *The War of Art: Break through the Blocks and Win Your Inner Creative Battles.*

Robbins, Tony. *MONEY – Master the Game: 7 Simple Steps to Financial Freedom.*

Talbot, Betsy and Warren. *Married with Luggage: What We Learned about Love by Traveling the World.*

Viscott, David. *How to Live with Another Person.*

# Endnotes

## Chapter 1 – The Happy Couple

2. Taryn Hillin, “New Research Says Living Together before Marriage Doesn’t Lead to Divorce,” *The Huffington Post*, March 11, 2014, accessed July 31, 2015, http://www.huffingtonpost.com/2014/03/11/divorce-cohabitation-stud_n_4936928.html.

3. Casey E. Copen, et al. “First Premarital Cohabitation in the United States: 2006 – 2010 National Survey of Family Growth,” Report. April 4, 2013, Division of Vital Statistics, http://www.cdc.gov/nchs/data/nhsr/nhsr064.pdf.

4. McKinley Irvin Family Law, “32 Shocking Divorce Statistics,” accessed July 5, 2015, http://www.mckinleyirvin.com/Family-Law-Blog/2012/October/32-Shocking-Divorce-Statistics.aspx.

5. Theresa E. DiDonato, “The 3 Simple Habits That Predict Long-term Love,” accessed July 5, 2015, https://www.psychologytoday.com/blog/meet-catch-and-keep/201411/the-3-simple-habits-predict-long-term-love.

6. O’Leary, K. D., Acevedo, B. P., Aron, A., Huddy, L., & Mashek, D. (2012). “Is Long-Term Love More Than a Rare Phenomenon? If So, What Are Its Correlates?,” Social Psychological and Personality Science, 3(2), 241-249.

7. J.A. Lavner et al., “Psychology of Close Relationships,” accessed July 5, 2015, http://isites.harvard.edu/fs/docs/icb.topic1214378.files/March%2011%20Readings/Psychology%20of%20Close%20Relationships%203-11-13%20Slides.pdf.

8. Roko Belic, "Things I Learned While Making a Movie About Happiness," accessed July 5, 2015, http://mariashriver.com/blog/2012/02/things-i-learned-while-making-movie-about-happiness.

**Chapter 3 – Communication: Kindness and Love Languages**

9. Emily Esfahani Smith, "Masters of Love," *The Atlantic*, June 2014, accessed July 5, 2015, http://www.theatlantic.com/health/archive/2014/06/happily-ever-after/372573.

10. The Gottman Institute, "Research FAQs," accessed July 5, 2015, http://www.gottman.com/research/research-faqs.

11. Harriet Lerner, "Why 'I Love You' Isn't Enough," *Psychology Today*, May 2014, accessed July 5, 2015, https://www.psychologytoday.com/blog/the-dance-connection/201405/why-i-love-you-isnt-enough.

**Chapter 5 – The Division of Labor: Fairness and Respect**

12. Pew Research Center, "Record Share of Americans Have Never Married as Values, Economics and Gender Patterns Change," accessed July 5, 2015, http://www.pewsocialtrends.org/2014/09/24/record-share-of-americans-have-never-married.

13. Brigid Schulte, "Couples Who Share Housework Have the Most Sex and Best Sex Lives," *The Washington Post*, August 14, 2014, accessed July 5, 2015, http://www.washingtonpost.com/news/local/wp/2014/08/14/couples-who-share-housework-have-the-most-sex-and-best-sex-lives.

**Chapter 6 – Hygiene: Behind Closed Doors**

14. BusinessWire, "New Survey Reveals the Lasting Power of Attraction", accessed January 17, 2017, http://www.businesswire.com/news/home/20110513006237/en/Survey-Reveals-Lasting-Power-Attraction.

**Chapter 7 – Money, It's a Kick (in the Ass)**

15. Robi Ludwig, "Why Is It So Hard to Talk about Money?" *Today*, 2013, accessed July 7, 2015, http://www.today.com/id/43543561/ns/today-money/t/why-it-so-hard-talk-about-money/#.VN3-2_nF-So.

**Chapter 9 – Living Together versus Marriage: How Committed Are You?**

16. Alan Edmunds, "Marriage Success Related to How Long You Dated", San Diego Divorce Centre, January 25, 2011, accessed February 20, 2017, http://www.sandiegodivorcecenter.com/marriage-success-related-to-how-long-you-dated.

**Chapter 10 – Covering Your Ass(ets)**

17. CommonLawRelationships.ca, accessed July 16, 2015, http://www.commonlawrelationships.ca/alberta.

**Chapter 11 – Sex and Desire: The Science of Falling in Love**

18. BBC News, "Falling in Love Drives You Mad," BBC Online Network, July 29, 1999, accessed July 7, 2015, http://news.bbc.co.uk/2/hi/science/nature/407125.stm.

19. Samantha Cleaver, "5 Reasons Men Cheat – and How to Stay Faithful," *Men's Health*, March 30, 2015, accessed July 7, 2015, http://www.menshealth.com/sex-women/avoid-infidelity.

**Chapter 12 – Sex and Desire: The Science of Staying in Love**

20. Craig Mackenzie, "Nose for Happiness: Doctors Discover Nasal Spray That Can Stop Couples Having Heated Arguments," *Daily Mail*, August 5, 2012, accessed July 7, 2015, http://www.dailymail.co.uk/news/article-2183953/Oxytocin-Nose-happiness-Doctors-discover-nasal-spray-stop-couples-having-heated-arguments.html.

21. Lee T. Gettler, et al., "Longitudinal Evidence That Fatherhood Decreases Testosterone in Human Males," *Proceedings of the National Academy of Sciences of the United States of America*, vol. 108, no. 39, September 12, 2011, accessed July 7, 2015, http://www.pnas.org/content/108/39/16194.full?tab=author-info.

22. Patricia Love and Steven Stosny, *How To Improve Your Marriage Without Talking About It* (New York: Harmony Books, 2009).

23. Victoria Ward, "Cuddling Is More Important to Men Than Women, Survey Says," *The Telegraph*, July 10, 2011, accessed July 7, 2015, http://www.telegraph.co.uk/women/sex/8628620/Cuddling-is-more-important-to-men-than-women-survey-says.html.

24. Sara Gottfried, "50 Shades of Better Sex: Secrets of a Harvard Gynecologist", accessed July 7, 2015, http://sexybacksummit.com/dr-sara-gottfried.

25. Harvard Health Publications, Harvard Health Medical School, "Glycemic Index and Glycemic Load for 100+ Foods," accessed July 19, 2015, http://www.health.harvard.edu/healthy-eating/glycemic_index_and_glycemic_load_for_100_foods.

26. T.G. Travison et al., "A Population-Level Decline in Serum Testosterone Levels in American Men," *The Journal of Clinical Endocrinology and Metabolism*, vol. 92, issue 1, 2007, accessed July 7, 2015, http://press.endocrine.org/doi/full/10.1210/jc.2006-1375.

27. Trust for America's Health, "F as in Fat: How Obesity Threatens America's Future," August 2013, accessed July 7, 2015, http://healthyamericans.org/report/108.

**Chapter 14 – Trust**

28. Miss Fran Jan, "I Wasn't Treating My Husband Fairly, and It Wasn't Fair," December 28, 2014, accessed March 25, 2017, http://www.sunnyskyz.com/blog/610/I-Wasn-t-Treating-My-Husband-Fairly-And-It-Wasn-t-Fair.

**Chapter 17 – Mental Health**

29. Alex Kecskes, "Higher Education, Higher Income Couples Less Likely to Have Marital Problems," divorce360.com, January 9, 2017, accessed March 25, 2017, http://www.divorce360.com/divorce-articles/statistics/us/more-education-less-chance-at-divorce.aspx?artid=436.

30. John Carvel, "Cinderella Said to Be a Poor Role Model for Later Life," *The Guardian*, April 23, 2005, accessed July 20, 2015, http://www.theguardian.com/uk/2005/apr/23/books.booksnews.

31. Mental Health America, “Co-dependency,” accessed July 17, 2015, http://www.mentalhealthamerica.net/co-dependency.

**Chapter 18 – Heal Your Wounds. Claim Your Power. Get More Love.**

32. Nick Carpenter, “Rock Climbing Saved My Life: A Veteran’s Struggle with PTSD,” *Rock and Ice*, July 15, 2015, accessed July 19, 2015, http://www.rockandice.com/lates-news/rock-climbing-saved-my-life-a-veteran-s-struggle-with-ptsd.

**Chapter 20 – Spiritual Matters**

33. According to a survey and workshops led by secular parenting expert and author Dale McGowan in his blog, parentingbeyondbelief.com; Dale McGowan, “The Chill Grandma,” accessed July 9, 2015, http://parentingbeyondbelief.com/blog/.

**Chapter 21 – Kids, Stepkids and Furry Kids**

34. Marco Albertini and Martin Kohli, “What Childless Older People Give: Is the Generational Link Broken?” ResearchGate, April 21, 2014, accessed July 9, 2015, http://www.researchgate.net/publication/231948092_What_childless_older_people_give_is_the_generational_link_broken.

35. The Guardian, “Childless couples have happier marriages, study reveals,” January 12, 2014, accessed January 27, 2017, “https://www.theguardian.com/society/2014/jan/13/childless-couples-happier.

36. Arild S. Foss, “Older People Just as Happy without Children,” *ScienceNordic*, November 24, 2012, accessed July 9, 2015, http://sciencenordic.com/older-people-just-happy-without-children.

37. Joshua Becker, "21 Surprising Statistics That Reveal How Much Stuff We Actually Own," accessed January 27, 2017, http://www.becomingminimalist.com/clutter-stats/.

**Chapter 22 – Vulnerability**

38. The Brenda Stafford Centre, "I Am Courage Program," accessed July 19, 2015, http://www.brendastraffordsociety.org/i-am-courage.

39. The City of Keller, "Dating/Domestic Violence," accessed March 25, 2017, http://www.cityofkeller.com/services/police/public-education/assaults-violence/dating-domestic-violence

40. Maire Sinha, "Family Violence in Canada: A Statistical Profile, 2010," Statistics Canada, accessed July 9, 2015, http://www.statcan.gc.ca/pub/85-002-x/2012001/article/11643-eng.pdf.

**Chapter 24 – Resolving Conflict**

41. Zig Ziglar, "Keeping Your Marriage Strong," accessed July 19, 2015, http://podbay.fm/show/192820274/e/1230563940?autostart=1.

CPSIA information can be obtained
at www.ICGtesting.com
Printed in the USA
BVHW081955170119
538104BV00012B/204/P

9 781634 923088